The Internet for Women

THE
INTERNET
FOR WOMEN

Rye Senjen and
Jane Guthrey

SPINIFEX

Spinifex Press Pty Ltd
504 Queensberry Street
North Melbourne, Vic. 3051
Australia
email spinifex@publishaust.net.au

Home Page http://www.publishaust.net.au/~spinifex

First published by Spinifex Press, 1996
Copyright © Rye Senjen and Jane Guthrey 1996
Copyright on illustrations © Jane Guthrey 1996

Edited by Janet Mackenzie
Typeset in Sabon and Gill Sans by Claire Warren
Cover design by Liz Nicholson (Design Bite)
Made and printed in Australia by Australian Print Group

National Library of Australia
Cataloguing-in-Publication data:
Senjen, R. (Rye), 1957– .
The Internet for Women
Includes index
ISBN 1 875559 52 3
1. Internet (Computer network) – Handbooks, manuals, etc.
2. Computer networks. I. Guthrey, Jane, 1960– . II. Title.
004.67

Contents

Introduction

New technologies continually appear and become integrated into our society, often leaving us no choice but to submit to their promise of a happier, healthier or less stressful life. Occasionally we put our foot down and steadfastly ban them from our homes and our lives. For a year or two. Then resignedly we relent. After all the answering machine *is* convenient and it doesn't hurt anybody. Does it?

However, neither the answering machine, the fax machine nor the portable cappuccino machine have aroused the controversy and often heated debates that have accompanied the arrival of the Internet. To some, the Internet is an unnecessary evil (preceded by the computer) – a haven for pornographers, full of bomb-making recipes and unscrupulous multi-national companies, which threatens to further alienate people and communities. To these people the Internet offers no solution to the problems faced by developing countries, to ending poverty, to environmental degradation and to improving women's lives.

Others have described the Internet optimistically, as a medium that offers hope and the possibility of real change for the better. They experience the Internet as a collection of services which can bring individuals and groups together, in friendship, to offer assistance or to carry out the work that is necessary for change to occur.

Services available through the Internet have much to offer women. We have experienced email as a wonderful, convenient and cheap method to communicate with our friends and allies. It is especially useful for women living in remote areas and for those hindered by disabilities. Researchers and those in the field of education find their work made easier through the plethora of information available on the World Wide Web. Recently we spent an amusing hour on an IRC channel chatting "simultaneously" with two other writers, one in New Zealand and the other in England. Chat lines provide a useful and inexpensive networking medium for organizations.

Women's access to the Internet does not require that we all must have computers and modems in our homes. In some Australian States, public libraries provide Internet access free. You may have access through your workplace, or university. A group of friends could easily share the equipment – after all it's not necessary to be on-line all day! Despite what the media says, Internet access is not going to set you back thousands of dollars: you can buy an old computer and a second-hand modem in Australia for less than $350.

We believe it is vital for women to help shape the Internet so that we can create a place where women feel a sense of belonging. We need to take ownership of a technology that has immense potential for social change. Internet services bring together groups of people with common interests and common situations including support groups and professional, political and grassroots organizations. Mailing lists, IRC and email are well suited to the communication needs of non-hierarchical organizations as they encourage shared thinking. The World Wide Web offers individuals and small organizations the opportunity to publish their story, their point of view or their grievances, on the Internet. This material has the potential to reach a huge audience, cheaply, without media or government intervention.

When thinking about what the Internet has to offer women it is necessary to look beyond our own individual needs. We need to ask ourselves questions regarding the usefulness of Internet technology for all women, not only in our own economically advantaged countries but those living in the so-called developing countries as well. Can Internet technology improve women's lives materially, emotionally and spiritually, and if so which women and where? Can the technology build individual women's self-respect, strength and confidence? Can the Internet be used by groups to build structures for change? Does it educate women? Does it have the potential to increase women's power and influence? When you make decisions about your own use of the Internet we ask you to think about each of these questions, in order that you use the technology wisely and usefully. We believe that the Internet has the potential to be liberating and empowering; however, it's up to individual women to make it so.

What this book is about

By writing this book we hope to demystify the Internet and put it into a context that makes it relevant and accessible to as many women as possible. This book is for women who are just starting to explore the possibilities of the Internet, as well as seasoned Internet users. We have tried to strike a balance between practical "how to" advice on using the most common Internet services, and explanations on how the technology works and what its implications are. You will learn about email, mailing lists, the World Wide Web, chat programs, how to retrieve files from the Internet, and Internet-based role-playing games. We have deliberately kept the technological explanations to a minimum as they are rarely necessary in order to use a particular Internet service successfully. We have included a chapter that explains the equipment which you need to get Internet access, what types of Internet access you can obtain, and what questions to ask a prospective Internet service provider.

This book also covers topics not covered in more general books on the Internet: gender issues, pornography, sexual harassment, anonymity, privacy and security. To put the Internet into a more women-centred perspective we have included a chapter that introduces our computing foremothers and describes how some women have already begun to make the Internet an integral part of their lives. And in the final section of the book you will find a collection of Internet resources of special interest to women. Internet addresses are still relatively unstable and will change without warning. For this reason we have placed all resources mentioned throughout the book on our Web page

(http://www.publishaust.net.au/~spinifex).

All addresses will be checked on a regular basis and the site will contain the latest address for a particular resource.

We hope this book will inspire and assist you in your first steps into cyberspace. We also hope it can be a companion to which you can refer when in need. This book cannot answer all your technical questions: there are simply too many possible software programs that one could use for any given Internet service. We have tried to select software tools that illustrate how to use a particular Internet service. The tool that you are using may be different, but we hope that our explanations are sufficiently detailed for you to understand the necessary steps that are required to use a particular Internet service.

How to use this book

Conventions used

Throughout the book where instructions on using Internet facilities are specified, the following typographical conventions have been used.

"Courier" typeface is used to indicate a word or phrase to be typed, e.g.
You can join a channel by typing: `/join #cybergrrl`

Sabon Bold indicates a command: either to select a menu; to select an option from a menu; or to activate a button, e.g.
Select **Mail and News Preferences** from the **Options** menu.
Press the **Send** button to post the article.

Internet addresses

All addresses on the Internet can be specified as Universal Resource Locators (URLs). These addresses follow a general format. For example an FTP address might look like:

ftp://ftp.lighthouse.com.au/woolf/orlando.txt

> **ftp://** indicates the access method. Other access methods are Gopher, World Wide Web (http), Usenet News and Telnet.
> **ftp.lighthouse.com.au/** is the address of the computer, followed by a /
> **woolf/** is the file directory where this resource is located on the computer, followed by a /
> **orlando.txt** is the filename itself.

URLs *never* end in a full stop. However, they sometimes end in a slash (/). Because they are often very long and complex, we do not use a full stop at the end of a sentence which ends in a URL, even though this is grammatically incorrect.

URLs *never* include any gaps between the text. They will usually have a colon and two slashes after the access method e.g. **ftp://** and they may include slashes, dots, numbers, tildes (~) dashes (-) or underscored dashes (_).

A more detailed description of Universal Resource Locators can be found in Chapter 7.

Animal icons

The parrot has a useful tip she'd like to share with you.

Don't forget. The elephant reminds you not to forget to follow her instructions.

Beware! The crocodile asks you to pay attention to her warning, otherwise you may have serious problems.

Thanks

We wish to formally thank some of the many people who have made this book possible. Firstly we wish to thank the women who appear in chapter 2 and who graciously permitted Jane to interview them (using email of course): Kathryn Turnipseed, Jo Sutton, Scarlet Pollock, Rosie Cross, Christene Capel, Barbara Ann O'Leary and Amy Goodloe. Thanks also to the people who reviewed and commented on various drafts and chapters of the book: Michael Flower, Sheridan Power, Wendy Mee, Margaret Netherwood (http://www.werple.net/~margaret) and Jenn Vesperman. The production of the book was smoothed by Ross Garner's printer and the discussions on various Internet services with Paul Elliot and many other of Rye's colleagues in the Artificial Intelligence Systems Section, Telstra Research Laboratories. Thanks to Cate Kennedy for allowing us to use her poem "Relative Complexity" in chapter 2. Thanks also to Ailbhe Smyth for pointing out the Charlotte Bunch reform tool kit.

The book would have never seen the light of day without Renate Klein and Susan Hawthorne (Spinifex feminist publishers extraordinaire) and their realization that this was the book women everywhere had to have. To all the hardworking women at Spinifex Press we owe our thanks.

We are grateful for the assistance of our editor Janet Mackenzie who provided a much-needed eye for detail and Jo Turner who calmly saw us through the difficulties. Special thanks also to Claire Warren for her typesetting witchery.

Thanks to The Fruit Pedallers of Northcote for always being on hand with a fresh supply of healthy, organic food, and to the team across the road at the Alphabet City Café, who provided tasty meals when we didn't have the energy to cook. Special thanks to Shirley for cups of tea and company, and to all our friends for their continued encouragement and for bearing with us while we were writing "the book".

Rye Senjen and Jane Guthrey
Melbourne, June 1996

Chapter 1

Introducing the Internet

What is the Internet?

The Internet is a vast network of networks which literally connects millions of people world-wide via their computers. The Internet is like a huge web, extending into almost every part of the globe. To be part of the Internet, computers become physically connected to each other using special-purpose cables, ordinary telephone lines, radio connections, or satellites.

These physical connections enable us to send information between computers. This information can take the form of images, text and sound. You can use the Internet to exchange information or to communicate with people all over the world.

A key aspect of the Internet is its decentralized nature: no one owns it and no central organization controls its content or its running. Information is moved around the Internet using so-called "packet-switching" technology. A message is broken into its parts or packets which travel independently. Often the individual packets use different routes to get from sender to receiver. Each Internet site or subnetwork looks after its own associated network of computers and formulates its own code of conduct. When a message travels for instance from Germany to Australia, it may be retransmitted en route by sites with rules of conduct very different from those in Europe or Australia. Something that may be legally transmitted in Europe may be illegal in sites that retransmit the information. As yet no international laws have been formulated to deal with this problem. Maybe the Internet will eventually operate beyond the laws of nation states, becoming subject to international laws, like the oceans and air space.

Connecting computers together, of varying types and in different geographical locations, and making sure they speak to each other, are aspects of the technical and engineering issues associated with the Internet. Knowing about these is important and sometimes even useful, but not essential to using it. However the Internet is not just a physical network of computers, it is also a concept in people's minds. How to represent the idea of the Internet and utilise it are as important as its technical details.

Who uses the Internet?

Groups of people using the Internet fall into four major categories: the military; educational and research institutions; businesses; and the general public. In the 1970s the US military set up a data network connecting key strategic sites and universities with the aim of protecting the USA against a nuclear war. The US military has a tradition of financing research projects, and the data network was one such project. This network eventually evolved into the Internet. Educational and research institutions were connected right from the beginning. Researchers and students have long used the Internet to exchange information on the latest research in their chosen field. The use of the Internet next spread to engineers in commercial research facilities and then slowly to business in general. Electronic mail was found by some businesses to be an effective tool for communicating with customers, suppliers and between different business divisions. Today business increasingly sees the Internet as a vehicle for commercial purposes, selling everything from beer to computer equipment. The Internet has proven especially attractive to small and specialized companies, because a potentially very large consumer base can be reached without a huge advertising budget. Finally, people in their homes are starting to use the Internet as a means of communicating with each other world-wide.

The Internet has become a powerful tool of communication enabling grassroots organizations to consult with each other and mobilize public opinion. Greenpeace and other environmental organizations use the Internet to keep the public informed about their actions. During the August 1995 protests against French nuclear testing in the Pacific, green groups from sixty-two countries communicated via the Internet. They used the Internet to draft a petition, to discuss and agree on its content, and finally to sign it.

What does the Internet have to offer?

Want to make new friends, find others that share your interest in medieval women's poetry, find information for your research project, get advice on how to communicate with your cat, repair your computer – the Internet has it all and more. There are two types of things you can use Internet services for: firstly, to help you communicate with others, and secondly to find, obtain and provide information. You can treat the Internet like the mass media: consume it, digest it and spit out the parts you don't like, or you can participate and shape parts of the Internet in your image. The choice is entirely your own.

Let's have a closer look at the most common Internet services.

Talking to friends and strangers:
email, mailing lists, IRC and MUDs

The Internet enables you to meet and communicate with friends and strangers in many parts of the world. Using both communication in real time and email, you can be part of a community that centres on a common interest, rather than geographical location.

You have probably heard about electronic mail (email for short). Email is an Internet service that functions similarly to postal mail, except there are no stamps, no envelopes and no trips to the post office. What is required is that you and the recipient of your message each have an email address. Your email address functions a bit like a post office box. If I send an email message to your email address, the message gets stored at this address, until you read it. As most people connect to the Internet via an Internet service provider, the Internet service provider's computer is usually the physical location of this "post office box". There are many delightful things about email: it is fast – a message sent to a friend in Germany can take between a few minutes and a few hours; email is also fairly informal, like a cross between a telephone conversation and a postal letter; and sending an email always seems less arduous to me than sending a postal letter because I can perform the whole transaction sitting at my computer.

Another use of email is electronic mailing lists. Think of a subject you feel passionate about and then imagine communicating with people all over the globe

3

about your passion via your computer. Mailing lists help to bring together people who share a common interest but live geographically apart. The list has a central address to which all members of the list send their messages. At this address the message gets copied (usually automatically by a program) and a copy is sent to each participant of the list. There are thousands of mailing lists covering every conceivable topic from crime writing to breast cancer support to lesbian Buddhists. If you can't find a list that gets you in contact with others who share your interest, you can always start your own.

A variation of mailing lists are Usenet News groups. There are some important differences between Usenet News groups and mailing lists. With mailing lists you automatically receive other list members' postings in your mail box. However with Usenet News groups you retrieve the postings from the news groups you are interested in from your Internet Service Provider (ISP)'s Usenet News storage. There are several thousand news groups covering a large variety of topics. Usenet news groups can be less civilized than email lists and, while covering a large number of useful and important topics, you will also find the bizarre, the ugly and the pornographic.

If you would like something more immediate, something that is similar to going to your favourite café and chatting to friends, try Internet Relay Chat (IRC). It is similar to a telephone conference call, except you type in your responses. IRC consists of more than a thousand channels. When you connect to IRC you join a channel and any messages that you type into your computer are delivered automatically to all other participants of the channel. You can join established channels with topics ranging from the esoteric and the blatantly sexual to the hard-core technical. IRC is mostly about meeting strangers. Many channels function like singles bars, but you can easily create your own private channel and use it to meet with your friends from around the world.

If you feel attracted by the notion of creating a living story, you like role-plays and are fond of science fiction, fantasy or medieval storylines, you can join one of the hundreds of Multi-User Dimensions (MUDs) that exist on the Internet. MUDs are vivid text-based virtual environments that started as role-playing adventure and fantasy games. Today an increasing number of MUDs are solely used for social or educational purposes: you can learn a foreign language, take creative writing courses, or simply play out your fantasies. MUDs operate in a similar way to IRC, except you can move around a virtual environment (usually text-based). You use special words to interact with the environment and its inhabitants. As you gain experience in a particular MUD, you can take part in creating the environment and shaping the storyline.

Providing, finding and obtaining information: the World Wide Web

The Internet has been with us for more than twenty years, but not until the advent of the World Wide Web did it become of interest to a large section of the population. The World Wide Web provides us with an exciting and powerful tool to provide, find and obtain information. Increasingly, Web browsers (the software programs that you use to access the World Wide Web) are becoming the only software package you need to surf the Internet and interact with others.

How does the Word Wide Web work? It functions by connecting together, via computers, geographically distributed Web pages. Embedded bits of text, also known as links, tell the computer where to go to find the next page. You can recognize a word or section of text which functions as a link because it either appears in a different colour (often blue) or is underlined. Each page can contain any number of these links. The World Wide Web thus becomes a giant spider's web with all pages ultimately connected to each other.

Starting at a particular page, you follow down the different path that each new link suggests and quickly travel to many different parts of the globe. Minutes become hours and you often find yourself at exciting locations obtaining information you never suspected was available. But the World Wide Web not only makes information more accessible, it also allows everyone to become an author and to publish their own views of the world. If you want to share your knowledge on your favourite or specialist subject, you can easily prepare your own Web page and let the world know about it.

The Internet is not the only network

The Internet has evolved to become the major network to connect computers world wide. However in the 1970s and 1980s, when the Internet was still developing, other independent networks were also built. These included bitnet (the network of educational institutions), commercial networks such as CompuServe and grassroots networks such as Fidonet. Each of these networks represents a different design philosophy and came into existence in response to different needs in the community. In recent years these independent networks have connected to and been incorporated into the wider Internet. Still it is interesting to know something about these networks, because they may present themselves to you as possible Internet providers. If you live in one of the so-called developing countries, or in a rural area, they may be your only access to the Internet.

Commercial networks

Commercial on-line information services were developed in the late 1980s to provide information to subscribers of the service. Using paid information providers, these services were able to guarantee a high level of accuracy of information. One of the design principles of the Internet is to decentralize all network resources; in contrast, commercial on-line services are controlled in a hierarchical, top-down fashion. Commercial on-line services have central sign-up administrative facilities and often central databases where all information is kept.

Some commercial on-line services such as CompuServe have extended their network from the USA to almost anywhere in the world. They allow you to retrieve your email wherever you are, as long as you have access to a modem and a computer, and are one of their customers. Naturally, you pay substantially for this privilege. Commercial on-line services have only recently provided their customers with Internet access, and some of these so-called gateways are still fairly clumsy and unreliable. Remember, behind every commercial on-line service is a company that hopes to make additional money by providing customers with "value-added" services. The main advantages of commercial on-line services are their wealth of easily accessible and reliable information, their often easy-to-use software, and their sometimes helpful customer service. Well-known commercial on-line services are CompuServe, Prodigy, Delphi, America Online (AOL) and the Microsoft Network.

Grassroots networks

In the late 1970s grassroots political and activist groups around the world developed networks of their own, independent of the military-industrial complex in the USA. These early networks were usually developed by computer enthusiasts as a means of connecting small local on-line communities. Early community-based Bulletin Board Systems (BBSs) often specialized in a particular topic, such as science fiction or computer games. They offered freeware and shareware, local programs, local electronic mail and conferencing, and the opportunity to meet other like-minded computer enthusiasts electronically and often in real life as well.

Users and operators of local BBSs eventually wanted to connect with other BBSs across the USA and worldwide. To solve the problem of connecting computers that did not have a permanent connection with each other, a store-and-forward scheme was developed. This scheme involves computers calling each other at predetermined times, using the telephone network, to exchange information. One of the most popular store-and-forward schemes was developed by Tom Jennings, a gay activist and skate-boarder, and it became known as Fidonet. Fidonet operators take advantage of late-night cheap telephone tariffs to pass messages to each other. It is a very low-cost, easy-to-use, decentralized technology that put the power of computer communication into the hand of grassroots operators. Fidonet now spans the globe and in some developing countries is still the only means of connecting to the Internet.

To start your own BBS all you need is a PC, a modem, a telephone line and some specialized software. BBSs are still very popular today and many are connected to the Internet as well. BBS are provided by people of every cultural, religious, political and sexual persuasion. Unfortunately, pornographers and paedophiles have increasingly used BBSs to spread their wares, but many BBSs provide a worthwhile community service. Many now also have a dial-up connection to the Internet and they provide, often, the cheapest way of accessing all or parts of Internet services. Other BBSs have grown into fully fledged Internet providers with permanent Internet connections and access to all Internet tools.

An interesting development in Germany is the existence of women-only BBSs. FemNet and WOMAN (**http://www.woman.de/** and **http://www.zerberus.de/org/femnet/index.html**). These are associations of BBSs that offer a communications forum for women only. FemNet is a more commercially centred, but women-focused organization, while WOMAN is a loose federation of essentially independent women-only BBSs (ADA, CONNECTA, ELEKTRA, FEMAIL, FENESTRA and SIRENE). Both nets have regional access points and, because they totally exclude men, are ideal for state-wide communication and networking of women's projects, such as domestic violence shelters, women's holiday homes and other women's groups. Of course they are also used by individual women who want to connect with others in a completely safe and women-centred environment. They both carry many discussion groups, covering such topics as human rights, women's studies, migrants, racism, dreams, science and many more, as well as mailing lists and other services from the Internet. Women-only BBSs also provide a safe and supportive environment for women to learn how to run computer networks. In May 1996 WOMAN had about 300 users in Germany and was administered by a collective of fifteen women.

Political activists increasingly use email, Usenet News and the World Wide Web (see the human rights web at **http://www.traveller.com/~hrweb**) to monitor human rights violations and to pressure governments. Using these different Internet services facilitates communication between activists separated by thousands of miles and provides instant access to news and information not available though the mass media. Equally important, the Internet helps to knit together diverse communities around a particular issue. For example the East Timor Action Network (email **cscheiner@igc.apc.org**) uses the Internet to disseminate information and calls for action against the occupation of their country by Indonesia. Similar "action networks" exist for China, Vietnam, Mexico, Guatemala, Burma and Tibet, to name just a few. Some of these action networks find a digital home with PeaceNet (http://www.peacenet.org or email to peacenet@peacenet.apc.org), others are the creation of a few committed individuals. PeaceNet is a project of the Institute of Global Communication and provides BBSs like conferences and email lists to its subscribers. It is represented in many countries and has a lot of women-related information and conferences. It often functions as a cross between an Internet service provider and an alternative on-line service.

Understanding how Internet services work

Very few small aircraft pilots are nowadays able to service and repair their own aircraft. Yet in the 1930s and 1940s when Amelia Earhart and Beryl Markham were pilots, every pilot was expected to be able take apart an aircraft's engine and put it back together. Beryl Markham describes how on her flight from Kenya to England she needed to perform an emergency landing in deep sand in the desert near Kosti (halfway to Khartoum). After "fiddling" with her aircraft engine to find out what caused it to misfire, she left for Khartoum the next day. These were the early and adventurous days of flying.

In some ways we are still in the early days of computer and Internet technology. With a little bit of knowledge you can repair and upgrade your own computer and install its software. While not essential, it does help to know, at least roughly, how computers work and how they communicate with each other. Internet services will make more sense to you if you understand how they operate.

Client-server relations

Internet services such as email, FTP, Gopher, IRC and the World Wide Web use an arrangement called client-server architecture. It sounds frightful, but it is actually a very straightforward system. The client part (also called client program) of this arrangement is played by your home computer. Servers (also called hosts) are larger, more powerful computers that house the Internet service that the client wants to use. One server may be communicating with many clients at the same time. Client programs display, either in text-form or graphically, the information that the server has sent them. Client programs also manage the communications between your computer and a server. Each Internet service uses different conventions for their client-server communications. These conventions are called protocols. For instance the World Wide Web uses a protocol called **http** or hypertext transfer protocol. It is not usually necessary to have a deeper understanding of these protocols.

Just to make things a little confusing, World Wide Web clients are usually called browsers.

Figure 1.1 Client-server architecture

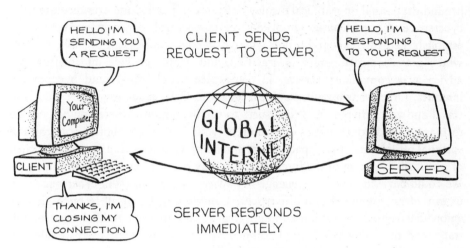

Metaphors of the Internet

The Internet has been described in a variety of ways. The most commonly used metaphors are: cyberspace, the information superhighway, and an electronic marketplace. Each of these terms captures a particular flavour of the Internet, but leaves out large chunks of facilities and possibilities. How we describe something is important because the description has an effect on how we experience reality. When thinking about your vision of the Internet it is useful to reflect on the visions that already exist. The metaphors used to describe the Internet all describe the same physical reality, but what they evoke is very different.

Cyberspace

"Cyberspace" sounds futuristic. Science-fiction enthusiasts relate well to this term as it conjures up the mystery of intergalactic travel and probing the unknown. The term "cyberspace" was invented by the science-fiction writer, William Gibson. In his own words cyberspace is "the consensual hallucination of visually realized data achieved through plugging into a global data network". Gibson imagined that, rather than using a computer to connect to this data network, a direct physical link between a person's brain and the data would be made. Of course this is not yet possible.

Currently the term "cyberspace" refers to the imaginary place created by electronic networks. It is essentially a space in your mind, a packaging you create around the textual or graphical display on your computer. Some commentators see cyberspace as a new frontier removed from state control: a space where people can establish their own law and order; where new communities can be built. A space where grassroots democracy is practised, and people provide information and advice as a community service. In cyberspace people are bound by common interests, rather than by geographical location. Cyberspace is a place were you travel and visit different sites (or "surf" to use the jargon), where you can belong to many varied communities according to your interests, hobbies, political and spiritual affiliations. It is a space where spreading your ideas is as easy as the click of a button. Thinking of the Internet in this way provides us with an opportunity. We could develop new rules, engage in new sets of actions. Will cyberspace help us in understanding cultural differences? Can we forget that all technologies are embedded in a socio-cultural context? Realistically it seems unlikely that nation states and the military-industrial complex will relinquish their need to rule and their desire to determine "their" citizens' lives. As commercial interests start to dominate cyberspace, will the Internet become another large supermarket? As mass media feels its grip slipping, will cyberspace be another straightjacket of mind control?

The Information Superhighway

You are entering the Information Superhighway. Fasten your seatbelts for a fast, efficient and uneventful ride. Make sure you bring plenty of cash. Cyberspace is about meeting people, the metaphor of the Information Superhighway stresses the distribution and access of information. As on a real highway, goods (i.e. information) are carried from information provider to user. The term is popular with politicians because highways need to be planned, built and administered by a central body. This is something politicians can understand and become involved in. Telecommunications companies and the mass media like to talk about the Information Superhighway because they can envision themselves as the providers of the information that travels this highway. In their view the Information Superhighway is a simple extension of current broadcasting. The telecommunications and broadcasting industries hope to provide multimedia on-line shopping, banking, videos, audio and music on demand.

This metaphor of the Internet almost totally leaves out people and their communications needs. This is interesting when you consider that email and other

When thinking about your vision of the Internet it is useful to reflect on some of the visions that already exist ...

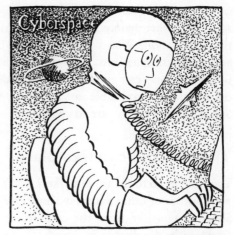

Cyberspace

The Electronic Marketplace

The Information Superhighway

The Reality

communications services are the most used and popular Internet facilities. If we see the Internet mainly as a source of information, then who will have access to the information? Who will create and who will own information on the Internet are important questions. One of the exciting things about the Internet at present is that anyone can publish and provide information to others. Much of the information is available at no cost. With the Internet as an Information Superhighway this is sure to change.

The electronic marketplace

Too tired to go to the supermarket? Can't be bothered fighting for a parking space with hordes of other Saturday shoppers? Welcome to the electronic marketplace. Shop all you like from the comfort of your home. Visit a computer store in Germany, a bookstore in North Queensland or a kite shop in Canada. The electronic marketplace is all about commerce. Information becomes a commodity to be bought and sold. The Internet itself can then be used to perform the transactions of commerce. This vision of the Internet clearly shows that it will not be enough to have access to the Internet, but that you also need the funds to purchase the information available. Will you be able to afford this information? If the network is used to perform financial transactions, using digicash, cybercash or emoney, how do you prevent fraud? Who is going to be held accountable if transactions go wrong? Will everyone be able to use this marketplace for selling (as is the case now) or will access to a selling booth be too expensive for most?

The Internet is certainly moving into the direction of a marketplace. Business is slowly recognizing its enormous potential for reaching customers. But as many would-be sellers have found out, you can only attract customers on the Internet if you provide at least something free. At present the Internet is mainly used by business to provide information to customers in the form of multimedia catalogues; however, you can already buy anything from computer hardware to pizza via the Internet.

Chapter 2

Women are doing it for themselves

RELATIVE COMPLEXITY

In my parents' loungeroom after Christmas dinner
I am talking to my brother the computer programmer.
He is explaining to me the principles of cyberspace.
"It is only relatively complex," he says finally, peeling the icing off his fruitcake,
"It is mainly a system of binaries, permutations of zero and one.
So the data may be stored as, say, zero, zero, one, one one, zero, zero one."
My mother sighs.
She is next to us, half-listening.
She is knitting a fair-isle sweater.
"I'll never understand how you get your brain around it," she says.
"It's beyond me," she says, and turns half her attention back
to her fair-isle pattern:
Purl purl plain, plain plain plain purl purl.

Cate Kennedy

Our computer foremothers

Calculating devices

People have been making machines for calculating and doing simple repetitive tasks for thousands of years. One of the earliest calculating devices was the abacus, which is still used today throughout Asia. In the Middle Ages cities and states vied with each other to have the most magnificent and complicated clocks. Musical boxes with spiked drums, that plucked metal combs in pre-set sequences to make a tune, probably inspired the earliest use of machines in industry. Punch cards were invented in the late eighteenth century for use in the production of patterns to be printed on cloth. A thread could be seen or hidden depending on whether there was a hole in a card or not. This method uses binary notation – 0s or 1s – which is essentially how computers work today. The mathematician and philosopher Pascal, in 1642, produced a small calculator which could add and subtract. Gottfried von Leibnitz invented a calculator which could divide and multiply in 1673. These inventions played an important role in the development of data processing – the mechanical processing of information. The computer makes decisions based on the information it has stored and is able to act on those decisions. The first machines that could do this were designed by Charles Babbage in the early 1820s. He designed a small machine, which he called the Difference Engine, which was able to calculate logarithmic tables. In 1834 he unveiled his plans for the Analytical Engine which, though mechanical, worked on the same principles as the modern electronic computer.

The first programmer and her friends

Ada, Countess of Lovelace (1815–52), was a visionary mathematician who worked with Charles Babbage on the Analytical Engine and therefore played a key part in the development of the computer. Ada's mother Ann Isabella Milbank, who was also a mathematician, married Lord Byron in 1815 but was separated from him a year later after the birth of Ada. Although they were fascinated with each other at the time of their marriage, it became apparent that the glamorous, romantic and highly sought-after poet was not a suitable partner for a young woman regarded as being sensible, cautious and virtuous. Byron nicknamed her the Princess of Parallelograms in reference to her mathematical genius. Ann was able to relieve herself of her husband and become a single parent with her reputation and status still intact – quite a feat at this time.

Ada Countess Lovelace

Even as a small child, Ada had obviously inherited her mother's talent for mathematics. Ann, who devoted her life to her daughter, was delighted, and became Ada's first teacher. Ann surrounded her daughter with learned friends, just as her parents had done. In those days, in the circles they mixed in, it was not unusual for girls to be encouraged to study and excel in mathematics. Frequent visitors to the house included an eccentric mathematician, Augustus de Morgan, and Mary Somerville, the famous scientist and mathematician.

Mary Somerville discovered algebra by accident in a fashion magazine. She became determined to learn about the curious x's and y's which were a complete mystery to her circle of friends. Despite having a family which thoroughly disapproved of women being educated in anything other than sewing, and an equally unhelpful husband, Mary was able to acquire the resources she needed to study mathematics in depth. She went on to publish a number of important works on physical, molecular and microscopic sciences. She is known as one of the greatest women scientists England ever produced, and during her long and vigorous life (she was still studying mathematics until the day of her death at the age of ninety-two) Mary worked actively for women's rights. It was Mary Somerville who first introduced Ada to Charles Babbage. When she took Ada to see Babbage's Difference Engine, Ada immediately understood its workings and recognized it as a valuable tool for science and mathematics.

Babbage was greatly impressed with Ada and asked her to help him on the machine he was working on known as the Analytical Engine. Unfortunately the engine's design was so far ahead of its time that it was impossible to build. The thousands of moving parts (which nowadays would be replaced by silicon chips) could not be manufactured accurately enough, so the machine could not be completed. Ada's contribution was to provide conceptual programming ideas for Babbage's machines. She published "Sketch of the Analytical Engine" in 1843, essentially describing the world's first software program and the first set of sophisticated coding instructions. Ada Lovelace was in fact the world's first computer programmer. Ada went on to develop in her writings the "loop" and "subroutine" concepts – a century before electronic computing machines appeared.

Ann Milbank was continually on the look out for any of the nasty traits of her estranged husband which her daughter Ada might have inherited. Mathematics was considered to be a suitable antidote for the overheated imagination of the adolescent. As Mathematics and Natural Philosophy (also encouraged) have "no connection with the feelings of life; they cannot, by any possibility, lead to objectionable thoughts" (Stein: 1995, 5). Despite this underlying repressiveness, Ada found in mathematics not only a connection to her mother through logic and reason, but also a connection to her intuitive and playful side – mathematics in fact encouraged the so-called Byronic influence which bothered her mother so!

Ada did not regard mathematics as a science of cold hard facts, distant and authoritative, as her mother encouraged her to. Instead she preferred to look for relationships between numbers, referring to algebraic symbols as "mathematical sprites and fairies" (Lewis: 1992). She saw mathematics as a language and herself as the translator. She described it "not merely as a vast body of abstract and immutable truths" but rather as the vehicle through which humans "express the great facts of the natural world" (Lewis: 1992). She related to mathematics in a playful and interactive way and realized in her later years that "her greatest mathematical achievements had come, not from the exercise of pure reason, but from insight, imagination, and intuition" (Lewis: 1992).

Ada Lovelace was remarkable in the way that she anticipated the role that computers would play in society, a hundred years before the electronic computer was invented. She understood that the computer would always be limited in that it could not originate ideas for itself, but would be a tool for assisting people to do whatever they wanted. Ada even anticipated computer-generated music – she may well have envisaged a network for gathering and dispersing information which today we call the Internet. Unfortunately, scandal marred the last few years of Ada's life. She and Babbage, both avid horse-racing followers, developed a code for a betting system. The scheme ended disastrously and Ada lost a great deal of money. She was forced to sell the family jewels and suffered deeply from remorse as a result. Ada Lovelace died in 1852 of cancer of the uterus. She was only thirty-six years old. After her death she was virtually forgotten until computers started to play an important role following World War II, and her work was rediscovered. In 1977 Ada Lovelace's memory was honoured when a computer programming language was named after her. "Ada" was built for the US Department of Defense for use in control systems, such as aircraft navigation.

The first computer

During World War II teams of scientists were working in the United States, Germany and Britain on ideas for an electronic computer. Electricity and the vacuum tube had been available from the 1890s but the war generated a renewed interest in technology.

They were working on inventions which were supposedly closely guarded secrets, but the teams located in different parts of the world came up with the same ideas at the same time. Amongst the first computers to be built were ENIAC, at the University of Pennsylvania, and Harvard Mark I and Mark II at Harvard University. The Harvard Mark I was an electromechanical tabulator built by Howard Aiken. Aiken was assisted by a mathematics professor named Grace Hopper, who had joined the military section of WAVES (Women Accepted for Voluntary Emergency Service) after a surge of patriotism, and graduated as a commissioned lieutenant. Grace was assigned to work at Harvard with Aiken on the Bureau of Ordnance and Computation Project. Here she learned to program the first large-scale digital computer. The Mark I was really a recreation of Babbage's Analytical Engine, except that it was an electromechanical device which used an electric current to operate switches. The large machine was considered most unsightly and computations were very slow and very noisy. In keeping with the times, an attractive art deco façade was created which gave the Mark I a futuristic appearance and brought computers to the attention of the wider community.

Portable calculator carried by young woman, 1920s. *Burroughs Corp. Records Collection at the Charles Babbage Institute.*

Meet the grandmother of COBOL

Grace Hopper was working on the Harvard Mark II on the day a moth got caught up in the circuitry. The poor moth caused a malfunction and had to be removed, inadvertently introducing the term "debugging" into computer language in reference to incidents where a function needs to be put right. The deceased moth was saved and it now rests in the Naval Museum in Dahlgren, Virginia. However Grace is not remembered only for her part in the "debugging" incident: she was a visionary in the field of computer programming. At the time, computers were being programmed to use mathematical symbols, not words. In 1959, while Grace was working on the ENIAC project at the University of Pennsylvania, she suggested an idea which was previously thought to be impossible. She proposed that programs could be written in English and then translated into machine code. She and her co-workers were able to build a pilot model which was subsequently developed and came to be known as COBOL. Grace Hopper is often referred to as the grandmother of COBOL, the first program which used English words instead of mathematical symbols.

Grace Hopper's technical vision made her a pioneer in her field. She foresaw the application of artificial intelligence and contributed many ideas and tools

Grace Hopper, named "Man of the Year", 1969.
TAPs Photo Gallery of Women and Computers.

which are now commonly used in computing. She was admired and respected also for her tireless energy and her willingness to teach and support young people. She was one of the most requested speakers in computing. In 1986, at the age of eighty, Rear Admiral Grace Hopper was the oldest commissioned officer in the US Navy on active duty.

Grace Hopper has received numerous awards for her work, including honorary degrees from some fifty universities. In 1969, the Data Processing Management Association named her "Man of the Year". As a tribute to this inspiring and brilliant woman, the Grace Hopper Celebration of Women in Computing, a highly successful conference for women in the computer industry, was held in the spring of 1994.

Programming: a job for women?

During World War II, when the computer revolution really took off, the programmers were nearly all women. Programmers were called either "calculators" or "computers" and women were often stereotyped as being good candidates for the job. "Programming requires lots of patience, persistence and a capacity for detail and those are the traits that many girls have" (Seligsohn: 1967, 47).

The earliest computers, including the Harvard Mark I and Mark II, could only store and run one program at a time. By the late 1950s the ENIAC project developed the EDVAC computer which could store and run more than one program. Kathleen McNulty was one of ENIAC's first programmers. The war gave women a great opportunity to work in technical fields like computing, when previously the only work open to them had been teaching or nursing. Women like Kathleen, though respected, were not expected to achieve higher professional ratings unless there were no available men to fill the posts. As the war drew on, fewer and fewer men were available and women took up senior positions. It was an exhilarating and exciting time, and a wonderful opportunity for the enthusiastic and innovative women involved. Judy Clapp, a programmer for Whirlwind, and Mildred Koss of UNIVAC felt themselves to be at the forefront of a new era. Judy Clapp notes that they were "working day and night, inventing as we went" (Seligsohn: 1967, 48). Mildred observed "There were no limitations on what you could accomplish. There was lots of vision and new ideas as to where the computer might be used . . . It had some rules and operating system, but it was up to you to do whatever you wanted it to do" (Seligsohn: 1967, 48). With Grace Hopper as her supervisor at UNIVAC, it is not surprising that Mildred Koss was caught up in the pioneering spirit of the time. In later years Mildred was employed by the Control Data Corporation where she worked with a team which developed the first graphics algorithms.

Patsy Simmers, Gail Taylor, Milly Beck and Norma Stec holding early computer boards.
US Army Photo 163-12-62.

From the 1950s onwards, smaller and cheaper computers were being developed. One of the first computers, the ENIAC, used 18,000 valves (which generated a great deal of heat and only lasted a short time) and weighed 30 tons. The invention of the transistor revolutionized the entire science of electronics. In 1958 the development of the semi-conductor chip made of silicon resulted in the printed or integrated circuit board (containing hundreds of millions of tiny transistors) which is integral to any electrical appliance. Early computers could not be connected to each other as they are today. A technique called "time-sharing", which used special telephone lines using on/off pulses, made it possible to connect several typewriter terminals to one computer. This allowed one computer's power to be spread to several others. Whirlwind, developed by Massachusetts Institute of Technology, was the first computer to use time-sharing. There were several women involved in its initial development and Judy Clapp was one of them. In the early fifties Judy received an M.Sc. degree in applied science from Harvard and she went on to work as a programmer on the Whirlwind. She helped to program a prototype of an air defence system that received impetus from radar, tracked flying aircraft, and directed the courses of other aircraft. This was one of the first non-numerical applications for computers. Judy Clapp went on to be part of a team which developed the first set of software tools for large teams of people to co-ordinate writing, integrating testing and maintaining a large system.

Ester Gerston (standing) and Gloria Gorden
wiring the right side of ENIAC with a new programme.
US Army photo from the archives of the ARL Technical Library.

In the 1960s engineers devised a way to connect a computer's digital data into a form which could be carried by ordinary telephone lines. Hence the Modulator-Demodulator or the "modem" was invented, causing another revolution in computer communications. A modem is the piece of hardware which enables anyone with access to a computer and a telephone line in their home or workplace to be connected to the Internet. It helps also to have a personal computer, a computer which is small enough to sit on a desk in your home or office. The PC, as it is known, came into being in 1972 when MIT released a portable computer costing only $US397. Other companies quickly took up the challenge and soon the Apple computer took the world by storm with its "friendly" design and relative ease of use. In 1981 IBM developed its own version of the PC and the PC has continued to stay in the forefront of the technology. MS-DOS, developed by Bill Gates, became the first successful operating system for PCs. The Apple Macintosh arrived in 1984 and it is still favoured by many home users. Apple built the first battery-powered portable computer in 1991 and nowadays many computer users rely on small "laptops" which can be used unobtrusively in cafés or on a park bench by the sea.

Women using the Net today

Statistics tell us that women represent a significantly lower percentage of Internet users than men, although the gap is slowly closing. Computer technology still has the power to intimidate women (or bore them) but more importantly, women are under-represented because we have less opportunity to have access and information enabling us to make use of the Internet. The situation is changing all the time. In Australia there is talk of giving all children laptops and Internet training as part of their school curriculum. It seems unlikely when the reality is that many disadvantaged children do not even receive adequate education. However, it is a fact that children in economically advantaged countries are on the whole accustomed to having computers in their homes and schools, and girls and boys alike are confident using them as both learning tools and for entertainment. Many of the next adult generation won't be burdened with a lack of knowledge and understanding of computer technology and many of the "experts" and Internet gurus will be women. (For a more comprehensive discussion on this subject, see Spender: 1995).

The good news is that many women are already experts, making innovative use of the Internet, and they are making it their business to inspire others to do the same. Ever heard of Vsisters, Lesbian.org, Geekgirl, Women'space or the Electronic Witches? Perhaps not, but by the end of this chapter you'll know all about these five adventurous enterprises as well as a host of others – women who have been empowered by the Net and who delight in passing on their knowledge to others as quickly as they can – and you can't get information around the globe much faster than via the Internet!

Electronic Witches:
Internet training and activism in Croatia

The international mass media has allowed people throughout the world to be regularly informed about the political violence which has devastated former Yugoslavia. Television allows us to "see" how it really is, and radio and print media give us first hand accounts from "fearless" reporters. However, the mass media are notorious for presenting only part of the story and for leaving out the experiences of 50 per cent of the population. Women's voices are rarely heard during times of war and when they are mentioned at all it is usually in the context of "women, children and the elderly". Women are usually seen in the context of their victimization, as victims of rape or displaced as refugees. Sensationalist pictures aimed to shock and horrify appear on our television screens, but these photographers' and reporters' interpretations of women's lives seem only to separate us from the reality of each individual's unique situation. Fortunately we don't need to rely solely on the mass media to bring us accurate information and a broader perspective. Thanks to the Internet, reliable information and intimate accounts of life in a war torn country, can be dispersed throughout the world.

The Internet is alive and well in the former Yugoslavia, and email services allow friends and families, separated by blockades, to communicate freely. Electronic Witches, which operates from Zagreb, was set up in 1994 by two women to broaden women's access to electronic mail. The project has been phenomenally successful, due to the hard work and resourcefulness of its remaining co-founder, Kathryn Turnipseed, and to the willingness of the women of the former Yugoslavia to embrace new technology.

In the short time I have been acquainted (by email) with Kathryn Turnipseed I have developed an enormous respect for her. A woman who can give up a successful career as a commercial banker in New York to take on the task of working for women's human rights and information technology training in Croatia, in the midst of a full-scale war, is a woman to be greatly admired. Actually, I'm dying to meet her! As a commercial banker, learning about corporate finance and the ways that multi-national corporations operate, Kathryn came to realize that she wasn't suited to the meaningless environment of the banking world. She became active in the feminist Women's Action Coalition (WAC) and, in 1992, helped to organize a street demonstration in New York protesting against the use of rape as a weapon of war. She then worked with MADRE, bringing together women from throughout the world to speak out on the issue. Through WAC and MADRE Kathryn met a wide group of women working on human rights, including those involved with groups in Bosnia and Herzegovina, Serbia and Croatia. The opportunity to change her life came when the bank "downsized" in 1993 and Kathryn volunteered to be made redundant.

Thus, with money saved from her job and time on her side, Kathryn set off for a tour of Eastern Europe. At that time she had no intention of going to the former Yugoslavia: after all, "there's war going on" (Turnipseed: 1996a). A chance meeting with a young man from Zagreb resulted in a serious change of plans. He persuaded her to visit his country, saying "war is localised, it is not all over Croatia. He invited me for a holiday on the Island of Hvar" (Turnipseed: 1996a). On their way to Hvar, on the Dalmatian coast, the pair stopped in Zagreb. Here Kathryn found the women she'd met in New York through MADRE. She agreed to help them out at the Women's Information and Documentation Centre for a couple of weeks, with translation and fundraising. More than two years have gone by and Kathryn's still in Zagreb and writes, "I have yet to experience the island of Hvar" (Turnipseed: 1996a).

In June 1994, after six months at the centre, Kathryn left to establish (with co-founder Cecilia Poulson, who unfortunately had to return to England to study)

Electronic Witches and B.a.B.e. (Be active Be emancipated – the women's human rights group), in Croatia. The Electronic Witch project was set up to give women the opportunity to learn about email, to give them access to equipment, and to set up a network whereby those who had learned the ropes could go on to train others. They have trained more than one hundred women who represent the Centre for Women War Victims, Arkadia and the Centre for Girls in Serbia, the Anti-War Campaign in Croatia, Doctors of the World, and the Council for Defense of Human Rights and Freedom, to name just a few organizations. They produced gender-sensitive training materials and co-authored a user's guide to the communications software. Electronic Witches provided modems for six groups, and installed software and set up user accounts for many others. They work closely with the Zamir network, the email network originally set up by anti-war campaigners in Zagreb and international activists, which now provides vital communication links throughout the former Yugoslavia. Kathryn writes "the establishment of the Zamir Network is a testimony to individual creativity, commitment and perseverance" (Turnipseed: 1996b).

Women's use of and access to email technology is fundamental to the Electronic Witch project. Kathryn writes, "As is common throughout the world, email technology on the Zamir network reflects the masculine culture of technology. The system was designed and developed by men and then the services were made available to women. Male dominance of this technology is not the same as purposeful discrimination against women and availability is not the same as access" Turnipseed: 1996b). She identifies three components to having access to email technology: "Hardware and software must be obtained, motivation and ownership must be developed, and confidence raised" (Turnipseed: 1996b). I was surprised to learn that equipment is not in short supply in most cities in the former Yugoslavia. Although there are difficulties in getting many kinds of goods, people have become very resourceful. International aid and grassroots organizations have provided a great deal of support, often enabling non-government organizations in the region to acquire the most up-to-date equipment available. If you have the money, you can buy computer equipment. However, Kathryn points out that "women's groups – as everywhere in the world – are challenged to get funding for their projects". Kathryn is dismayed that issues concerning censorship and the possibilities of the World Wide Web dominate discussions in North America and Western Europe while "so many people I know would be thrilled to have access to email!" (Turnipseed: 1996c).

Women generally have had little support in accessing traditional forms of media and therefore in giving public expression to their views. Feeling alienated from the mass media, we are understandably suspicious of electronic forms of communication and this has contributed to our under-representation in email communities. Kathryn's work with Electronic Witches has allowed a core group of women throughout the former Yugoslavia to become contributors to email communities and therefore to help change the gender balance. Kathryn encourages her core group of email users to harness other forms of communication to distribute and share ingoing and outgoing information. Networking and creating links in this way allows electronic communications to become a powerful tool for all, rather than just for those in privileged positions with access to the equipment.

Kathryn is optimistic that women can move into the centre of electronic networks in a way that has not been possible with other communication media. Electronic Witches has been successful in a region where women suffer extreme marginalization and where any form of communication has been, until recently, fraught with difficulties. Motivation is the key. Kathryn's experiences in Croatia show how with training and access to equipment and the encouragement to overcome our fears, women can use the new communications technology to make a difference to the way society views

You can email Electronic Witches:

electronicwitches_zg@zamir-zg.ztn.apc.org

Virtual Sisterhood: a support network and vital link to women's resources

Virtual Sisterhood is a network dedicated to supporting and strengthening women's use of electronic communications. Primarily focused on women organized in groups, Virtual Sisterhood works as a meeting point for sharing strategies, overcoming problems and broadening our understanding and use of the technology. Virtual Sisterhood aims to assist the global women's movement by promoting the many women-created on-line resources already available and encouraging women's organizations to make fuller use of electronic communications. Since it was formed, in January 1995, Virtual Sisterhood has proven to be an invaluable resource for women throughout the world. It is accessed by women's organizations in countries as widespread as Nicaragua, Bulgaria, Japan, Poland, the former Yugoslavia, and Sweden. If you are part of a group, large or small, and haven't already visited Vsisters (as they are fondly known), be sure to do so. You'll get advice, you can join discussion forums, and read the latest publication of Sea Change, Vsisters' newsletter.

Vsisters' founder, Barbara Ann O'Leary, hails from Metuchen, a town in the state of New Jersey. She lives with her husband in a 130-year-old former farmhouse. With a background of ten years as a professional stage manager, Barbara Ann is well accustomed to organizing and networking people. During our recent email conversation, Barbara Ann wrote, "I've always had a strong interest in facilitating communication, in freedom of expression" (O'Leary: 1996).

After working for three years with the international women's advocacy organization, WEDO (Women's Environment and Development Organization)

Barbara Ann saw the need for a resource enabling women's groups to make better use of the Internet. She realized the potential electronic communications held for women activists to organize themselves and to communicate more effectively with each other and the wider community. Women face many difficulties when it comes to making use of the electronic media – for instance, lack of training and access to the Internet are real problems – but these can often be addressed and tackled head on. Barbara Ann does just that through effectively networking women with particular needs with those who have the skills or knowledge to give assistance. She creates links throughout the world with women who otherwise would have had no way of communicating with each other, and perhaps no other way of resolving their problems.

Vsisters is helping to break down language barriers on-line by giving assistance to women's groups worldwide to make resources available in their native languages as well as in translation. Volunteers offer their time and expertise to make this project, and many other Vsisters' initiatives, work effectively. Vsisters assists the Electronic Witch project in former Yugoslavia and helped *Women'space*, the feminist newsletter from Canada, get off the ground. Vsisters travelled to Beijing in 1995 where it participated in the Fourth World Conference on Women. Discussions, conference resources, accounts from various participants and linkages to other "Beijing" related sites can be found by clicking on *What's New At* at Vsisters' Web site. *Sea Change* is a newsletter available in print and on-line which shares stories about how women throughout the world are using electronic communications technology "to network, publish and change the world" (O'Leary: 1995).

Vsisters is affiliated to Womensnet which is a member of the Association for Progressive Communications (APC). Other members are EcoNet, ConflictNet, PeaceNet and Labornet. The APC provides training, support and information for its members. You can obtain more information on Womensnet by emailing to

womensnet-info@igc.apc.org

Barbara Ann believes that the Internet can help to strengthen communities. She writes "Online communications encourage a new sense of community – across boundaries of time, geography and other barriers. It does not replace or impede other methods of community building. In fact, it can be a real strengthener of local community ties" (O'Leary: 1996).

Find friends and allies at Vsisters

The number of women's groups using the Internet grows daily. Knowing they're there, somewhere, is encouraging but it's useful to know where to find them, and that's often the hard part. To make life easier, Vsisters is encouraging women's groups and organizations to make use of their Global Directory (*Women's Organizations and Electronic Communications – A Global Directory*). It's distributed on the Web and via computer disc, and is available in print also. The more groups make use of this global network, the more useful it becomes. If you're part of an organization or you have a project you'd like other women to know about, why not become part of the Global Directory. To see who's already listed and to find out how to get on board yourself, visit Vsisters' Web site at

http://www.igc.apc.org/vsister/

Virtual Sisters Online Strategies – a mailing list

Many women are using Virtual Sisters Online Strategies mailing list (known as vs-online-strat) as an open forum to discuss their group's involvement with electronic communities. It's a great place to meet others with similar interests, to work on strategies, and to discover a diversity of views and experiences. You'll get help with technical problems and advice on making the Internet work better for you. Vs-online-strat is about networking – soon you'll be sharing your experiences, helping one another out with sticky problems, planning strategies for development and discussing how to link up with other media. The idea is to broaden our understanding of on-line communications and to learn from each other. Rhonda Sim was lurking on vs-online-strat for weeks before she took the plunge and posted a request for help. She works in Nicaragua and Costa Rica for women's NGOs and she's investigating the possibility of getting all of their fifty volunteers throughout South America on-line. It's a big project, but with Virtual Sisters' help, no doubt the task will be made easier.

To subscribe to vs-online-strat email to: **majordomo@igc.apc.org**
Put this text into the body of the message: **subscribe vs-online-strat**

Rural women: combating isolation, strengthening ties

The Internet can make a huge difference to women living in remote and rural areas. Christene Capel lives 100 kilometres north-west of Longreach, Queensland, in such a remote area that her twice-weekly mail service simply stops when it rains and stays that way until the roads dry up sufficiently for the mail van to get through. Keeping informed and in contact with the outside world for political, professional and friendship reasons is vital for women like Chris who are living in isolated parts of the world. Since being introduced to the Internet, Chris now taps into a resource which is a great deal cheaper than the telephone and a lot more efficient than a mail service. Now she regards it as a critical communications medium for people living in remote areas.

When Chris embarked on a graduate diploma in teaching and librarianship, she found she couldn't get by without using a computer at home. As part of her course, she was introduced to the Internet (electronic mail). Having regarded computers with disdain and scepticism, Chris found the advantages of being connected to the Internet in a remote grazing district a good reason for reassessing her attitude. The prospects for communication were immediately apparent. Now she hopes all her family members will eventually have email. Her parents, sister and brother live in Kempsey, Perth and the Snowy Mountains respectively, so telephone bills tend to be huge. Chris is dreading the day that her daughter and son leave to attend boarding school in Toowoomba (1200 km away). "I would love to see email contact between home and boarding school . . . This would be one cheap way to overcome the gap between home and school while kids learn vital computer skills and mothers are kept sane!!!" (Capel: 1995). Interesting to note that the computer so recently disdained by Chris is now regarded as vital for her children's education!

Chris believes that there are very few rural women as yet on-line in Australia because the technology is relatively new and women are only now beginning to realize the benefits. Inadequate phone-lines are a major hurdle. There is a scarcity of technical knowledge, as with any new technology, and for a group notorious for "making do" under difficult conditions, it is understandable that people quickly become disenchanted with a system that may require support from an "expert". In isolated conditions "technophobia" can be overpowering to some people, leading them to deny the benefits of the Internet. Although, as Chris points out, "rural women have proved to be quick to adapt to the usage of new technologies such as fax machines for business and other purposes" (Capel: 1996). She believes that information about the Internet and how it can be useful for people living in the country has been badly disseminated to rural women (and men also). There's the factor too, of women simply not having enough time to learn the skills. Women tend to take on a huge workload in the country. There may be children to tutor during the day, off-property work and unpaid community work, meals to prepare for family members and hired workers, secretarial and management tasks as well as outdoor mustering and gardening, to name but a few of the daily tasks. There's not a lot of time left for learning new skills!

Despite the problems, women in remote rural areas are slowly being converted to using on-line communications. Many, like Chris, were forced to use the Internet as part of university courses done by correspondence. Some Distance Education centres are hooking up children to their teachers through email, with mothers often taking on the task of being their home tutors. This way mums (or sisters) learn all about the Internet and become enthusiastic as they realize the possibilities for gathering information and communicating with people more easily not only on nearby properties but throughout the entire world.

A number of women in rural Queensland had the opportunity to learn more about the Internet as a result of a research project (funded by Telstra) conducted by Margaret Grace and two colleagues at the Queensland University of Technology. The project trialled the use of interactive TV and email for providing information to rural women. They had video link-ups throughout Queensland and one in Canada, where a similar trial was being conducted, and a panel of information specialists in Brisbane. During the TV program they looked at legal and health issues as well as communication for rural women, and an email trial was advertised. While many women were unable to get on-line and participate fully in the email trial (due to phone problems and a lack of confidence with the technology), Chris was one of the lucky ones and she found the experience extremely useful and thoroughly enjoyable. Women learned to "talk" to each other using mailboxes. Some have formed on-line friendships and continue to "talk" to each other regularly this way. Chris' daughter found herself a French-speaking Canadian "keypal".

Margaret Grace's research reveals that rural women have been eager to embrace new technologies, but technical problems and the lack of a supportive infrastructure continue to be major obstacles when it comes to taking up computer-mediated technologies. Fortunately, the research project has been funded, under a grant by the Australian Research Council, for another two years which will give more rural women the opportunity to have an Internet experience (Grace: 1996).

As a result of the trials, the women were contacted by the Women's Policy Unit from the Queensland State Government, which gave them information and support. Chris has been asked to be part of a women's email group called Women-in-Touch which will help direct the unit's policy. Previously it would have been impossible to participate in such a group, but now Chris and other rural women have the opportunity to be part of ongoing discussions and ultimately to influence policy – without having to leave home.

Chris subscribes to several mailing lists relating to teacher-librarianship, gender issues in computer-mediated communication, sheep and various rural women's interest groups. Through Vsisters' mailing list vs-online-strat, Chris participates in a lively discussion on the difficulties of rural women's access to the Internet. Unfortunately, those in rural areas pay a lot more for their Internet connection than those of us who live in the city. Some areas have their own local service provider, but otherwise country people find the gulf between city and rural prices steadily widening. When you consider that in remote places mail services are irregular and telephone calls expensive, it is clear the people living there are the most in need of a cheap, reliable communications network.

Despite high access charges and the problems of lack of technical support and inadequate phone-lines, Chris is a complete advocate of the Internet. "It really can break down some barriers . . . Without it [Internet] I would shrivel and die quite frankly. The Internet has been a godsend for me!" (Capel: 1995).

Women'space: a feminist zine from rural Canada

We're moving now to Canada to visit Jo Sutton and Scarlet Pollock on their organic farm in rural Nova Scotia. Here Jo and Scarlet publish *Women'space*, amid the idyllic surroundings of 40 acres of farmed land set amidst an endless forest of spruce, fir, maple and poplars. Always on hand to give assistance when needed are three dogs, seven cats, ten goats, four cows, three sows and an assortment of ducks, geese and chickens. Women's issues, particularly the prevention of discrim-ination on the grounds of race, class, sexual orientation disability and age, are the focus of *Women'space*. It's a news-sheet by, for and about women. It started out as a resource for the local area, but now focuses on a larger community, while still aiming to be Canadian-centred. *Women'space* is published on the Web as well as on paper and is distributed to women's organizations throughout Canada.

After discovering the Internet and finding loads of information and a supportive women's network already in place, Scarlet and Jo were motivated to share their positive experiences with others. They volunteered to help local women's groups get on the Net. Living in a rural area, they experienced the usual difficulties – lack of equipment, little support for women in a male-dominated field, technophobia, and so on. However, with encouragement and tutoring from Virtual Sisterhood's *WWW Development Team*, particularly Barbara Ann O'Leary and Mary Trounstine, three months down the track Scarlet and Jo proudly published their first newsletter.

December 1995   Volume 1 Number 3

Women'space reflects a long association with radical feminism. Jo and Scarlet have been active feminists since the early days of the Women's Liberation Movement. In the last few decades the feminist movement has undergone changes in emphasis and many setbacks. Jo and Scarlet have found that amongst sisters in cyberspace the spirit of generosity is reminiscent of those heady days of the 1970s. In their Web page they write, "Networking, activism and support are interwoven as we push ourselves to learn to work with the new electronic tools we are encountering" (Pollock and Sutton: 1995). Women grappling head on with new technology, being involved right now as a new phase in communication takes off, gives us a sense that "there is reason to hope, to raise our expectations" (Pollock and Sutton: 1995).

Looking through the four volumes of *Women'space* on the Web it's clear that, unlike some of the new breed of sisters I've encountered on the Net, these two don't fit into the "netchick" or "cyber grrrl" category. There's no hype, they're not trying to impress us with smart tough-girl talk or liberal views. Take a look at *Netchick*, a recent book about Internet resources by Carla Sinclair described as being for "young, hip and post-feminist women" (Simpson: 1996), and you'll immediately see the difference. The work of Jo and Scarlet is grounded in activism for real change, for women and society as a whole, addressing issues like violence and poverty. Carla and her admirers appear to have embraced the new technology in order to be outrageous, to shock, and to ultimately behave in the same ways that men do – and they imagine they're being radical.

Volume 3, which appeared in January 1996 starts with a general rundown on feminist culture in cyberspace, discussing the Net's potential for democracy, where a diversity of women's voices can be heard. There are useful discussions on the use of the Internet in schools, with a piece from Nancy Barkhouse who teaches at Atlantic View Elementary School. Nancy tells us how her kids put together a Web page, and we share something of the pride they felt in being the first class in Nova Scotia to do so. Education for grown-ups, deaf kids, science for girls, Indian schools on the Web, computer games designed for girls – these are a few exciting areas discussed. As Scarlet and Jo write, "If you've ever had doubts about whether it's worthwhile to get on the Internet, these sites will be more than convincing.

They are dynamite! Packed full of ideas, resources and geared to extend your global knowledge horizons, they will knock you flat" (Pollock and Sutton: 1996).

Other articles include "Making Diversity Work", where Doreen of the Nova Scotia Advisory Council on the Status of Women has the opportunity to write about her role as a council member. Doreen has been involved in setting up a local women's centre, she's worked on a program for men to change their abusive behaviour, and she co-ordinated the pilot "Barriers" project, which addresses "the barriers faced by black women in dealing with violence in their everyday lives" (Doreen: 1996).

Justine Kiwanuka, from Disabled People's International, attended the UN Fourth World Conference on Women which was held in Beijing during September of 1995. Justine's article, "The Disability Network in Beijing", discusses the Network which was formed in preparation for the conference "to unite and build a strong voice of women with disabilities around the world" (Kiwanuka: 1996). Disabled people faced many challenges at the conference, including access problems (which were compounded by the incessant rain), but the opportunity to network with others and deal with the many issues that had brought thousands of women together at the conference made it worthwhile. The Beijing Conference unfortunately received a lot of negative press in Australia. The mass media chose to highlight divisions, and to ridicule workshops like "Lesbian flirting techniques"; male reporters seized the opportunity to expound their misogynist views. If you want to know what really happened, you'll find many first-hand accounts on the Net, and you'll discover women who found the connections they made at the conference invaluable.

Volume 4 of *Women'space* features an expanded editorial board and focuses on violence against women in the community as well as issues on developments on the Net and across the country. Scarlet's article "What Do Women Activists Do Online?" discusses the ways in which activists can use the Internet for brainstorming and networking, for showing our care and concern for others via email letters, for promoting resources and ultimately to take action. Scarlet makes the point that "Because we do not physically see each other, what matters is what women say. This leads to a greater diversity, where contributions are equally weighted as they would be in an ideal group" (Pollock: 1996). Judy Michaus writes in "Why Run a Web Site?" that the time for women to use the Internet as an activist tool is now and "If you don't, the peril belongs to all of us: women may well lose the opportunity to profoundly affect the nature of the Web, the world and the quality of our lives" (Michaud: 1996). It remains to be seen whether the advent of new information technology will actually result in a real difference in women's lives, but the Internet does seem to have generated a great deal of hope. With a feeling of hope comes a new outpouring of ideas and actions, and the possibility of change.

Also discussed in Volume 4 are resources available in support of battered women, with Web addresses and an overview of the best sites. Because of the element of secrecy inherent in the Internet, women who are victims of abuse may find it the safest medium for securing vital help and advice. Already some public libraries around Australia are offering free Internet facilities, providing women with a safe place to search for information, without any evidence of them having done so.

Women'space is published quarterly in paper form and can be mailed throughout Canada ($15) and the US ($14) and also to international subscribers at a cost of $19 Canadian. Jo and Scarlet sent us a copy of Volume 4 and we have to say it is the most comprehensive and useful Internet magazine for women we've found. *Women'space* has its home at: **RR#1, Scotsburn, Nova Scotia, Canada B0K 1R0.**

One of the things I like about the *Women'space* Web site is that they've put all the articles on one "page". Rather than making a list of linked addresses, as is the usual format for newsletter-style pages, *Women'space* has retained a more linear format. You can save the newsletter as one file or document and print it in one go. *Women'space* on-line magazine can be found on the Web at:

> http://www.softaid.net/cathy/vsister/w-space/womspce.html

You can email Scarlet and Jo at: **diamond@fox.nstn.ca**

Geekgirl: an inspirational zine

Have a look in your local newsagent and you'll be surprised at the number of glossy (and often expensive) magazines devoted to the Internet. Some of them have incredible graphics, and most have useful articles regarding how to use particular Internet services. The controversy over censorship of the Internet is hotly debated in these magazines, while at the same time the topic of sex on and off the Internet is widely featured. Addresses for on-line pornographic magazines as well as places to find prostitutes are divulged. Sex sells, and the producers of these magazines are more than happy to take advantage of this. While appearing to take issues seriously surrounding the availability of explicit and offensive material on the Internet, they show their true colours by actively promoting this material. Don't expect many women writers to feature in these mainstream magazines and don't expect much of specific interest to women. Luckily, one talented and driven young woman has taken on the boys in a highly successful way with a magazine she calls *geekgirl*. Rosie Cross lives in Newtown, a suburb of Sydney where, according to Rosie herself "everyone looks feral and smells!" (Cross: 1995). Not surprisingly, Rosie spends most of her time in front of her computer, putting together her magazine which appears on-line as well as on paper.

Rosie describes *geekgirl* as "an inspirational zine which aims to inspire aspiring geekgirls to hop on board" (Cross: 1995). Each issue takes on a direction of its own and includes a diversity of feminist comment. Rosie thinks of *geekgirl* as "a persona and publication which more than anything else opened up the debate about gender online at the same time offering a broad-ranging wicked read for both men and women" (Cross: 1995). *Geekgirl* is featured in Internet magazines not only in Australia but also in the United States, and Rosie is widely acclaimed as a true pioneer and an inspiration to others.

Rosie has been on-line for six years, almost as long as the Internet has been available to the public in Australia. Like many women who now embrace the Internet as a communication and information-sharing resource, Rosie had no background at all in computing. She's been involved in community radio (she has a B.A. in communication, majoring in radio) video and "wanky art stuff" (Cross: 1995) as well as a variety of women's groups and women's welfare services.

Geekgirl has sustained Rosie's interest for two years, which is pretty phenomenal considering she usually loses interest in a project after only three months. *Geekgirl* and the World Wide Web have allowed Rosie to incorporate into one package her three major interests – print, radio and video. New developments in Internet technology will no doubt open up more exciting opportunities. For a woman like Rosie, who has a constant thirst for new geekish things, the possibilities for developing the *geekgirl* project are as boundless as the technology itself.

geekgirl

issue five - hysteria

issue four - mermaids and myths

issue three - broadband

Geekgirl is virtually a one-woman band, though boyfriend, Rob Joyner, "a real geek, known affectionately as Mr. Wallpaper helps out with some of the real nifty graphics" (Cross: 1995). It's a project which requires money (bandwidth charges, printing costs for the hard copy) and one which doesn't as yet generate much on its own. In order to make it all possible, Rosie spends all of her time working on *geekgirl*: she not only puts together the zines but she also manufactures *geekgirl* Tshirts, computer covers and stickers. The reality is she needs sponsorship and advertising to keep going "til the new mechanisms of digicash or e-money are put in place, and people can trust and rely on them in terms of security and reliability" (Cross: 1995).

Geekgirl does not have a particular target audience and feedback seems to show that it attracts around a 60:40 female–male ratio. "I am not out to create an audience, largely geekgirl has created its own, and I am delighted to say it's huge, global and 99.9% of that audience is thrilled with each issue and leave encouraging remarks and motivate me to push on" (Cross: 1995). Putting out a quality product is high on Rosie's agenda and, judging by the feedback, she is certainly achieving that. For Rosie it is "blissfully pleasing that my publication has allowed the cyberfeminist agenda to be high on the list of netizens to talk about and be aware of" (Cross: 1995).

Geekgirl has something for everyone

Rosie Cross has a way with words: she's smart, she's hip, and she's not afraid to say what she likes. Don't be fooled by the "cyberchick" attitude (Rosie is a self-confessed brat!), *geekgirl* offers an enjoyable read, even for the more conservative reader. Rosie recently interviewed the first female professor of information technology in Australia, Professor Joan Cooper of the University of Wollongong. Joan carried out a survey on "Australian Women on the 'Net" and made some interesting and revealing discoveries. According to Joan, women throughout Australia are using the Net and loving it! Joan's advice to those who are holding back, often because of negative propaganda generated around problems such as pornography and harassment, is to just get on and do it. You'll find this interview in Volume 4 of *geekgirl*.

While visiting Volume 4, entitled "Mermaids, Myths and Tales", you'll discover an array of interviews and articles, some quirky and fun, others (like the one with Joan Cooper) more serious and educational. I especially enjoyed "The Mermaids of Sarah Parker" in which Sarah, a painter, shares stories of mermaids through the ages. Did you know they were once revered and worshipped by the people of ancient Greece and Egypt? There's an article on flaming, and another called "Women Who Surf", which reveals that the first Australian surfer was a woman. In case you're wondering, that's surfing with a surfboard, not a keyboard!

Kaz Cooke, a cartoonist and Australian feminist icon, whose work regularly features in Melbourne and Sydney daily newspapers, appears in Volume 5 of *geekgirl*. She talks to Rosie about her new CD and the impracticability of high-heeled shoes for women. Stories from a variety of writers appear including a first-hand account of the diet/beauty trap that so many young women fall into, often resulting in severe illnesses like anorexia and bulimia.

Rosie's fascination and skills with new Internet technologies mean that each issue of *geekgirl* includes the latest features the technology offers. This makes for a visually exciting experience each time you click on to a new issue. All the better that *geekgirl* brings with it a feminist agenda which aims to inspire women and provide us with an alternative. You can find *geekgirl* at:

http://www.geekgirl.com.au

Lesbian.org and Women Online: meet the multi-talented Amy Goodloe

Amy Goodloe is a very busy woman. Her house in Oakland, California, is alive with the constant humming and whirring produced by four computers, four modems and three phone-lines. Amy, her partner (a comic-book publisher) and a beagle named Wimsey have nine Internet connections and three domain names between them. What, you might well ask, do they do with all this technology? The answer is – a great deal. Wimsey has her own Web page, which she invites you to visit at any time. Meanwhile, Amy runs a non-profit organization on the Net she calls Lesbian.org, she operates an Internet consulting business called Women Online, and she hosts a number of women's Web sites as well as running nine women-only mailing lists.

For such a "wired" household, it was interesting to learn from Amy that she and her partner are avid book readers, with interests ranging from science fiction to medieval literature to feminist theory to physics, and they're serious writers too. Amy has a background in English literature and education, she has two master's degrees and taught at college level for four years. Two years ago Amy combined her growing interest and expertise with Macintosh computers and the Internet along with her skills as an educator to become a Macintosh and Internet consultant. As her business picked up "she realized she had tapped an important and previously unreached market: women who wanted access to computer and Internet technology but lacked adequate training" (Goodloe: 1995). In January 1995, Amy was inspired to form a Web site on the Internet called Women Online, which provides quality, affordable and woman-friendly training, as well as valuable information and extensive links to other women's Web sites.

promoting lesbian visibility on the internet

For those who live in the San Francisco area, Women Online offers extensive computer and Internet training. You can learn all about email, newsgroups and mailing lists, you can attend classes on "How to Keep Your Mac Happy", "How to Buy a Mac" and "Find It on the Internet". Amy has assisted a number of women and lesbian and gay businesses in establishing a presence on the Web, and individuals can take classes on designing their own Web pages. Such women-only Internet training enterprises are sprouting up in major cities throughout Australia, New Zealand and North America. They are usually advertised in local newspapers or magazines for women and lesbians. Because the Internet is relatively new and ever evolving, the quality of the teaching and information you'll receive will depend largely on the experience and skill of the course operators. It's probably wise to do some investigative work first before you hand over your money. Amy has designed a number of Web pages, including her own Lesbian.org, all of which are extremely well organized and visually attractive, so if you're living in San Francisco and need some training you can't go wrong.

Amy has been supported with the marketing aspects of the Women Online project by Roberta Kane, who has ten years of marketing, sales and speaking experiences up her sleeve. Roberta assisted Amy in "forging creative partnerships with Women-Owned businesses and organizations" (Goodloe: 1995). The two are now working together on a non-profit Mac Lab called Compuwomen. Amy gets help from a team of volunteers to run Lesbian.org, while she acts as director and Web designer.

Lesbian.org is, in my opinion, the most useful Web site for lesbians on the Internet. This should be the first stop for anyone wishing to discover and experience the large and growing lesbian and gay presence on the Net. As well as providing an extensive listing of lesbian links, Lesbian.org includes a number of Amy's own initiatives. Visit *Sapphic Ink*, a lesbian literary journal which aims to bring quality lesbian writing to a broader audience via the Web. You can submit your own work and enjoy the prospect of having it appear on-line. A large selection of poetry, fiction and non-fiction books are reviewed as well. The Lesbian Information Exchange provides a "notice board" where messages and announcements can be posted. If you're looking for a friend, need some help with a project or have an inkling someone may be looking for you, this is the place to go.

Amy's collection of mailing lists is worth visiting just for the sheer excitement of discovering the vast and varied subjects for discussion which are available on-line to lesbians. Amy maintains some of the lists herself, including *lesbian-studies* which provides a forum for academic research and discussion into lesbian studies world-wide. On a more technical level the *Internet-women-help* list provides help on a variety of Internet functions and issues.

Lesbian-owned businesses, products and services; Web pages for lesbians; virtual salons; humour; film reviews; travel; health and sexuality – the activities and initiatives found at Lesbian.org are too numerous to list in full. I suggest you visit Amy Goodloe's excellent Web site as soon as you've read this book, if not sooner!

Women Online can be found on the Web at
    http://www.women-online.com

Lesbian.org, your onestop lesbian Web site, can be found at
    http://www.lesbian.org

Discover quality lesbian writing and submit your own to **Sapphic Ink**
    http://www.lesbian.org/sapphic-ink/

Where to from here?

These seven women and their activities are a small example of how women have made the Internet their own. At the end of this book and at the Spinifex Home Page at http://www.peg.apc.org/~spinifex/ you will find an extensive list of resources relevant to women. Best of all, why don't you establish a presence on the Internet yourself? Become a regular contributor to email lists. You may want to establish your own on-line zine. Create some hot links. Design your own home page. The possibilities for those with enthusiasm and a little time on their hands are boundless.

Chapter 3

Gender issues
on the Internet

As women become more visible on the Internet, issues of gender are increasingly raised. These issues include sexual harassment, the different ways women and men communicate, the different value systems men and women often subscribe to, and issues of power, control and identity. After all, the Internet is just an extension of the real world. All of these issues can and do arise on the Internet and it is useful to know when, where and why problems occur and what you can do about them.

Let us have another look at what the Internet is. The Internet provides services to find information and retrieve it once found. More importantly, it provides mechanisms and opportunities for people to communicate with each other. You can send email to a friend, participate in online discussions through mailing lists, or hang out in multi-user environments (MUDs) or chat with people on-line (IRCs).

Your user name (the name you use to log-on) may not reveal your gender, your social status, or your appearance. You might be the director of a large organization or a busy mother at home. You may be small and blond or tall and brunette; you may be gay or straight, female or male. The Internet lacks what some call social contextualization. It is often hard to attach to a written message a stereo-typical image of the person who wrote it. However, this anonymity has its downside. Anonymity allows people to forget social conventions and to behave in ways that are normally unacceptable. As social conventions are less clear and some social cues are missing, politeness and concern for others decreases.

Harassment on the Internet

A common myth of Internet communication is that it is friendly and free of gender bias. Some women (and some men) have found that if their user name identifies them as female they are subjected to verbal abuse and even sexual harassment.

Women report getting messages from more or less unknown males ranging from invitations to join them for coffee, offers of help on various topics, to sexually explicit messages. You may welcome an offer of help with a problem, or an invitation to have coffee, but when these offers are persistent and continue without your consent, you are being sexually harassed. Sexual harassment has only recently been exposed (by feminists) for what it is, and what was once accepted is now viewed as unacceptable and unlawful behaviour in many countries. There is no reason why it should be permitted on the Internet (or anywhere else).

What are the reasons for (sexual) harassment?

Because sexual harassment uses the discourse of sex, it is easy to assume that it is about sex. Many definitions of sexual harassment specify that the harassment is of a sexual nature. This may imply that the harasser in some way has a sexual interest in the person he harasses. It is easy to come to this conclusion in real life, but the Internet exposes the real reason for sexual harassment: the need to feel or exert power over another person (usually a woman). Because at present there are still too few active women participating in Internet communities, men feel strangely threatened by their presence. A locker-room mentality and the atmosphere of a boys' only club still pervade some Internet communities. When certain men are confronted by women on the Internet, they feel enraged by this "intrusion". It appears the only way these men can deal with it is by putting women in their "rightful" place. The tool used by men world-wide to put women in their place is sexual harassment.

Developing community standards

As more and more women become active members of Internet communities, our presence will reach a critical mass and demand a certain level of community standards. Community standards and ways to deal with deviant behaviour can be established either by the systems administrator (the person who looks after the day-to-day running of a particular Internet community) or by a particular Internet community as a whole. Acceptance of these standards can then become a condition of participation in that community. It is already common for mailing lists to have a statement of purpose, outlining expected types of behaviour. Additionally, many mailing lists are moderated. In a moderated list, the moderator reads every message and makes sure that they all comply with the purpose of the list. Other types of Internet communities, such as MUDs, are also establishing community standards and methods of dealing with unwanted behaviour.

You can deal with unwanted behaviour yourself by having "filters" installed in your email program, which remove all messages from a particular individual. In IRCs the "ignore" command also acts as a filter. Community solutions, such as banning individuals from further participation in a particular Internet community, are also used successfully.

Enforcing community standards on Usenet News (also known as NetNews), the giant bulletin board on the Internet, is a different issue. Usenet News is not controlled by a single person or group and has virtually no established policies or rules of behavior. Each Usenet News group is a separate entity. The only way to enforce standards in this situation is by peer pressure. In its early years Usenet News was a valuable resource for dissemination of knowledge and an aid to researchers. Of course this is still the case, except there are some areas of Usenet News were anarchy rules and anything goes. Other Usenet News groups are moderated and function similarly to mailing lists. The key to enjoying Usenet News groups is to read only subject matter that really interests you and to discontinue your involvement if you find the group offensive.

What is sexual harassment on the Internet?

If you are, without your consent or invitation, sent lewd messages, suggestive graphics, sexual jokes or comments, or are propositioned in a sexual manner, you are being sexually harassed. Sexual harassment is any form of unwanted, repeated attention of a sexual nature. While it may initially seem easiest to ignore such advances, this is a poor strategy in the long term. If a person harasses you, it is likely they will do it to others.

What to do about sexual harassment

Remember you are not responsible for acts of sexual harassment. They are not your fault. Sexual harassment is not about sex, but about power.

Every Internet community needs a grievance procedure for dealing with sexual harassment. Members of the community need to be told that sexual harassment is unacceptable and will not be tolerated. Prohibited behaviour needs to be clearly defined and punishment spelled out. Details on how, when and where you can complain about sexual harassment need to be made available when you join a community.

Here are some initial steps to take if you experience sexual harassment or any form of harassment on the Internet.

Take precautions
Do not put your home address and phone number on mail messages. On-line harassment can lead to real-life harassment and stalking.

Say no clearly
Inform the harasser that the attention is unwanted.

Document the harassment
Save all messages you receive and any replies you send in a special file.

Look for other victims
If you are on a mailing list, ask other members on the list if they have had similar experiences.

Bring the issue to the attention of the ISP used by the harasser
If you are being harassed, send a carbon copy of the offending email or Usenet News posting to the postmaster of the site where the item originated from. Simply replace the username of the harasser with the word post-master (e.g. postmaster@siteoftheabuser). If you don't get a response from the post-master, contact the people who supply the site. Keep going up the chain until you receive a satisfactory response.

Bring the issue to the attention of the wider Internet community
Start discussions and educate other on-line users on the issues surrounding harassment.

Pornography on the Internet

In the United States, pornography is an $8 billion trade in sexual exploitation. Pornography is the graphic, sexually explicit subordination of women in pictures or words. It presents women as dehumanized sexual objects, apparently enjoying pain, humiliation, rape, torture and abuse. Pornography is easily available on almost every street corner. This is not entirely surprising: sex in general is used as the prime advertising medium for selling goods and services in the Western world. It is not surprising that pornography is readily available on the Internet. Nor is it surprising that paedophiles and hard-core pornographers use the Internet to disseminate their wares. Pornography is degrading for everybody – it's not just children we should be worried about. Many "ordinary" women and some men find pornography offensive. It is important to protect children, but it is equally important to protect ourselves and to let others know of our opposition to pornography.

The media response to the Internet has been to expose it as a hotbed of pornography and paedophilia. Women and children have been warned off the Internet by the scaremongering of the media. Some may view this as another plot to keep women in their present place and to prevent them from using the Internet as a powerful tool of communications. It is true that pornography can be easily found on the Internet, especially if you use one of the powerful search engines to search for this kind of material on the World Wide Web.

Probably the most readily available sources for pornographic material on the Internet are the Usenet News groups in the alt.sex and alt.binaries.erotica Usenet hierarchies. Under these subgroups of Usenet News you can find such interest groups as alt.sex.necrophilia, alt.binaries.pictures.erotica.children, and alt.binaries.pictures.erotica.bestiality. These groups contain megabytes of pornographic pictures and stories, and addresses of suppliers of pornographic material. However these groups only represent a very small part of all available news groups (around 200 out of an estimated 15,000). Most of the pictures available are simply scanned in from pornographic magazines, rather than produced specifically for the Internet. As picture files are usually very large, downloading them into your home computer can take a very long time. Pornographic pictures are not only degrading for women, but their transfer also chews up enormous Internet resources and clogs up the available transport channels. Increasingly, employers who find employees downloading this kind of material take a step in the right direction: they sack them.

As the Internet becomes a marketplace, pornography is offered for sale directly on the Internet. Both *Playboy* and *Penthouse* have immensely popular Internet sites that you can visit. There are now Internet sex shops from which you can order anything from condoms and adult sex toys to pornographic videos. As a quasi-information service there are Internet sites that provide information on availability and location of prostitutes and escort agencies in Canada, the United States, Thailand, the Philippines and Europe. Undoubtedly this trend will only increase. However, there are also some very important services available on the Internet that fit into a sexual category, such as mailing lists and Usenet News groups which provide support and information to survivors of sexual abuse, sexual harassment and rape.

Should you be worried? At present the vast majority of pornographic material resides mainly on adult bulletin boards (stand-alone computers that are not connected to the Internet, but that you can connect to through a modem and a phone-line). These services usually require a password in order to connect to them. A password is issued after the user has supplied a credit card number or faxed some sort of identification (such as a driver's licence). Pornography can be found easily enough on the Internet, but you have to go looking for it. Many pornographic World Wide Web sites have clearly displayed warning messages that indicate to the viewer what they are about to see. Increasingly the trend is to grant access to these sites only to users with a password. It is unlikely that pornographic material will arrive uninvited in your mailbox.

Pornographic images as screen backgrounds

Another effect of the availability of pornography on the Internet is the use of these images as a screen background. A screen background or "wallpaper" stays permanently on your computer while it is turned on. All text, images, icons, etc. are placed on top of it. These images vary from a rainforest scene to hard-core pornography to pictures similar to those found in pin-up calendars. Sometimes, rather than displaying just one image, multiple smaller copies of the image are displayed. The effect is that the complete image is always at least partially visible.

Using pornographic images as screen backgrounds is a form of sexual harassment. If you encounter such images, assert yourself and if possible make an official complaint. Many educational institutions and companies have policies prohibiting the use of such images. Demand that your company or educational institution develops, implements and uses policies that deal with sexual harassment in any form!

Making sure children don't have access to objectionable material

What about children's access to unsuitable material? Imagine you have a 14-year-old son and he has downloaded pornographic pictures using his own Internet account (you thought he was using the Internet to boost his schoolwork). Who do you hold responsible? Is it the Internet provider who should have screened the files that a 14-year-old can access? Or is it the people who put this kind of material on the Internet in the first place? What if there are laws that prohibit the uploading of pornographic material in Australia, but your son obtained the files from a site in Italy? Are the countries that transported the files from Italy, perhaps via France, England, USA and New Zealand, at least partly responsible? Or is it your own responsibility for not supervising your child better? When providing Internet access at home for your children, you must be aware of these issues. How you deal with them is for you and your children to work out.

It appears that a legislative approach does not offer an easy solution. A number of other solutions are being developed to try to solve the content problem. The proposed solutions fall into a number of categories. Software programs are available which permit access only to certain sites or deny access to objectionable sites. The problem with this approach is these programs tend to include or exclude whole sites rather than deal with individual files. These programs are also hard to maintain and require constant updating. This is a service for which you are charged, in addition to the initial outlay for the program. Another approach is to get the author of a file to rate and then label the file accordingly. Alternatively a third party (similar to a censor) could perform this activity: for instance, you could subscribe to a commercial, educational, church or political ratings service. A number of other suggested solutions include options like allowing access to the Internet only through password accounts or via credit card numbers, and the development of an industry code of conduct and enforcement.

One approach that is gaining momentum in the USA is PICS (Platform for Internet Content Selection). PICS is a cross-industry working group whose aim is to devise a set of standards and technologies that facilitate self-rating, third-party rating, and ease of use. Self-rating allows content providers voluntarily to label the content they create and distribute. Third-party rating allows multiple, independent labelling services to attach labels to content created and distributed by others. PICS considers first- and third-party rating of content as the way to give users maximum control over the content they receive, without requiring new restrictions on content providers. PICS is supported by large sectors of the computer industry. Version 3.0 of the Microsoft Internet Explorer will contain filtering capabilities based on PICS. Netscape Navigator, and access control/rating programs such as CyberPatrol and Surfwatch will also incorporate the PICS standard.

An example of an Internet rating system (again US-based) is RSACi (Recreational Software Advisory Council on the Internet). RSACi claims to provide a non-judgmental, voluntary content-labelling system by relaying the precise content of Web pages. It uses a questionnaire to rate the level, nature and intensity of sex, nudity, violence and offensive language (vulgar or hate-motivated) on a particular Web page, and then sends a rating tag to the webmaster to incorporate into the Web page. Parents and teachers can then use any Internet browser or blocking device that can read the RSACi tag to restrict their children's access to any single rating or combination of ratings. One advantage of the RSACi system is that it offers the ability to rate each page separately, rather than blocking whole Web sites.

Cybersitter, Netnanny and Surfwatch are examples of rating/filtering/control programs that you buy over the Internet or at a software shop and then install on your computer. I expect, however, that many World Wide Web browsers will in the future come with these capabilities. Which program you prefer depends entirely on your requirements.

- **Netnanny** is a control/rating program that monitors all activities and applications on your computer, rather than just online material. To control on-line access, it uses a database of World Wide Web addresses (URLs) and scans Web pages for objectionable words and phrases. The user can define her own words and phrases. Netnanny can also be used to block access to certain types of files such as image files.

- **Surfwatch** can control access to Usenet News, ftp, Gopher, IRC and the World Wide Web. It uses a blacklist of Internet resources and blocks more than 200 Usenet News groups and about 2000 World Wide Web sites. The company offers a service that automatically adds new "offensive" sites to your databases of sites.

- **Cybersitter** monitors all activities on your computer and can block and report access to forbidden sites. It uses a database of resources and a list of objectionable phrases. It claims to be able to check for the context in which these phrases are used. The filter can be updated free of charge and can operate in "stealth" mode.

Here are the addresses of control/filtering programs available on the Web:

PICS:	http://www.w3.org/pub/WWW/PICS/
RSACi:	http://www.rsac.org
Netnanny:	http://www.netnanny.com/netnanny
Surfwatch:	http://www.surfwatch.com
Cybersitter:	http://www.solidoak.com/

Regulating the access of material on the Internet?

The above approaches are not without problems. It would be easy for governments to harness ratings and programs that exclude objectionable sites in order to institute political, religious or cultural controls on Internet users. Considering that the Internet spans many different cultures and political systems, it seems inevitable that some nation states will want to control what their citizens can access. For instance, China has decided that the most effective way of stopping citizens from using the Internet is by making it prohibitively expensive to connect. In contrast, the Singapore government is keen to embrace the Internet, while at the same time trying to stop its citizens gaining access to certain information. The Singapore broadcasting authority is instructing Internet service providers to block any content that will undermine the country's political and social "stability".

Increasingly online information services, such as AOL (America On Line) and CompuServe, are taking it upon themselves to act as moral guardians for their subscribers. In a widely published incident, AOL decided that certain words must not appear in the messages that customers send from within its network, including private email. One of the offending words was *breast*. A number of breast cancer survivors tried to form a chat room called "breast cancer survivors" in the summer of 1995. They were told that the chat room name was obscene. Someone tried variations, such as "boob cancer" and "hooter cancer". AOL accepted these as not "obscene". Two months later, a breast cancer survivor scanned through user profiles to find other women who described themselves as breast cancer survivors. She found that all these posts had been purged because of their allegedly obscene content. Needless to say, many AOL subscribers cancelled their accounts.

The question of how to regulate the access of objectionable material on the Internet is not an easy one to answer. The Internet is a network of networks; there is no single person or institution in control. It is more like a loose federation. Some say the Internet is the perfect example of anarchy working. With no one in control and a network that spans large parts of the globe, it is hard to decide who should be held responsible for the dissemination, transport and downloading of objectionable material. Ultimately the responsibility lies with the people who produce the material, the organizations (men) who profit hugely from its dissemination, and the "ordinary" people who continue to allow its existence in society to go unchallenged. If we are concerned, as women and perhaps as mothers, about objectionable material being accessible on the Internet, we should be concerned about its very existence and campaigning against its proliferation.

Gender communications

Early commentators of computer networking technology believed the new technology to be a challenge to conventional hierarchies of control. Computer networks were viewed as convivial and participatory, and opposed to the centrally controlled nature of other electronic media such as television and print media. However, studies of computer technology and computer-mediated communication increasingly reveal that, like all technologies, it is embedded in economic, political and cultural structures of domination.

Because Internet communication is largely text-based, it is easy for people to forget about social conventions. When you start to participate in Internet services such as Usenet News, IRC, MUDs and email lists you will find some new friends and make some new enemies amongst all the strangers that you have contact with. You may be surprised how blunt and impolite some messages are. Electronic discussions seem to deteriorate easily into name-calling and posturing. For example, you have subscribed to an email list for Burmese cat enthusiasts. After responding innocently to somebody else's comment on what to feed Burmese cats, the next time you log on you find one, two or maybe twenty email messages that point out rudely that your comment was incorrect, stupid and a waste of time. This sort of activity is called "flaming".

Flaming occurs as the result of a person forgetting who s/he is talking to. Because tangible reminders of the audience are missing, it is tempting to make the message stronger than necessary. In face-to-face conversations we use moderation and adjust the tone and content of our words according to the body language of our listener. On the telephone, long silences and subtle voice changes are cues which tell us when we've gone too far. When writing a letter, the time-lapse between writing and posting the letter gives us an opportunity to reconsider the contents. Electronic messages tend to encourage people to be more extreme and impulsive than they would normally be. People often feel less constrained by convention and less concerned with the consequences of their messages. Before you know what has happened, angry messages fly back and forth, and a full scale "flame war" has broken out.

Depending on where the flame war erupts, it can be extremely disruptive to the community concerned. I have participated in mailing lists where flaming has resulted in several members of the community feeling so hurt that they have left the community permanently and in disgust. At other times, flames are a minor irritation. Their major effect is that the number of messages created for the mailing list increases. Remember you do not have to read inflaming messages (check the "subject" field of incoming messages first), nor do you have to participate in "flame wars".

Sometimes you may read a message that contains the phrase "flame follows". The writer is indicating that the message that follows might be upsetting to others and is sending out an early warning signal. In contrast, sentences like "please don't flame me" or "no flames please" indicate that what follows might appear silly or stupid to others, and the writer is requesting the reader to be understanding and maybe even a little indulgent.

I believe flaming is also the result of gender-specific communication styles. Susan Herring (1993) analysed male and female participation in two academic mailing lists and found two discourse styles: adversary (usually adopted by men) and attenuated/personal, (usually adopted by women).

The adversary style of communication is characterized by the use of strong assertions, self-promotion, exclusive use of pronouns (*I, we*) and the use of imperatives. It is commonly used by men and rarely by women. Such a style can deteriorate easily into angry opinionated posturing (flaming). In contrast, women tend to focus on personal aspects of communication and use a culmination of hedges, qualifications and apologies. This style does not easily result in "flaming". Consequently, women tend not to contribute as often as men to adversarial exchanges. Unfortunately, the downside of women's "lack of interest" in this communications style is that women may not be recognized as peers in professional on-line groups. Women's tendency to use a non-adversarial style may inhibit their ability to successfully participate in on-line discussions and may even affect future professional opportunities. Is the alternative to adopt the masculine/adversarial style?

Not necessarily. You can choose to participate in Internet communities that are exclusively or predominantly female (see Appendix for a list of women-only and women-centred mailing lists). While flaming does occur in these groups, the overall atmosphere tends to be more caring and oriented towards sharing personal experiences and feelings.

Unfortunately gender-related Internet problems do not stop with the communication style you choose. Susan Herring (1993), in the same study, observed that if women did try to participate in on-line discussions dominated by men, they risked being either ignored or belittled by the men on the list. However, we should not attribute this male behavior to the technology itself: it is clear that it simply continues pre-existing patriarchal patterns of dominance and hierarchy. Studies by other researchers also confirmed that women often feel ignored, silenced and sometimes abused in electronic conversations.

Gender identity

When you use a telephone, differences in time and space seem to disappear. When it is midnight in Melbourne, it is lunch time in Munich and early evening in Iceland. The person you speak to on the end of a telephone line could be next door or on the other side of the globe. Not long ago, before the telephone was commonplace, speaking to a person just a few hundred miles away meant days of arduous travel on horseback, in a horse-drawn carriage or even on foot. The telephone changed the social boundaries associated with time and space forever. Using the Internet to communicate with others dissolves a different sort of social boundary: identity. It is possible using the Internet to take on any persona. Identity deception can of course happen in real life, but it's a lot easier on the Internet and happens frequently in MUDs (Multi-User Dimensions, role-playing and game environments) and associated environments.

The first thing you do when you participate in one of these environments is to create an identity: a name, a character, roles the character will play, its/her/his gender. Gender is not always restricted to a choice of male or female, on some MUDs you can choose to be an it (neuter) or a swarm of it's/he's/she's. For instance a Japanese MUD called Habitat has 1.5 million participants and a real-life ration of four males to one female. On-line the ratio is three male characters to each female. Why do many tens of thousand of male users crossdress on-line? Undoubtedly it is a lot less trouble to pretend to be a woman online than to actually walk the streets dressed as men imagine women (should) look: high heels, miniskirt and make-up. Online all a person needs to do is to express in writing the way he or she thinks the other sex communicates and relates experiences. This is, of course, not as easy as it sounds and most men have considerable trouble keeping up the fiction for any length of time.

Trying out a different gender does sounds interesting, until you discover that choosing a female character may mean a barrage of sexual innuendoes, explicit flirtations or outright sexual harassment.

At present the largest category of recreational players in MUD environments are 17–23-year-old males. Their obsession with violence, identity play and sexual innuendo (or worse) is not surprising. What is surprising though, is that such a large proportion of male players take on female characters that female characters are often assumed to be males in real life.

What do young males get out of impersonating female characters? Some clearly enjoy deceiving others. When I was a teenager hitchhiking around Europe I would regularly invent personas for myself and it gave me great pleasure to play out different roles and stories. As an adolescent living in a society which tries to mould you and control your actions and even your thoughts (you should be straight, feminine looking, passive etc.), role-playing games offer a way of exploring other ways of thinking and acting. MUDs evolved out of role-playing games and it can be fun behaving in ways that you would not be able to choose in a real-life situation. Some males take on female characters in order to initiate sexual talk. Common MUD wisdom has it that any flirtatious female is in real life male. Also, some men simply want to experience how the "other half" lives. It can be very enlightening for these men to experience the effects of sexual propositioning that are part of some MUDs.

Sherry Turkle (1996) in her book *Life on the Screen: Identity in the age of the Internet* discovers some interesting things about the above phenomenon. When she questions Case, who plays a female character in a medieval MUSH, he reveals that "playing this woman lets me see what I have in my psychological repertoire

. . . And I can see how some of the things that work when you're a man just backfire when you're a woman." He likes to play several Katharine Hepburn type roles, describing them as "strong, dynamic and out there". Case has decided that being assertive as a man is coded as "being a bastard". However, if you are assertive as a woman, it is coded as "modern and together". In Sherry's interview with Zoe, we find that her experience is exactly the opposite. Zoe has played a MUD man for two years. "First I did it because I wanted that feeling of an equal playing-field in terms of authority, and the only way I could think of to get it was playing a man." Zoe was was accepted as a man by the other men in the MUD. They talked to her "guy to guy. It was very validating. All those years I was paranoid about how men talked about women. Or I thought I was paranoid. Then I got a chance to be a guy and I saw I wasn't paranoid at all." Zoe experiences that being aggressive is only acceptable in male behaviour. Sherry writes that "these stories share a notion that a virtual gender swap gave people greater emotional range in the real". I would suggest that while some players may learn something useful and even be transformed by their gender-swapping experiences, others may just enjoy the deception and the power derived from getting away with behaviours they would be punished for in real life. For example a college student interviewed by Sherry says, "quite frankly I'd rather rape on MUDs where no harm is done". Surely there is an element of harm even if a rape only occurs in text form. The words, after all, represent this young man's real-life fantasies.

MUDs and other kinds of virtual meeting places such as Internet Relay Chat can breed a kind of easy intimacy. New relationships appear to deepen rapidly and time seems to speed up. Unfortunately when these relationships are taken from the virtual to real life, disappointments are not uncommon.

A cautionary tale

MUDs are not the only Internet services were people play out their fantasies and create imaginary selves. Here is a cautionary tale from the world of Internet Relay Chat:

In October 95 I became a regular on a semi-private IRC channel for lesbians. My nickname was Shaz and others had cute nicknames like Elf, Ratty, Lark, Screamer, Lion and the like. The channel was welcoming and there was a regular core of about 25. Of course we developed a system of recognizing people we thought may be men. Mostly men are so transparent, entering a chat area saying who wants to suck my ———. Others are not so easy to detect and require a few questions to be unmasked. Some women developed close friendships with other women, some even began relationships.

One person, Sam I am, began a friendship with Vic. They began emailing each other privately and outside of the IRC channel. One day Vic asked Sam I am to telephone her, but Sam I am didn't. Sam I am also began emailing other women to "get to know them more personally". Sam I am sent Vic a photo of herself. Sam sent Vic some flowers on Valentine's day. Shortly after this event, Sam I am confessed. He was in fact a man and the photo was of his wife. His name was Steve and he claimed to be in love with Vic.

As you can imagine, everyone on the channel was very angry with Steve. Many women emailed him asking for explanations. Steve replied with abusive emails calling the women "man-hating lesbians". His outbursts and his confessions were recorded and sent to his system operator. Vic was devastated, but is now recovering with the help of the other 25 IRC regulars. I was not on IRC at the time of the confession, but I knew within 2 hours. It was amazing how all of us knew within a very short time and were there to support Vic (Shaz: 1996).

What I personally find heartening about the story is that Vic had the support of other women: she was not left to deal alone with this betrayal. It is a cautionary tale because it points out clearly that on the Internet you cannot be 100 per cent sure who you are dealing with and that it is important to take precautions. Keeping a record of your on-line interactions is always a good idea. Many IRC clients, for instance, come with a log option. If you turn the log option on, a copy of the chat session will be saved in a special file called log file. It is also a good idea to keep copies of all email sent and received.

Chapter 4

Getting connected from home: the nuts and bolts

Connecting to the Internet

To connect yourself to the Internet, the information in this chapter is essential reading. Some aspects of getting connected, such as modem speed, modem standards, the difference between PPP and SLIP, may seem unnecessarily technical. Try to persevere through the seemingly boring bits and pick up at least some of the language: it will make it a lot easier to communicate with the technical experts you'll encounter along the way.

To use the many varied Internet services you need a connection to the Internet. Most connections from home require:

- a phone-line
- a computer
- a modem
- an Internet account with an Internet service provider (ISP)
- appropriate Internet software
- some basic computer knowledge.

Ideally you also need a large dose of patience, a friend who is already on the Internet for support, and belief in your own abilities. Connecting to the Internet can be rough at first and it is important to remember that when things go wrong (believe me they will) it is not necessarily your fault. Some of the items in the list above come in a variety of options; which options you choose depend on how much money you can spend and which Internet services you decide to use.

Cheap Internet access?

The price of Internet access varies enormously from country to country. In the USA and Canada you can get unlimited graphical Internet access for as little as $US20 a month. In Australia you are more likely to pay by the hour, usually $A2–10 for graphical Internet access depending on your geographical location. If you live in one of the major cities, you can get a dialup shell/text Internet account with one of the hobbyist ISPs (Internet Service Providers) for $A50–100 per year. This will give you 1–3 hours Internet access per day, depending on the ISP. However, you will need extra amounts of patience, willingness to explore and fiddle with software, and plenty of time. In return, you will become an Internet witch. Prices in Great Britain are fairly similar to Australia, but in New Zealand you can expect to pay twice as much for one hour of Internet access. You will also need a computer that is capable of supporting dialup IP/graphical Internet access (cost around $A2000) and a fast modem (around $A300–500). If you are happy to have text-only access (no graphics, sound or video) and you have access to a reliable phone-line, $A200 should buy you an old 286 or 386 PC and a slow modem.

How does an Internet connection work from home?

Any Internet connection has two elements: the physical elements or hardware required to establish a connection; and the software to establish the connection and manage the information flow, once the connection has been established.

Figure 4.1 shows all the physical elements of an Internet connection. Your home

PC is connected to a modem, which in turn is plugged into your telephone jack. The telephone line carries your commands and information to your ISP's modem. The ISP's modem is in turn connected to the ISP's computer. The ISP has a variety of options for connecting its computer to the Internet. It may have a permanently leased line connection to the Internet, or an ordinary telephone line like yours.

Figure 4.1 Physically connecting your computer to the Internet

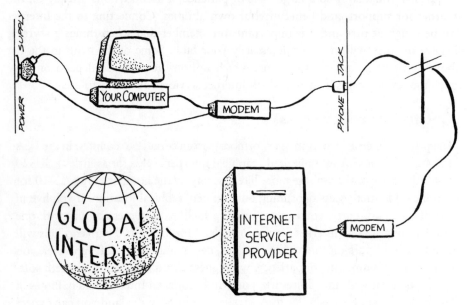

As well as the physical hardware, you need software that establishes and manages the connection and performs the exchange of information between your computer and the ISP's computer, and ultimately the wider Internet. There are a number of different ways of connecting to the Internet: dial-up shell/text account or dial-up IP/graphical account (SLIP, PPP). The software you need to connect to the Internet will depend on the connection you choose. Most ISPs have all the software you require for a particular connection. The connection you choose will largely depend on your personal requirements, how much money you are prepared to spend per month on your connection, the type of computer you have and, often, where you live. If you live in a remote part of Australia, for instance, you may not have a very reliable telephone line. Also, the number of ISPs available to you and the type of connection they offer may be severely restricted. Let's have a look in detail at all the elements involved in an Internet connection.

Elements of an Internet connection: what to look for

The phone-line

A reliable telephone line is a basic requirement for establishing an Internet connection. Lack of a reliable line may limit the speed of your Internet connection, or may make it impossible for you to connect via the telephone network at all. If you live in a major city or even in a smaller regional centre a decent telephone line should not present a problem. However, if you live in a remote area or in a so-called developing country, a reliable telephone line may be next to impossible to obtain. Still there are ways to overcome this problem. It is possible to connect to the Internet via satellite or mobile phone. However both types of access are expensive and not available everywhere. With the advent of low-orbit satellites just over the horizon, this type of access may one day become affordable for the average user. I also expect the access charges for mobile phone users to decrease over time.

Once you have made sure you have a reliable telephone line, there are a few things that you need to look out for:

- Check whether you have touch-tone dialling. Touch dialling is the preferred operating mode used by modems. If you only have pulse dialling, you will need to instruct your modem with special commands.
- Check if your telephone is connected to the telephone network via a PBX. This is very important. Connecting a modem to a PBX can destroy the modem unless you use the prefix required to dial out. If your telephone doesn't look like an ordinary telephone, make enquiries. Modems work properly only with standard analog telephones.
- Disable any call-waiting and similar features for the duration of your Internet session.

Telephone adapters around the world

Telephone adapters vary from country to country. The RJ-11 jack is common, but before you go on an overseas trip it's best to check which telephone adapter is used in the country you are going to visit. Here is an URL (see chapter 7 to find out more about URLs) that tells you about adapters used in different countries:

http://www.warrior.com/cpplus/adapters/index.html

The computer

Almost any computer will allow you to connect to the Internet. It doesn't make much difference whether you use a PC, a Macintosh, or something more exotic. Some of the older PCs that do not run Windows will give you only a text-based connection to the Internet. Using an older computer also means that you won't be able to run some of the more up-to-date Internet software, but do not despair. You can get by with surprisingly out-of-date hardware, it all depends how important it is to you to have pictures, sound or video (full graphical Internet access). Table 4.1 shows the minimum hardware requirements to get full graphical Internet access.

Table 4.1 Hardware requirements for graphical access to the Internet

Element	PC	Macintosh
Processor	386 or better	68030 or better
Operating system	Windows 3.1	System 7 or above
	Windows for Workgroups	
	Windows NT	
	Windows 95	
	OS/2 Warp	
Ram	4–8 MB	8 MB
Disk space	several MB	several MB

Types of Internet connections

As a home Internet user you usually have a choice of two types of account: dial-up shell/text account or dial-up IP/graphical (using either SLIP or PPP) account. It is also possible, either by choice or by circumstance (location, finance, etc.) to have email-only access to the Internet. Many Internet services can be accessed using email alone, but it is more cumbersome and slower than a dial-up shell or IP account. At the other end of the spectrum is direct permanent access to the Internet. While this option is still out of reach for most of us (due to the inflated cost structure of most national telephone companies), I think it will be the norm within a few years. Your Internet service provider will offer a number of possible ways of permanently connecting to the Internet. You can lease a telephone line, have an Integrated Services Digital Network (ISDN) connection – a special digital telephone line with a capacity of 64 kilobits per second (Kbps), or a T1 connection (1.544 megabits per second – Mbps). All of these options are currently very expensive.

Dial-up shell/text or terminal account

A dial-up shell/text or terminal account provides text-based access to the Internet. You will not be able to see the images that are part of most World Wide Web home pages, nor use any of the Windows or Macintosh graphical software programs. There is no support for any kind of multimedia. You dial into the text-based interactive system of the service provider, using a communications package that includes terminal emulation software (usually VT100). Terminal emulation software translates any characters you type on your home computer into characters your host computer understands and vice versa. Your home computer becomes a remote terminal of the host computer, and hence you have to use the same commands your host computer uses to access Internet services. If your host computer is a UNIX machine you have to use UNIX commands, if it is a VAX you have to use VAX commands. Once you are logged in, you are usually greeted by the system prompt or a menu. Even if there is a menu, you need to learn some of the commands of the ISP's operating system (usually UNIX). Finally, because your computer is not directly connected to the Internet, file transfer from the Internet to your home computer involves two steps. First you need to transfer the file to your host computer and then transfer the file to your home computer using a special program such as Xmodem, Ymodem, Zmodem or Kermit. If you want to send a lengthy email, you may want to compose the text on your home computer. The process of sending the message is almost the reverse of obtaining a file from the Internet. You need to transfer the text to your ISP's computer and then – using a special command, which depends on the email package you are using – into the email package. Finally, you can send the email (for an example of the commands, have a look at chapter 5).

Figure 4.2 Dial-up text-based or shell accounts
Your computer becomes a remote terminal when connected to your ISP

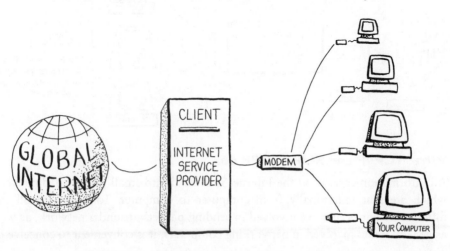

Although a dial-up shell/text account is limited (no graphics, more cumbersome), it has some good points. Shell accounts are often a lot cheaper than dial-up IP/graphical accounts. If you are using a PC with Windows, you can use a SLIP emulator to "pretend" graphical Internet access. However, it does require that you delve a little deeper into the technical aspects of the Internet. It is a bit like being able to change the spark-plugs in your car. Text-only access to the Internet is also a lot faster than graphical access. If you only want to receive email and download the occasional file, a shell account is all you need. Setting up a shell account is very easy: all you need is your ISPs dial-up phone number, your username and password. There are usually on-line help files that teach you the basics of the operating system.

Dial-up IP/graphical accounts using SLIP or PPP

When you use a dial-up IP/graphical account, your home computer temporarily connects to the Internet. With this type of connection you have graphical, multimedia access to the Internet through applications that are stored on your home computer. Files are directly downloaded to your computer, rather than being stored first on your ISP's computer. However, you need special software that manages your temporary connection to the Internet: TCP/IP (often referred to as a TCP/IP stack – the letters of the first word are pronounced separately, but the slash is not mentioned) and either SLIP (pronounced *slip*) or PPP (pronounce *pee-pee-pee*).

Figure 4.3 Dial-up IP or graphical accounts

What TCP/IP and SLIP or PPP do

All information carried on the Internet is divided into small parts called packets, which are sent individually from computer to computer. To deal with all the different activities that are involved in sending packets around a network, as well as general issues involved in networking computers, it is convenient to conceive of these activities as divided into layers. These layers are named, from bottom to top, physical, logical, network routing (which way to send packets) transport, session, presentation and, lastly, the application layer. In the physical and the logical layers we specify the operation of the actual cabling. In the middle layer – network routing, transport and session – we define how to handle the actual connection between the computers and how to send the data packets. The remaining two layers – application and presentation – are used to define how the software communicates with other software.

TCP/IP is the Internet protocol that deals with the first four layers of this conceptual model. When we want to use telephone lines to transmit packets, either SLIP (Serial Line Internet Protocol) or PPP (Point to Point Protocol) are used to deal with the physical and logical layer of this transport medium. TCP/IP is used for addressing and routing the information. If you are using a PC, then TCP/IP and SLIP/PPP are combined into one program called winsock.dll. There are numerous implementations of the winsock.dll, but one of the most popular is Trumpet Winsock. If your computer is a Macintosh, you'll have two separate programs: MacTCP and the dial-up IP program of your choice (MacSLIP, InterSLIP, MacPPP etc.).

SLIP or PPP?

Which of the two protocols you choose to use depends in the first instance on what your ISP supports. SLIP is the older, less sophisticated protocol. CSLIP (Compressed SLIP) is a variation of SLIP that is slightly faster because it uses compression techniques. PPP provides improved error correction and packet assembly when compared to SLIP. PPP should be your protocol, if possible.

Ideally your ISP should provide you with a partially set-up TCP/IP and SLIP/PPP package. If you have problems setting up your Internet connection, ask your ISP for help. It is beyond the scope of this book to explain in detail the ins and outs of setting up dial-up IP. There are, however, an increasing number of specialized books that deal with this topic (e.g. Miller and Keeler 1995) and there is plenty of help to be found on the Internet.

SLIP emulators

As already mentioned, if you have only a dial-up shell/text account, a SLIP emulator will still give you full Internet access. How is that possible? A SLIP emulator resides on your ISP's computer. This program relays the data packets arriving from the Internet to your home computer. You may wonder how this is different from ordinary SLIP. If you use SLIP, your home computer becomes a temporary part of the Internet, and it has a temporary IP address. If you have a temporary IP address your home computer can be a server to other computers on the Internet for the duration of the connection. Some Internet applications such as CU-SeeMe (a video conferencing package) cannot be run using a SLIP emulator. However, most Internet applications require your home computer to play the role of the client, so a SLIP emulator will do the job just as well.

To run a SLIP emulator, you will need the following:

- A dial-up shell account that permits you to get to the operating system's prompt. This means you need to be able to leave a menu system; if you are unable to do this, you cannot run a SLIP emulator.
- Permission to run a SLIP emulator on your ISP's computer. Some ISPs provide SLIP emulators for their customers; others forbid their use, because they will want you to use SLIP/PPP for which they can then charge a premium.
- SLIP emulator software. If you have to install the SLIP emulator on your ISP's computer (it is not hard), you need to know what type of computer it is and what operating system (Sun OS, SCO/UNIX, Linux, Ultrix, etc.) it uses.
- A software package that contains TCP/IP.

This all sounds fairly complicated. It is certainly not as straightforward as getting a ready-made software package from your ISP that is already set up for you. However, the SLIP emulator is not more complicated than setting up ordinary SLIP. And if you have no other option, it is certainly well worth the effort. Much of what you have to do is similar to setting up SLIP. Also, make sure your ISP is prepared to assist you.

Two well-known SLIP emulators are SLiRP and TIA. The SLiRP or TIA binaries (the executable program) need to be installed on your ISP's computer. They may already be installed; otherwise you can obtain the binaries and information on how to install them from these addresses:

SLiRP: http://blitzen.canberra.edu.au/slirp
TIA: http://marketplace.com/0/tia/tiahome.html

Here is what you do from home once, for example, SLiRP is installed on your ISP's computer:

1. Dial your Internet service provider and log in as you normally would. If you are in a menu, exit the menu to the system prompt. You are at the system prompt when you see something like >
2. When you are at the system prompt, type `slirp -b modemspeed`, e.g.:

   ```
   slirp -b 38400
   ```

3. You can now activate the Internet application of your choice by double-clicking on the appropriate icon.

4. When you want to finish, you type 00000 in the window where the operating prompt is located.

Instead of going through this rather lengthy manual process, you can set up a script that will do it automatically for you. Your ISP might provide you with a sample script; otherwise, you can find one on the SLiRP home page.

Other "emulators": SlipKnot, Icomm

If you have only a dial-up shell/text account, there is another type of program that you can use to gain at least some graphical access to the Internet. SlipKnot and Icomm are programs that act as converters of text-based World Wide Web browsers (usually Lynx). SlipKnot and Icomm do not use TCP/IP: consequently, they are a lot easier to set up and use and they are not expensive. Because you can also use FTP and Gopher with Lynx, you can also use them with SlipKnot or Icomm. However, other Internet services are not available. Slipknot and similar software packages cannot be detected by your ISP. Unfortunately, at present they are available only for PCs.

Internet software

What sort of Internet software you need depends entirely on the type of Internet account you have chosen. If you decide on a dial-up shell/text account, all you need is a communications and terminal package. Commonly available packages are Windows Terminal, Crosstalk, Telix, ProComm, etc. When you buy a modem, a communications and terminal package is often part of the deal. Anyway, most terminal packages are very reasonably priced, especially considering that they are the only bit of software you will ever need for this type of Internet access. All the other Internet software already resides on your ISP's computer. The communications and terminal package manages the communication between your computer and the packages that you are using on your ISP's computer. Make sure the terminal package you buy comes with a number of different terminal emulations. These allow your computer to communicate with a variety of different host computers. The most common terminal emulations are VT100, ANSI and TTY.

If you choose the multimedia experience of a dial-up IP/graphical account, most of the software that you use resides on the hard disk of your computer. Instead of using a communications and terminal package, you need a program that manages your communication with the Internet directly, such as Trumpet Winsock for a Windows PC, or MacTCP and MacPPP for the Macintosh. Windows 95 and OS/2 come already with all the necessary software as part of the operating system.

Additionally, you will need at least a Web browser such as Netscape Navigator or Microsoft Explorer. You can use both of these Web browsers to access many Internet services, including email. Depending on your needs, you may still want to get specialized client programs for Telnet, IRC, Usenet News and email. Each of these has to be obtained and purchased separately. Many are available free over the Internet, or are very cheap. Your ISP may also provide you with some of these programs when you sign up. Don't feel you have to stick with what your ISP gives you. The Internet is ever-changing and new programs are being released daily. Make sure you use the latest version of a program.

Internet Service Providers: what to look for

Internet Service Providers (ISPs) seem to have sprouted out of nowhere in the last couple of years. Their numbers seem to be ever increasing, and in many major and even regional centres there are a number of ISPs to choose from. ISPs fall into seven major categories:

- regional or statewide networks
- educational institutions
- mass-market online services, such as CompuServe, Prodigy and Microsoft Network
- telephone companies
- vendors of wireless access networks
- specialized firms providing only access to the Internet
- non-commercial groups providing access to the Internet, such as computer users groups and BBSs

Depending on your location, needs and money, you may be able to choose an ISP from any of these groups, or you may be restricted to one or two choices. Regional and statewide network providers usually do not offer access to home users. Their access options are targeted towards large companies and ISPs that need permanent access to the Internet. If you are a student, access via your educational institution may be your cheapest option. Many universities provide email and other Internet facilities to their students either free or for a nominal fee. Mass-market on-line services also offer access to the Internet to their customers. Because such services have a presence in many countries, if you like to travel overseas, an on-line service as your ISP might be a good choice.

However, there are still several serious problems with on-line service providers. These services were designed to be entirely separate from the Internet, and they only recently made Internet connections available to their customers. Electronic mail is usually exchanged with the Internet through a gateway, and browsing the World Wide Web and reading Usenet News is also possible. Many of the leading-edge Internet applications are simply not available to on-line service customers. This is because the on-line services are rarely fully connected to the Internet. Additionally, you usually have to use the software they provide, rather than being able to use the Web browser or email package of your choice. Because these companies offer more than just plain access to the Internet, they are often quite expensive. Overall, unless you are particularly interested in the information they carry, I would not recommend them.

Telephone companies are thinking about offering Internet access to the general public. In some countries, including Australia, a telephone company actually runs part of the national Internet. Vendors of wireless access networks have started to offer Internet access to satisfy the needs of people who are constantly on the move and who want to read their email on the way to the airport or while in a business meeting. This type of access is destined to become more common as the Internet starts to pervade more areas of our lives. Wireless access is still quite expensive and you also need specialized wireless modems or a mobile phone with a special cable to connect to your laptop or palmtop, or a personal digital assistant like the Newton. Most people however, choose an ISP that has Internet access as its only business offering. In Australia many of these firms have evolved out of hobbyist ISPs. Non-commercial groups are probably still the best choice if you want cheap Internet access from home. They are usually run by people who really know what they are doing and are often very friendly places to hang out. However, commercial activities are usually not allowed if you connect via one of these groups to the Internet.

Strategies for finding an ISP

Here are some strategies for finding an ISP which you may want to explore before you actually sign up with a particular one:

- Ask a friend who uses the Internet if you can visit and have a look.
- Visit an Internet cafe and try out the Internet.
- Talk to friends about their experience with different ISPs.
- Read the trade press (the various computer and Internet magazines).
- Get a list of ISPs from the Internet (either via a friend who is on the Internet or by visiting an Internet café).

Here are the addresses of some lists of ISPs:

Australia

http://www.cs.monash.edu.au/~zik/netfaq.html

ftp://archie.au/usenet/FAQs/alt.internet.access.wanted/Network_Access_in_Australia_FAQ

New Zealand

ftp://archie.au/usenet/FAQs/alt.internet.access.wanted/Internet_access_in_New_Zealand_FAQ

Worldwide

http://thelist.com/countrycode/countrycode.html

Some of the bigger ISPs periodically offer free or near-free Internet access for a limited period. This can be a good way of exploring the Internet, but there have been occasional reports that it can be difficult to escape from these "free" offers.

Questions to ask your ISP

Performance varies considerably between ISPs, depending on their connection to the Internet, the modem-to-user ratio, and the modems and software they use. Performance refers to the time it takes you to download a file from the Internet, the speed with which your email is delivered, or how often Usenet News is updated. Performance becomes an issue when you pay by the hour or minute. Common problems encountered with ISPs are constantly engaged telephone lines and poor customer support. If you are new to the Internet, customer support and preconfigured Internet software (a package of Internet software set up to work with a particular ISP) may be especially useful to you. Many ISPs provide an access package that makes it easy for you to get on the Internet.

Here are some questions you need to ask any prospective ISP. I have given what I consider to be the best possible answers in italics. For some questions, the best answer depends on your circumstances:

- What services and account types do you offer (shell, SLIP, PPP, permanent connections)?
  Shell, SLIP, PPP.

- If I choose a shell account, am I permitted to use a SLIP emulator?
  If they say no, go elsewhere, if possible.

- What are the initial sign up and account set-up fees?
  No initial fees.

- How long will you guarantee the present price level?

- What does a particular account cost per month/hour?

- Are there different charges for peak and off-peak times?
- How much data can I retrieve and store without extra cost?
  No extra cost for retrieving and storing.
- What are the payment options (credit card, automatic payment)?
- How many modems are used and at what speeds do they run?
  Modem speed is 28.8 kbps.
- What is the number of modems compared to the number of customers?
  Divide the number of modems by the number of customers. The smaller the ratio the better!
- Is there a surcharge if I connect to one of your faster modems?
  No.
- What Internet services are supported?
  All of the common Internet services, such as email, IRC, Telnet, FTP, World Wide Web, Gopher, should be available.
- Can I have my own home page and will it cost extra?
  Home page at no extra cost.
- What Internet software (Netscape, TCP/IP stack, etc.) is available?
  Software for all Internet applications that the ISP supports is available and can be downloaded from the ISP.
- What help is available via telephone or email?
  Both email and telephone support is available.
- Will you help me to set up for the first time?
  Yes.
- What is your connection to the Internet and how big is it?
  In this case bigger is better, but depends on the number of users.
- How often is your telephone line busy when I am trying to connect?
  Do a little experiment and ring their connection number during busy periods (any time during the weekend, and on weekdays between 6 and 10p.m.).

Dial-up IP information your ISP should provide you with

Unless you choose text-only dial-up, your ISP needs to provide you with certain information so you can connect to the Internet via your ISP. Ideally your ISP should provide you with software that has much of this information already filled in. Here is what you need to know:

- The ISP's dial-up telephone number.
- Your login name and password (initially you will be given a password which you will need to change the first time you log on).
- The dial-up IP protocol you can use (SLIP, PPP or either).
- Which type of IP addressing is used (static or dynamic). For static IP addressing you will be given a permanent number that you use every time you connect to the ISP. If the IP address is assigned dynamically for each session, you are given a new IP number for each session.
- If dynamic IP addressing for SLIP is used, is BOOTP (bootstrap protocol) also available? BOOTP makes your life simpler, because the program can not only work out the address assignment for itself, but also the TCP/IP related configuration information (gateway address, subnet mask and sometimes domain name information). If BOOTP is not available, you need a connection script. A connection script takes your computer through all the actions and responses that are necessary to establish a connection with your ISP. Explaining how to write such a script is beyond this book, but your ISP should really provide you with such a script.
- Gateway address used. This is the address of your ISP's computer that is connected to the Internet and you.
- DNS server addresses used. The DNS sever is a computer that translates an Internet address into its corresponding IP address. There are usually several DNS server addresses.
- Subnet masks used. This number makes sure that information is correctly transferred from your computer to the ISP's computer. It is not required by all client software.
- POP server address (for certain email packages).
- Usenet News, Gopher and Web server address for your Web browser.

Why is my Internet connection so slow?

You are retrieving a file on bird-watching in Peru from the Internet and wondering while you wait, and wait, whether you shouldn't take up knitting as well. It's so slow. You have been waiting for half an hour for this transfer to be completed and still all you see is a blank page. What are the possible reasons?

- The connection from your computer to your ISP's computer is slow.
- The connection from your ISP to the national grid is congested and slow.
- If you are retrieving something from overseas, then the overseas connection might be congested.

Modems

What is a modem?

The word *modem* stands for modulation/demodulation. The modem converts the digital data produced by your computer into analogue signals (the modulation part). These analogue signals are then transmitted down the telephone line and converted back to digital information by another modem on the other end of the telephone line (the demodulation part). If you would like to know more about how modems work and you have access to the World Wide Web, try:

http://www.myhome.org/modems.html

There are different types of modems. Modems can be external, internal and PCMIA card modems. PCMIA card modems are tiny, about the size of a credit card. Data modems transmit data, fax modems act as fax transmitters, and data/fax modems can do both jobs. In general, fax modems are not suitable for data transmission. Fax/data modems are data modems that have additional support for fax. The reason for this is that data modems and faxes use different modulation methods (tones) to communicate. Additionally, once data modems have negotiated a modulation scheme they will continue to use it till the end of the session. Fax modems, in comparison, switch before and after each page between a low speed modulation scheme (to exchange control information) and a high speed modulation scheme (to exchange the actual image of the page). Modems that combine the two functions of fax and data also need separate software for each function. This software is often included in the purchase of the modem.

External modems versus internal modems

An external modem is contained in a small plastic box and connected to the computer by a special modem cable. It may be as large as a video cassette or as small as a cigarette packet. Internal modems are attached directly to the computer's motherboard and do not require a modem cable. They are usually a little cheaper than external modems, but in my opinion they are not as versatile and useful as external modems.

External modems can be used with any type of computer. You can simply unplug the modem and move it from a Macintosh to a PC. All you need to do is buy different cables. However, it is not usually possible to move an internal modem from computer to computer. If the internal modem misbehaves, you usually have to turn the computer on and off, which is a nuisance if you are on-line at the time. External modems have a row of indicator lights that let you track the activities of the modem; this can be very useful when you are encountering problems. The only inconvenient aspect of external modems is that they require three electrical connections: for the electrical power, the telephone and the computer.

PCMIA cards

If you own a PC laptop you might consider using one of the small PCMIA card modems. PCMIA (PC Manufacturer's Computer Interface Adapter) is a new standard for peripheral devices like modems and network cards that allows you to attach and remove these devices easily through a special slot in the laptop. PCMIA modem cards can perform all the functions of a large modem and are a lot more convenient.

Modem cables (for external modems)

The modem cable connects into the serial port on the back of your computer. Serial means that the bits of information travel one after the other, rather than in parallel. The parallel port is usually used to connect the printer. A modem cable has on one end a 25-pin connector. This is plugged into the modem. For a PC, the other end of the cable has either a 9-pin or a 20-pin connector or both. The Macintosh uses 8-pin connectors. It is important to use the correct modem cable for high-speed modems; otherwise, the modem's transmission speed will be dramatically reduced. These cables are called *hardware handshaking modem cables.*

If your Internet connection seems too slow, the modem cable may be the culprit. The problem is that even with the correct pins at each end, some modem cables do not have enough wires to ensure efficient transmission. Unfortunately, you cannot tell whether your modem cable is properly wired or not. Bad performance and lack of reliability may be an indication that your modem cable is substandard. If you have any doubt about your cable, buy another one. They are not expensive.

Modem speeds

The transmission speed of your modem determines how fast you can communicate with your ISP and how fast you can download a file to your computer. Over time modem speeds have increased from 300 bits per second to 28,800 bits per second. The latter is the fastest transmission speed available to date. Rather than writing 28,800 bits per second it is more usual to see this number abbreviated to 28.8 kbps (kilo bits per second). Using a 28.8 kbps modem it will take six minutes to transfer 1 megabyte (MB) of compressed data, twelve minutes using a 14.4 kbps modem and seventy minutes using a 2400 bps modem.

How to estimate file size and transfer times

The simplest way to estimate the time it takes to transmit a file is by dividing its size by the speed of the modem and then divide the result by six.

(File size ÷ modem speed) ÷ 6 = Transmit Time

For example, transmitting a 1MB file at 14,400 bps takes 11.57 minutes:

(1,000,000 ÷ 14,400) ÷ 6 = 11.90 (approx. 11.57 minutes)

Modem standards

Modems are built and sold by many manufacturers throughout the world. To ensure that modems will successfully communicate with each other, standards for each transmission speed have been developed. It is important when you buy a modem that you ensure it complies to the appropriate standards for each transmission speed it is capable of. Check the documentation carefully. The standards define how the modem should communicate at different speeds and how it handles error correction and data compression irrespective of its speed.

Table 4.2 Standards for modem speeds, error correction and data compression

Name of standard	Purpose
v.32	Communication at 4.8 kbps and 9.6 kbps
v.32bis	Communication at 14.4 kbps and able to adapt to lower rates
v.34	Communication at 28.8 kbps
v.42	Error correction standard
v.42bis	Data compression standard

If you buy a 28.8 kbps modem it is important that it complies at least with the v.34 standard, but it is desirable that it complies with all of them.

Occasionally when data is sent, the pattern of one's and zero's arrives in a form slightly different to the original pattern. These data errors or discrepancies can be fixed by "on-the-fly" error correction. The v.42 standard provides for this type of error correction. Data compression is used to make the data transferred more compact and hence it speeds up data transfer. V.42.bis is the most commonly used data compression standard.

Cable modems for highspeed Internet access

Currently the fastest dial-up modem will give you a speed of 28.8 kbps. This is usually not sufficient for many of the newer Internet services such as video and audio-on-demand or Internet telephony. Even commonplace Internet services such as the World Wide Web are becoming slower and slower as more people add multimedia features (sound, video, images) to their Web pages. The larger the file size the longer it takes to download a file at a given speed.

One solution just appearing on the horizon is the cable modem. Cable modems use the cable-TV network rather than the telephone network to connect your computer to the Internet. Similar to dial-up modems they modulate and demodulate data, but the data is transmitted over TV channels rather than voice channels.

Theoretically speeds of up to 10Mbps can be achieved with these modems. This speed would reduce the download time of a 10 Mb file from 45 minutes to a few seconds. No more knitting or doing the dishes while you download Web pages! In practice there are still many problems to be sorted out before these speeds can be achieved. Field trials of cable modems are currently being conducted in a number of countries, including Australia. Cable modems should be commercially available in early 1997. Because the installation of cable modems is not as straightforward as dial-up modems, they will probably initially be rented out to customers. When they arrive, cable modems will give you highspeed Internet access 24 hours a day.

Buying a modem

Before you buy a modem, speak to friends about their modems and where they bought them. If you have any trouble setting up your modem, you will need a supplier who is ready to support you. Computer magazines conduct tests, from time to time, on modems and these tests can be worth consulting. Here are a few things to consider when buying a modem:

- Make sure the modem comes with a power supply, high-speed modem cable, telephone jacks and some communications software.
- Ask your supplier what sort of after-sales support they are prepared to provide. Installing modems is usually straightforward, but things do go wrong.
- Make sure you obtain all the documentation available for a particular modem (or any hardware or software). Too often modem suppliers fail to give women any documentation.
- Have a look at the documentation that is provided and check whether it has software that tests for hardware conflicts and software that finds the correct com port (see below).
- If you are using a PC, check whether you need to update your UART (see below).
- Buy the fastest modem that you can afford.
- Make sure the modem supports all of the above standards.
- Is the modem approved for use in your country? It is best to stick to approved modems for the obvious legal reasons; additionally, non-approved modems are often harder to set up.

Setting up your external modem (PC)

Checking for the 16550 UART chip

For the best possible performance, make sure your computer uses a 16550 UART (Universal Asynchronous Receiver/transmitter) chip. If you use an older UART (one with a lower number) then, even if you use a high-speed modem, your maximum transmission speed will be limited to 9.6 kbps. You can find out what UART you have by using a hardware diagnostic utility like Microsoft Diagnostics.

1. Double click on the **MS-DOS** icon from your Windows screen. You now see the DOS prompt, something like c:\ or c:\directory name, depending on how your machine is set up.

2. From the DOS prompt type `msd`

3. Microsoft Diagnostics is now examining your system. When it is finished, it will ask you to choose between OK and cancel. Press the **OK** button. You will now see a list of various information about your computer. Press **c** to get information on your com ports and the UART chip they are using.

4. When you have read the information on com ports, press the **OK** button to finish with this screen and then **F3** to leave the program.

5. To get back to Windows, type `exit`.

If you don't have a 16550 UART chip, consider updating at least one of your serial ports. It is not very expensive to do this.

Choosing a com port

Com (short for communications) ports are used by the computer to communicate with external devices such as printers, mice, scanners and modems. You need to identify a com port that is not being used for anything else and assign it for use by your modem. Your modem should come with a simple communications package that makes it easy for you to set it up. One of the things this software package does is to check for an available com port. Often com port 1 is available for use by a modem: the other com port is usually used by the mouse. Now you need to figure out which connector at the back of the computer is assigned to which com port. Sometimes the com ports are labeled. Otherwise the easiest way to find out is by looking at your manufacture's documentation. If all else fails you can always use trial and error.

Connecting the cabling

Take the high-speed modem cable and plug the end with the male (pins are sticking out) DB-9 or DB-25 connector into the appropriate com port on the PC. Plug the other end of the modem cable into the pin slot on the modem. Now attach the power supply (usually a small squarish box with two electrical cables attached) to the modem. Plug one end of the telephone cable into the modem and one end into the nearest telephone jack. It doesn't matter which end you use. If your modem has two jacks, one will be marked Line, the other will be marked Phone. Plug the telephone jack into the plug marked Line at the back of the modem. You can attach a regular phone by plugging it into the plug marked Phone or you can leave the Phone jack empty.

Setting up an internal modem (PC)

Ideally, your internal modem should be installed by a professional, because it can be a lot more tricky than installing an external modem. It all depends on how good the manufacturer's documentation and support is. The biggest problems arise usually from IRQ (Interrupt Request Line) conflicts. Make sure that your modem includes software that tests for possible conflicts.

Once the modem is installed on the motherboard, you can plug the telephone line into the modem connector (telephone adapter) on the back of the computer.

Setting up a PCMIA modem

Setting up a PCMIA modem is very simple. Simply plug it into the PCMIA slot on your laptop. Because of the small size of this modem, a telephone adapter is required (it should be part of the modem when you buy it); this looks a little like a rat's tail. One end plugs into the PCMIA card, the other end is attached to the adapter. Plug your telephone line into the adapter, the other end into the wall jack.

Setting up an external modem (Macintosh)

Plug the Din-8 pin of the high-speed modem cable into the Din-8 plug on the back of your Macintosh. This port is usually identified by an icon with a telephone on it. If you have a Powerbook 500 or later, the icon that identifies the correct port looks like a telephone and a printer. This is because the modem and printer are sharing the same port. It is best not to try to use a printer and a modem at the same time, even though many communications software packages allow you to do so. Next attach the power supply to the modem and plug it into an outlet. Plug the telephone line into the nearest wall jack and into the back of your modem. Turn on the power. Red lights should appear on the modem.

Setting up an internal modem (Macintosh Powerbook)

Ideally, your internal modem should be installed by a professional. Once the internal modem is installed, plug the telephone cable into the wall jack and the other end into the modem jack in the back of the computer. Make sure to select the Internal modem port in the dialog box of your communications software.

Chapter 5

Email: staying in contact with the rest of the world

Why email is so exciting

Email or electronic mail is one of the fundamental services of the Internet. In some ways it is similar to sending a letter through the postal system. To do that, you write the letter, put it in an envelope, and address it to the receiver. Once it is placed into a mailbox you probably don't know, or care, what exactly happens to it as long as it is delivered to the home or business of the person it was intended for. Email operates in a similar way, except on the Internet there is no postperson: computers pass your message to each other until it reaches its destination.

Email is most commonly used to send messages to other people, but you can also use it to send messages to computers and instruct them to do things for you. In fact, you can access most Internet services using email. You can, using email, retrieve a file that is located on a computer thousands of kilometres away, search databases and use various Internet tools such as Gopher and the World Wide Web, and read Usenet News. How to use email to access all these Internet services is explained in the chapter that covers the particular service.

The first step to sending an email is to use your computer to create a message. This is done within one of the many mail interface programs available. These programs generally provide functions to compose, address, read and forward mail items. Once written and correctly addressed, your message is automatically sent to the email address specified. The receiver's computer stores the message until the person is ready to read it.

Electronic mail is an easy and timesaving means of keeping in contact with friends and colleagues. It is not as formal or defined as conventional letter-writing. You'll probably find yourself dashing out many short messages rather than spending time composing long letters. I use it nearly every day simply to stay in contact with my friends, even those who live in the same city. It is more reliable and often easier than trying to contact someone by phone, especially if they don't have an answering machine. The comparative ease of communicating through email makes it less formal than letter-writing. There is no envelope to address, no stamp to affix, no trip to the post office and, best of all, it's lightning fast. To send a message halfway around the world, for example from Melbourne to London, typically takes only a few minutes.

By belonging to various mailing lists (see chapter 6) you may well find yourself corresponding with women spread out all over the globe. Non-government organizations have found it an excellent way of keeping up with campaigns worldwide. Increasingly, women's groups rely on email as an efficient way of "talking" to each other.

You can use email to send reports, files and, if you have the right software, pictures, sound and videos. It is easy to store the email you receive and use it as a reminder of agreements reached or things to do.

There are a few common hazards associated with email: mail may get lost or misdirected; only parts of a message may arrive; or mail may be forged. The first three problems are usually the result of slight addressing errors by humans, software, or hardware. Forgery of email is as yet uncommon, but encryption (a method of making the message readable only by you and the receiver of the message) can protect you against this possibility.

Because there is such a wide variety of common email packages available, it is impossible to cover them all in detail. Instead the aim of this chapter is to introduce you to the general concepts associated with email.

Email programs and what to expect from them

There are many different programs that you can use to send, receive and manage your email. Which program you will use is dependent on your Internet provider or organization and the type of Internet access you have. Common programs for dial-up shell/text access are mail, Pine and elm, and for graphical dial-up access Eudora and Pegasus. If you have dial-up IP/graphical Internet access your email program resides on your home computer. It operates by contacting the mail server on your ISP's computer and then bringing all the new messages to your home computer. If you have dial-up shell/text access you will have to use the email program your ISP has on its computer. The messages reside on the ISP's computer. If you want to download specific messages to your home computer, you need to use a special program that performs the transfer of the messages.

Addresses of graphical email packages from the World Wide Web are:

Eudora:	http://www.qualcomm.com/quest
Pegasus Mail:	http://www.cuslm.ca/pegasus

Pegasus is free, and a version of Eudora called Eudora Lite is also free.

Whichever program you use, you need to be able to do at least the following things:

- check for newly arrived email
- read your email
- reply to somebody's email
- forward email to somebody
- save email
- delete email
- write email
- organize email into folders.

Anatomy of an email

Before we look at how to read and send email, let's look at the different parts of an email. An email message has two parts to it, a header and the body of the message. Usually the two are divided by a blank line. The body of the message is where you type the text of your email. The header contains the addressing information.

The header

When you send an email, the header consists of a number of parts (known as fields):

To: This is where you type the email address of your recipient when you want to send an email.

Subject: Here you compose a short sentence indicating what the email message is about. This is an important line because when a person receives your message this is the part that appears, along with your address, in the list of newly arrived messages. At this point they can decide whether to read the entire message, save it to read later, or delete it unread.

cc: This stands for carbon copy. If you want to send duplicate copies of your message to other email addresses, this is the place to write these addresses.

When you receive an email the header may contain some additional fields. Some of these are used for administrative purposes, but there are a few that are important for you to know about:

Date: When the message was sent.

From: Here you can see the email address of the person who sent the message.

Sender: The From field and the Sender field may not contain the same email address. The sender may have sent the message on behalf of somebody else. This occurs for instance when you belong to a mailing list.

Reply-to: Lists the email address to which any replies to the message should be sent. Not all email programs can understand this field.

The body of the message

It is possible to type in your message directly, using your mail program. These programs are often limited in their functions, so you may prefer to use a word-processing package. Most mail programs provide a command that will allow you to import a file into the body of the message. However, if you do this you must take a little care. Unless you know that your mailer, and/or the mailer of the receiver of the message, is able to send and receive binary files, you should always send your message in text form (also known as ASCII or text-only). It is easy to write a file, for instance, in Word for Windows, but if the message recipient has an earlier version of Word for Windows, your message may be unreadable. Additionally, programs which encounter your message en route may have difficulties with it.

If you prepare an email using your word-processor, always save it as text-only with line breaks (Microsoft Word). Some word-processors may call this option save with no format, or save as ASCII text, DOS-text, plain text, or something similar. Make sure to also select the option that puts a line break after each line, otherwise you will end up with one very long, continuous sentence.

Software for email

Using Eudora with a dial-up IP/graphical account

Eudora is one of the most popular email packages for dial-up IP/graphical accounts. It is available for PCs and Macintoshes and you can choose between the free version (Eudora Lite) and Eudora Professional. The commercial edition of Eudora includes such extras as a spelling checker, filtering capabilities, colour-coded message labeling, multiple nicknames and signatures, Kerberos Password Authentication System support, and much more. But for many of us Eudora Lite is all we need, and it's free.

How Eudora works

When you use a dial-up shell/text account to read and send your email, you work with the messages on your Internet service provider's computer. This is not how it works with a dial-up IP/graphical account. A program like Eudora will, after you have connected to your ISP's computer, collect the messages that are waiting for you and transfer them to your home computer. A special kind of server, called a POP (Post Office Protocol) server, stores messages until you collect them. Once the messages are transferred, you can sign off from your ISP and deal with the messages at your leisure. When you want to send email, the process is reversed, except the messages go straight to the SMTP (Simple Mail Transfer Protocol) server. This is the server that handles all incoming and outgoing mail traffic.

Starting Eudora for the first time

Using Eudora Lite for the Macintosh or PC is very similar. If you come across an earlier version of Eudora you may find that different names have been used for certain menu items: for instance, in an earlier PC version the menu item **Options** was known as **Settings**. If there are discrepancies between your Eudora and the Eudora I have used, you will have to employ some lateral thinking, and consult on-line help or the manual. I have described here which menu items to click to receive the desired result. Instead of menu items you can also click on the appropriate icons. Again consult on-line help or the manual if the icons don't appear obvious, or experiment by clicking on the icons and note what happens.

Configuring Eudora for the PC

1. Connect to the Internet by connecting to your ISP. Double click on **Eudora** to start it.

2. When you use Eudora for the first time, you will need to fill in your email address, the address of your POP mail server, and a few other details. Select **Options** from the **Tools** Menu. Click on the **Getting Started** icon.

3. Type in the your email address in the **POP Mail** field.

4. Enter your name in the **Real Name** field.

5. Select **Winsock** as your connection method.

6. Now click on the icon **Personal Information**. A new screen appears, containing already some of the information that you have provided in **Getting Started**. Type your email address into the field **Return Address**.

7. Click on the **Hosts** icon. Type the name of the POP into the SMTP field. Your Internet service provider will give you the name of the POP server it uses.

8. There are a number of other icons that you can now select to customize Eudora, such as **Checking Mail, Sending Mail, Attachments, Fonts** and **Display**. You can look at each of these and change the attributes according to your need. In the first instance, stick with the default settings.

9. When you are satisfied with your options, click **OK**.

Configuring Eudora for the Macintosh

1. Connect to the Internet by connecting to your ISP. Double click on **Eudora** to start it.

2. When you use Eudora for the first time, you will need to fill in your email address, the address of your POP mail server, and a few other details. Select **Settings** from the **Special** menu. Click on the **Getting Started** icon.

3. Type in the your email address in the **POP Account** field.

4. Enter your name in the **Real Name** field.

5. Select **MacTCP** as your connection method.

6. Now click on the icon **Personal Information**. A new screen appears, containing already some of the information that you have provided in **Getting Started**. Type your email address into the field **Return Address**.

7. Click on the **Hosts** icon. Type in the name of the POP server into the SMTP field. Your ISP will give you the name of the POP server it uses.

8. There are a number of other icons that you can now select to customize Eudora, such as **Hosts, Checking Mail, Sending Mail, Attachments, Fonts** and **Display**. You can have a look at each of these and change the attributes according to your need. In the first instance you may want to stick with the default settings.

9. When you are satisfied with your options, click **OK**.

Reading your email

After you have set up Eudora, it's time to check if you have any mail:

1. Select **Check Mail** from the **File** menu.
2. A dialog box will appear that asks you for your password. Type in your password and click on the **OK** button. Eudora connects to the POP mail server and

checks if you have any mail. If you have, Eudora logs into the POP mail server and downloads the mail messages to your home computer. When the process is complete the **In Box** window appears.

3. You can read the full text of any of the email messages displayed in the In Box window by double clicking on the **subject field** of the message. Other information provided in this window includes the sender, date and length of a mail message.

Replying to email

If you already have a message from a person then it's very easy to reply to it:

1. Display the message on the screen or click on the subject of the message to highlight it in the **In Box**. Now select **Reply** from the **Message** menu. You will notice that this menu offers all sorts of other options, like forwarding email, redirecting it and resending it. Once you have mastered sending and replying to email, make sure to explore these options.

2. Eudora now displays a new message window. It has already filled in the sender's address (From:), the recipient's address (To:) and the subject of the message (obtained from the message you are replying to). It has also pasted in the message that you are replying to. All that remains for you is to write your reply and finally to press the **Send** button.

Writing a new email

1. Select **New Message** from the **Message** menu. A new message window appears. This time the only thing that Eudora has filled in for you is the **From:** field. Type in first your real name and then in brackets your email address.

2. In the **To:** field, type the email address of the recipient.

3. In the **Subject:** field, type the title of the message. Make sure to select a title that is meaningful and summarizes your message in two or three words. As the popularity of email increases, some women, including myself, receive hundreds of emails daily. Any email that looks irrelevant to me, is usually deleted unread.

4. Type your message in the empty window beneath **Attachments:**.

5. When you have completed your message, press the **Send** button, and the message will be on its way.

Deleting email

There are four ways to delete email. First, select the email you want to delete in the **In Box** by clicking on its subject field or open it for viewing. Then do any one of the following:

- Select **Delete** from the **Message** menu.
- Press the **Delete** key.
- Click the **trash can** icon on the main window toolbar.
- Select **Trash** from the **Transfer** menu. This will transfer the selected email to the trash can. Depending how you set up Eudora, the Trash is emptied every time you log out or you can empty it yourself by selecting **Empty Trash** from the **Special** menu.

Organizing your email into mailboxes

After you have used email for a while, you will start to wonder how to organize this flood of messages that will soon be a part of your daily life. Eudora provides you with mailboxes to organize your email. Here is what you do:

1. From the **Mailbox** menu choose **New**.
2. A dialog box appears. Type in the name you want to give the new mailbox.
3. Now click **OK**. A new mailbox has been created. You can now transfer mail from your In Box to your new mail box.
4. Select the email you want to transfer in the **In Box** by clicking on its subject field or open it for viewing.
5. Select the name of the new mailbox from the **Transfer** menu. This will transfer the selected email to the new mailbox.

Using Pine mail with a dial-up shell/text account

Let's have a look at a common UNIX mail program called Pine. Pine is used extensively in the UNIX world, and if you have a dial-up shell/text Internet account, you are likely to come across it, because many dial-up Internet providers are based on UNIX (rather than on Windows or Mac). The software your ISP makes available determines which tools you can use to read your messages.

Starting Pine for the first time

1. To be able to use Pine, you need to be connected to your ISP (logged-in, in Internet jargon). If new email is waiting for you, you will see the following message after you log in:

   You have new mail.

2. To start Pine, type pine at the operating prompt. Alternatively, if your ISP uses menus, select Pine from the appropriate menu. This is what you see:

```
PINE 3.91   MAIN MENU          Folder: INBOX  3 Messages

       ?    HELP            - Get help using Pine

       C    COMPOSE MESSAGE - Compose and send/post a message

       I    FOLDER INDEX    - View messages in current folder

       L    FOLDER LIST     - Select a folder OR news group to view

       A    ADDRESS BOOK    - Update address book

       S    SETUP           - Configure or update Pine

       Q    QUIT            - Exit the Pine program


  Copyright 1989-1994. PINE is a trademark of the University of
  Washington.

  ? Help    Q Quit    L ListFldrs    I Index    S Setup    B Report Bug
  O OTHER CMDS            C Compose         G GotoFldr       A AddrBook
```

The main menu screen is the starting point for all your email activities. One of the menu items will be highlighted. You can move between menu choices using your **up** and **down arrow** keys or the **tab** key. When you press the **Enter** key, you will go to the menu choice highlighted. Alternatively, you can type the character abbreviation at the beginning of each menu choice. Notice that the two last lines of the screen give you a quick summary of the commands available to you on this screen. The most important ones here are **?** for help, **Q** for quit, **I** to go to your new mail, and **C** to write a new message.

Leaving Pine

To leave Pine type Q from any screen. Pine will ask you if you really want to quit. Type Y if you do. Depending on how you set up Pine, it may also ask you if you really want to delete the messages marked delete from the InBox folder. Pine rather unfortunately calls this operation expunge. Type Y for yes or N for no.

Reading your email

1. To read your email move the highlighted line to **Folder Index – view messages in the current folder** and press **Enter**, or type I irrespective of where the highlighted line is.
2. A window appears containing a list of your current mail messages:

```
PINE 3.91   FOLDER INDEX           Folder: INBOX Message 2 of 4

+ N 1 Mar 1 Vita (3,357) Did you see Orlando?
+ N 2 Mar 3 Alice B. (2,637) Want to come to Paris for lunch?
+ N 3 Mar 1 Vita (11,906) Your text with my added comments
+ N 4 Mar 1 Orlando (1,192) re: trip to Paris

? Help    M Main Menu    P PrevMsg   - PrevPage    D Delete    R Reply
O OTHER CMDS V[ViewMsg] N NextMsg Spc NextPage U Undelete  F Forward
```

Again the last two lines of the screen contain a summary of the commands available on this screen.

3. Use the **up** or **down arrow** to select the message you want to read; then press the **Enter** key to view the selected message.

```
Date: Fri, 1 March 96 15:47:02 EST
From: vita@sissinghurst.com (Vita S.W.)
To: virg@bloomsbury.com
Subject: Did you see Orlando?

Virg,
Did you see the movie Orlando. Wasn't it fabulous. How about lunch
  sometime to discuss it. Cheers Vita.
```

Notice that the first line tells you when the message arrived; the second line reveals who it is from (first the address, then the name of the sender); the next two lines tell us who the message is addressed to and what the subject of the message is. Finally, we have the message itself.

Replying to email

What if Virginia wanted to reply to the message? To reply to an email that you have received:

1. Display the message you want to reply to on the screen and then type R, or highlight the message in the **Folder Index** window and type R. Pine will now display the **Message Reply** window. It has already filled in the recipient's address, the subject, and a copy of the message you are replying to.

2. Move your cursor to the line below **Message text** and compose your message. Depending on how Pine is set up it may include in your reply the message you are replying to. If you want to erase part or all of this message, position your cursor on the line you want to erase and type Cntrl K.

3. When you are happy with the message you composed, type Cntrl X (hold down the control key and type X) to send the message on its way.

Creating a new email

To create a new message:

1. Type C while you are either in the main menu, the index, folder list, or message text screens.

2. The **Compose Message** screen appears. This time it is up to you to fill the address of the recipient, the subject of the message, and of course the actual message. When you have finished type Cntrl X to send the message on its way.

```
PINE 3.91 COMPOSE MESSAGE          Folder:INBOX 11 messages

To      :
Cc      :
Attchmnt:
Subject :

----- Message Text -----



^G Get Help  ^X Send  ^R Read File  ^Y Prev Pg  ^K Cut Text    ^O Postpone
^C Cancel  ^J Justify  ^W Where is  ^V Next Pg  ^U UnCut Text  ^T To Spell
```

Again the last two lines of the screen list the commands available. For instance type Cntrl T to activate the spelling checker or Cntrl J to justify the text.

Including a text file in your email

No doubt many of your email messages will be quite short and you can easily write them while you are on-line. Occasionally you will want to compose a larger message at your leisure, or you may want to send a text file via email. How do you transfer the text that you have written with your word-processing package into your email message?

1. Save the text you have created with your word-processor as **text only with line breaks** if you are using Microsoft Word. Other word-processors call this option **save with no format,** or save as **ASCII text, DOS-text, plain text,** or something similar. Otherwise you will end up with one very long sentence. Take a note of this file name.

2. Connect to your ISP.

3. Your communications package will provide you with either **xmodem, ymodem, zmodem** or **kermit.** These are the names of different file transfer protocols that manage the uploading and downloading from your computer to your ISP (or any other computer that you can reach by modem) and vice versa. Which file transfer protocol to use depends on which protocol your ISP

supports. Consult your communications package online help or manual for the actual commands, as they vary from package to package. The communications software I use (Comit for Windows) has an easy-to-use menu system that guides you through sending and receiving files.

4. When you have successfully transferred the file to your ISP, start Pine. Type C to start a new message, R to reply to a message.

5. To include a text file in the message, place the cursor below the line message text and type Cntrl R (hold down the control key and type R). Pine will ask you for the name of the file to include. Type in the name and the file will be included in the message.

Abandoning a message

Halfway through writing your message you suddenly realize that you aren't ready to send it. You can abandon the process permanently by typing Cntrl C (hold down the control key and press c). Alternatively you can postpone writing a message to another time by typing Cntrl O.

Sending an email on to someone else (forwarding)

To forward an email, highlight the message to be forwarded in the Index screen or while the message is displayed and type F. A new message composition screen appears that contains the message to be forwarded (including the subject of the message). All that remains for you is to fill in the address of the receiver of the message.

A word of caution about using the reply function of your mail program. Always check that the return address the program has filled in for you is correct. The mail program obtains the reply address from the **From:** field of the message that was sent to you. This address may not be the address of the person who sent you the message, or the address may contain mistakes.

Deleting email

To delete an email, highlight the email in the Index screen or type D. Alternatively, if you want to delete the message immediately after you have read it, type D while the message is displayed on the screen. Once you have deleted a message, a D appears beside the message on the Index screen. During a session you can undelete a message by typing U after highlighting the message in the Index screen.

Saving email

To save a message type S. Pine will ask you to name the folder you want to store the message in. This is a good time to start creating various folders for your messages in order to keep your email organized. If you simply press **Enter** without typing a name, Pine will save the message in the **saved-messages** folder. Alternatively, you can type in a name and Pine will ask you if you want to create a new folder. Type Y to create the new folder.

Transferring an email to your home computer

Occasionally you will want to print out an email message, or you might have been sent an article or a story that you would like to be able to access at all times. You need to download a copy of the message that you have received to your home computer. This is what you do:

1. Connect to your ISP and start up **Pine**.
2. First you need to save the message as a separate file. Highlight the message in the **Folder Index** screen and type E. Pine asks you to type a name for the message to be copied to your directory. Type the name and press **Enter**.
3. Leave Pine by typing Q.
4. Now you need to activate **xmodem, ymodem, zmodem** or **kermit**. These are the names of different file transfer protocols that manage the uploading and downloading from your computer to your ISP (or any other computer that you can reach by modem) and vice versa. Which protocol to use depends on which ones your ISP supports. Most ISPs support the first three protocols. Also check which protocol your communications package supports and make sure to select the same protocol that your ISP supports. For example, if you are using xmodem type st filename to send text to a PC or sa filename to send text to a Macintosh at the operating prompt. Your ISP may have a menu system that includes uploading and downloading as a menu option. This will make it a lot easier for you.

You can give a command either in upper or lower case in Pine; the result will be the same.

Learning more about Pine

You can learn more about Pine by visiting the home page at http://www.cac.washington.edu/pine or ask questions by subscribing to the comp.mail.pine Usenet News group.

What about bounced mail?

You are going through your briefcase and find the business card of a friend you've not contacted for some months. You notice she has an email address (having recently acquired email yourself, you have found new meaning in those strange-looking addresses) and decide to send her a message. With some excitement you compose a lovely letter, expecting a happy reply. With the press of a button you send off your message, but, alas, the message reappears in your own mailbox with a comment like:

```
550 <stein.paris.edu.au>... Host unknown
```
or
```
- user name not known at this address -
```

The message has, as we say in Internet jargon, bounced. There are many reasons for messages bouncing. You might have made a spelling mistake in the address, the address may be out of date, or your friend may have left her job. Now you need to know how to find her current email address.

Understanding email addresses

When you write a letter, you know that in order for it to reach your intended receiver you need to include the person's name, street name and house number, town, country and postcode. What do you need to include in a person's email address?

An email address is in some ways similar to a postal address: it tells you and the computer the name of the person and exactly where the person's computer is located. An email address consists of two parts:

```
username.hostname
```

The username is the name a person is known under by the computer she uses. My username is r.senjen, but if my last name was more common it might have been r.senjen2 or senjen3. Depending on your ISP you might be able to choose your username or you may be assigned one by your system's administrator (the person who looks after your ISP's computers).

The hostname is the name of the computer you are using to connect to the Internet. Hostnames are created using the Domain Name System (DNS). Hostnames consist of several parts, separated by a full stop or period (pronounced *dot*). They are read from left to right, from the most specific to the most general.

At the most general level, the following names are used:

edu: educational institutions
com: commercial
gov: government
mil: military
net: networks
org: organizations that don't fit into the previous categories.

If one of these codes is the last letters of the email address, you can assume that it is a US email address. Otherwise you will see a two-letter country code (e.g. **nz** for New Zealand or **au** for Australia) as the last letters of the address. Once the country or general domain has been determined, it is entirely up to the system's administrator how to organize the rest of the host name.

So let's have a look at my Internet email address:

```
r.senjen@telstra.com.au
```

As we have seen, **r.senjen** is my username, and **au** is the country designation for Australia. The rest of my host name, **telstra.com**, refers to the fact that Telstra, the company I work for, is a commercial enterprise. What remains is an @ (pronounced *at*), which signifies that this particular username "belongs" to the address that follows.

You may also encounter other non-alphanumeric characters such as ! (pronounced *bang*) or %, or – in email addresses. These are just different forms of syntax, comparable to calling a road a street or a lane. All Internet addresses using the Internet mail protocol (SMTP) have @ as part of the address; it's simply a convention. If you encounter one of the other signs, it tells you that the person is connected to one of the associated "nets", rather than the Internet directly. Many of these "nets" provide Internet access as well, but this is only a fairly recent development.

Writing to somebody who uses one of the commercial on-line service providers used to be a little tricky, because their addressing system didn't always conform to Internet address standards. However these small problems have largely disappeared and most addresses now conform to the Internet standard.

How to find an email address

The simplest, most straightforward method of finding someone's email address is to ask the person in question to send it to you by snail mail (an old-fashioned letter in the post). If her address is a complicated one, it may be best to give her your email address and have her send a message to you to reduce the danger of errors.

If you are unable to ask your friend directly, you could try to guess her email address. Many companies and universities have standardized their addressing systems and it's often not hard to guess someone's address, especially if you already have an example of another person's address at the same place. For example, if I thought that Virginia Woolf worked at Monash University in Melbourne I might try

```
v.woolf@monash.edu.au
```

How did I make up the address? Well, I know that au stands for Australia, edu signifies educational institutions and Monash is the name of the university. More about how email addresses are made up in a moment.

If all else fails, there are various methods of using the Internet itself to search for an address. To use the Internet to find a person's email address you'll need to know more than just her name. You'll need to know where she works or the name of her ISP's computer. It's easiest to find people who work for academic institutions because these organizations have been using the Net for a long time.

If you have access to the World Wide Web than you can use one of the increasing number of Internet "white pages". These are similar to the Web indexes for subject-based information, but specialize in finding people rather than information. Here is a selection of "white pages" to try:

Four11 Directory Service: http://www.four11.com
Internet people: gopher://yaleinfo.yale.edu:7700/11/Internet-People
Netfind: http://www.nova.edu/Inter-Links/netfind.html

Using the Usenet address server to find an address

If you think the person you are looking for has access to Usenet and has posted messages to Usenet during the past year, try sending an email message to query the Usenet database.

send email to: mail-server@rtfm.mit.edu
in the body of the message type: send usenet-addresses/*name*

In the *name* part you can list all the possible words that may appear in the person's address (see the example below). You might try her first and last name, possible usernames (e.g. r.senjen, senjen), an abbreviation of the institution she works for, and a country abbreviation. The information can be written in any order and in upper or lower case. You can put multiple requests into the same email message, but put each request on a separate line.

So, let's try it. I sent the following message:

```
        send usenet-addresses/rye senjen au
to:     mail-server@rtfm.mit.edu
```

This is what I got back.

```
        rye@crl.go.jp (Rye Senjen) (Jan 15 95)
        rye@media.trl.oz.au (Rye Senjen) (Jul 14 94)
```

In addition, there were about forty unrelated addresses, some including the word rye, others bearing no resemblance to my first or last name whatsoever. This service can take a few minutes, hours or even days to answer your query, depending how busy it is.

Accessing the Internet by email

To find out how to use email to access Internet services such as FTP, Gopher, Usenet News, etc. send email to one of the following addresses:

Address	Send the following message
listserv@ubvm.cc.buffolo.edu	GET INTERNET BY-EMAIL NETTRAIN F=MAIL
mail-server@rtfm.mit.edu	send usenet/news.answers/internet-services/access-via-email
mailbase@mailbase.ac.uk	send lis-iis e-access-inet.txt

Dos and don'ts when using email

Email is a fairly new communications medium and the conventions for its use are still in the process of being established. They lie somewhere between traditional letter-writing and a telephone conversation. Here is a list of points to remember when writing an email message:

- Be concise.
- Make references clear.
- Use humour with caution.
- Be discreet (always ask permission from the original sender before copying and forwarding on a message).
- Don't waste bandwidth (some people have to pay for the email they receive and/or the time it takes to download messages).

You might like to use "smileys" or your own inventions to overcome the one-dimensionality of the textual messages, for example: :>) or :>(can indicate your emotional state. I tend not to use smileys much, but they are a good idea if you feel confined by the need to be concise and want your message to have a lighter, more personal touch (see chapter 6).

Chapter 6

On-line communities: how to participate

What makes computer-mediated communication different?

Until recently is was rare for people to communicate regularly with each other before they had actually met in person. Those with particular interests or hobbies would periodically exchange letters, but because letter-writing is time-consuming, friendships developed very slowly, if at all. Friendships usually emerge from a combination of physical proximity and shared interests or common goals. It seems we never really feel we know a person until we've met them face to face. However, once a physical connection has been made, friendships can be sustained over long periods of time on the basis of the occasional letter or phone-call. Because of its relative speed and affordability (to some), the Internet has changed the way that people communicate with each other. Many Internet users are claiming that they are in fact developing meaningful connections, through chat rooms, MUDs and email. People claim that "real" friendships are being made and some claim to be having romantic relationships via the Internet. Whatever your own personal feelings about Internet romances, it does appear that the Internet has overturned many assumptions about social context and behaviour.

Many women are sceptical about the possibility of meeting people and developing real friendships through the Internet. Do we really need to see a person or hear their voice to make a meaningful connection? Personally I haven't made any new friends, although I spend many hours per day on-line. However, there are women who claim that it can and does happen. There are instances of couples meeting in real-life after an extended period of on-line courtship and then continuing their relationship successfully. Other couples are satisfied with a "virtual" relationship. I have found, however, that an Internet connection enhances and deepens my already existing friendships. The convenience of using email, for instance, to communicate with an acquaintance also makes it easier to move to friendship with that person.

What are the characteristics that makes using a computer different from other forms of human communication? Some key differences are :

- an absence of regulating feedback and a lack of social context
- few widely shared norms governing the use of the Internet
- a lack of non-verbal cues
- a certain level of anonymity due to the lack of visual or aural signifiers.

The Internet has a number of services that are used to communicate with others such as email, Usenet News, chat programs (IRC), and Multi-User Dimensions (MUDs). Each of these offers different ways of communicating. All of these modes of communication are at present text-based. However, over time I expect video and two- and three-dimensional graphical representation of users to be added to some of these services. Email and Usenet News do not require the participants to be on-line at the same time; messages are stored and can be read at the users' convenience. IRC and MUDs are used in real time and are of special interest because they defy many of the conventional understandings of the difference between the spoken and the written word.

Using Internet Rely Chat (IRC) or MUDs, messages are directly transmitted to all participants. IRCers frequently use nicknames and MUDers can not only choose a name, but also a gender and a character. Both offer the opportunity to play with identity and extend a person's perception of herself and how others perceive her.

To overcome the lack of non-verbal cues, users of computers have developed a variety of textual equivalents such as the infamous smiley or by indicating laughter with *hahaha*. Here are some examples of smileys. If you have trouble recognizing them, turn the page on its side.

:-)	basic smiley
;-)	wink, wink – indicates sarcasm
:-|	indifference
:->	devilish grin
@:-)	curly haired person grinning
8-)	person with glasses grinning
:-D	shock or surprise
:-/	perplexed

Abbreviations are also frequently used; here are some common ones.

AFAIK:	as far as I know
BTW:	by the way
FAQ:	frequently asked questions
FWIW:	for what it's worth
IMHO:	in my humble opinion
RTFM:	read the —— manual
ROTFL:	rolls on the floor laughing

Despite the fact that on-line computer communication lacks most of the conventional social controls, a number of social sanctions have arisen to punish users who do not obey netiquette (the etiquette of the Internet). One method used to punish recalcitrant users is spamming, in which a person's mailbox is flooded with so many messages that the computer system that the mailbox is attached to collapses. Peer pressure is often used successfully to "punish" errant members of a particular computer community.

Electronic mailing lists:
talking to like-minded people world wide

Imagine you have a passionate interest in the poetry of Sylvia Plath. You'd love to be able to have discussions with other enthusiasts about her work, but the only other people you know of who share your interest live thousands of miles away. Luckily some of you have access to email and you start corresponding with each other through the Internet. After an especially inspiring interchange with one of your "Plath" friends you decide to send a copy of your discussion to all the others in your "group". This is how an electronic mailing list is born.

Electronic mail is a medium for one-to-one communication. By extending the concept of email and sending a duplicate of a particular message to each person on a mailing list, we have one-to-many communication – electronic mailing lists.

Mailing lists are an increasingly popular way for people with shared interests to stay in contact with each other wherever their geographical location, without the long delays of the postal service.

Topics already operating cover everything imaginable from origami to breast-feeding and beyond. There is no limit to the subjects we humans find to fascinate us, and it is always a pleasure to find others to share our interests.

You may be wondering if belonging to a mailing list is expensive. To my knowledge 99.9 per cent of all mailing lists are free. I have heard of one or two business-oriented mailing lists that are starting to charge an annual subscription fee, but this move has caused considerable discussion and even outrage in some Internet circles.

How does it work?

Participants of a mailing list send messages to a central address. At this address a special program (the mailing list processor) takes each incoming message and forwards it to all people on the mailing list.

There are three activities which a mailing list needs to allow for:

- subscribing
- sending messages
- unsubscribing.

A list usually has two addresses, one for administrative tasks and one for the actual messages that are to be forwarded to each person on it. It is very important to send requests for subscribing and unsubscribing only to the administrative address of a list. You can often recognize the administration address because it has the word "request" in the address.

There are numerous list processor programs available but probably the most well known are: LISTSERV, Majordomo, and Listproc. These programs completely automate the process of subscribing and unsubscribing. Your name is automatically added to or removed from a list without human intervention. These programs offer more that just a forwarding service: they respond to additional commands such as suspending/resuming mail, sending all of one day's email in one message (a function called digest), and searching archived messages.

Moderated versus unmoderated lists

Because some lists are very specialized and/or the topic is one that could lead easily to heated discussions, many mailing lists are moderated. This means that all incoming mail is first read by the moderator. This person decides whether a message fits the character of the mailing list. A list may have restrictions on who may join it. Some lists are for women only, while others allow only those of a particular profession to join.

Who is chosen to be the moderator? Mostly the person who decides to start a list is its first moderator. Sometimes lists have to look for new moderators, because the old ones change jobs or interests and others are called upon to volunteer their services. Moderating a busy list can be quite a time-consuming business. You not only have to read all the messages and decide whether they fit within the list's brief, but you also have to deal with bounced messages and email to people who are having trouble unsubscribing.

Which list processor does a list use?
The address of a list may tell you which list processor the list uses. Look out for the words LISTSERV, Majordomo or Listproc in the address. If none of these appears in the list, chances are it is processed by humans!

How to find a list to join

The number of mailing lists on the Internet is ever expanding. The LISTSERV program alone is used by over 1000 mailing lists, serving over 1 million subscribers with 2–6 million messages per day. The numbers are reportedly growing at 70 per cent per year. So, how do you find the list of your choice?

Visit the LISTSERV home page (**http://tile.net/listserv**) and search for the list of your choice by subject, host country, sponsoring organization or popularity. Of course, not all mailing lists use LISTSERV to manage mail distribution, but many do, so the LISTSERV home page is a good start. Another option is to use ftp to get lists of lists and you can also search Web sites that contain lists of lists. Another way of finding a list is by finding a Web page that covers the topic you are interested in: chances are that if a mailing list exists for it, it will be mentioned on the Web site. See also chapter 11 for lists of special interest to women.

I visited the LISTSERV home page to see if there were any lists dealing with crime writing. On the first page you can search the database for a list, or choose a folder. The folders contain lists ordered by subject, host country, popularity, name, description, or sponsoring organization. I chose the subject-based folder, rather than performing a global search on the list database. I double clicked on the folder, **Alphabetical listing by subject,** and was taken to a list of subfolders. One of these was **literature and writing.** After choosing this subfolder, I was presented with an alphabetical list of lists on this topic. One of these was DOROTHYL-MYSTERY LITERATURE E-CONFERENCE. When I clicked on this link it revealed more information on the list:

```
DOROTHYL-MYSTERY LITERATURE E-CONFERENCE
Subscribers: 2585
Archive searching: open to everyone
Who can join: anyone
Country: USA
Site: Kent State University, Kent, Ohio 44240
Computerized administrator: listserv@kentvm.kent.edu
Human administrator: dorothyl-request@kentvm.kent.edu
To send mail to the group, write to: dorothyl@kentvm.kent.edu

You can join this group by sending the message "sub DOROTHYL your
name" to listserv@kentvm.kent.edu
```

As you can see, DOROTHYL is popular, with over 2500 subscribers, and anyone can join. All you need to do is to email the message "sub DOROTHYL your name" to the administrative address of the list.

The LISTSERV home page is not the only place to explore. Here are the Internet addresses for some other lists of lists:

Standford Research Institute	ftp://sri.com/netinfo/interest-groups.txt
Some lists of lists:	email: listserv@vm1.nodak.edu in the body write: get list of lists
Liszt – directory of email discussion groups:	http://www.liszt.com
The Listserv home page:	http://tile.net/listserv
Kovacs scholarly list:	

http://vmsgopher.cua.edu:70/1gopher_root_mullen%3a%5b_general_elists%5d
http://www.mailbase.ac.uk/kovacs/
email to: listserv.kentvm.kent.edu
send the message: get acadlist index

Subscribing and unsubscribing to a list that uses LISTSERV

Let's now look in more detail at one of the common list-processor programs. LISTSERV is used by many mailing lists to manage all their administration automatically. After subscribing to a mailing list which uses LISTSERV, you automatically receive a welcoming message explaining the purpose of the list and a summary of the major commands. Each time you issue a command to LISTSERV (excluding sending your messages to the list), you will also be sent a status report letting you know whether or not your command was successful.

To subscribe to a list that uses the LISTSERV mail-processing package you need to send the following message to the address used for administrative purposes.

```
subscribe <listname> <firstname lastname>
```

For instance, if you want to join the list book-l, the administrative address would look something like this:

```
listserv@lighthouse.com.gb
```

You would send the following message to this address:

```
subscribe bookl <firstname lastname>
```

After you have subscribed to a list, you are ready to participate in discussions by sending messages to the main list address. As soon as your email address is added to the mailing list, you receive all messages sent out by all the other list members.

Each particular list you subscribe to will generate different numbers of messages. On some lists you may receive up to thirty messages a day, while others might average one or two. In your initial enthusiasm to gather information you will probably, like me, subscribe to many lists. Soon your message board will be overflowing and you'll be tempted to spend all day reading your mail. Luckily some lists offer a digest version, which is the accumulation of all the messages collected in one day sent out in one long file. This is a great arrangement if the lists are very active and you're short on time. Once you have subscribed to a list, the confirmation message usually tells you if a digest form is available.

If you are getting too much mail or you are finding a list less interesting than you expected, you can always unsubscribe. To unsubscribe send the following message to the address used for administrative purposes:

```
unsubscribe listname
```

For example, if you belong to the list called book-l, you send the following message:

```
unsubscribe bookl
```

There is no need to include your name when you unsubscribe. The automatic listhandler uses your return email address to recognize you.

Replying to messages received from a mailing list

When you reply to a message, you must take extra care. Do you wish your reply to be sent to all the list subscribers, or do you want to email the sender privately? When replying to mail it is easy to get into the habit of simply hitting the reply function. This is fine if you are replying to an individual's email message, because your message will be sent only to this person's address. However, if you are replying to a message which was sent through a mailing list of which you are one of many subscribers, you'll find that when you hit the reply function your message is then transmitted to each person on the list. This could be embarrassing!

If you use the reply function of your mailing program to reply to a message from a mailing list, take extra care. If you want your reply to go to the entire list, make sure the address for the list is inserted in the address field.

How to find out who else subscribes to the mailing list (LISTSERV)

Imagine you and your close friend are on the Sylvia Plath mailing list. You are at home, going through the latest news on the list and you find a pertinent comment, sent by your friend, about one of Sylvia's poems. You are reminded of the misery you have just experienced today at work and, without thinking, hit the reply button and pour out your heart to your friend. What an unco-operative miserable lot of workmates you have, what an inconsistent, intolerable boss you have, etc. You have forgotten something vital – the reply to contains all the other 150 mailing list addresses of Sylvia Plath fans all over the world – including your boss!

You probably didn't even know your boss was on the list. It is quite common for a list to have only a handful of active members and many more "lurkers" who just listen in and rarely or never contribute their own message. However, you can find out who all the people are on a mailing list, if they choose to be accessible.

To find out who has subscribed to a list send the following message to the administrative address of the list:

```
review listname
```

Table 6.1: Summary of mailing list commands

LISTSERV

Send all administrative commands to the administrative address. Send the following commands in the body of the message. Do not put anything on the subject line.

Process	Command	Comment
Subscribing	subscribe listname firstname lastname subscribe DOROTHYL VIRGINIA WOOLF	
Unsubscribing	unsubscribe listname firstname lastname unsubscribe DOROTHYL VIRGINIA WOOLF	Do not include your name when unsubscribing. The automatic list-handler uses your return email address to recognize you.
Suspending mail	set listname nomail set DOROTHYL nomail	This is very useful when you go on holiday. Again, do not include your name.
Resuming mail	set listname mail set DOROTHYL mail	Once you have returned you need to let the program know to start sending you mail again.
Who is on the list	review listname review DOROTHYL	This is a useful method of finding someone's email address.
Retrieving past messages and other files	index listname index DOROTHYL	
Obtaining a particular file	get filename filetype get ORLANDO.DOC REFDOC	Send this command after you have identified from the index which particular file you want to look at.

(Table continues)

Majordomo

Send all administrative commands to the administrative address:

listname-request@listaddress or Majordomo@listaddress

Send the following commands in the body of the message. Do not put anything on the subject line.

Process	Command	Comment
Subscribing	subscribe listname email address subscribe cybergrrl v.woolf@bloomington.com	
Unsubscribing	unsubscribe listname email address unsubscribe cybergrrl v.woolf@bloomington.com	
Getting a digest	subscribe listname-digest subscribe cybergrrl-digest	
Cancelling the digest	unsubscribe listname-digest unsubscribe cybergrrl-digest	
Obtaining help	help	
Finding out more about the list you want to subscribe to	info listname info cybergrrl	
Who is on the list	who list who cybergrrl	This is a useful method of finding someone's email address.
Getting an index of files related to the list	index listname index cybergrrl	
Obtaining a particular file	get listname filename get cybergrrl onlineNow.doc	Send this command after you have identified from the index which particular file you want to look at.
Stop processing commands	end	This is useful if your mailer adds a signature.

(Table continues)

LISTPROC

Send all administrative commands to the administrative address:

listname-request@listaddress or Listproc@listaddress

Send the following commands in the body of the message. Do not put anything on the subject line.

Process	Command	Comment
Subscribing	subscribe listname firstname lastname subscribe cybergrrl Virginia Woolf	
Unsubscribing	unsubscribe listname firstname lastname unsubscribe cybergrrl Virginia Woolf	
Who is on the list	recipients listname recipients cybergrrl	This is a useful method of finding someone's email address.
Getting a digest	set listname mail digest set cybergrrl mail digest	
Cancelling the digest	set listname mail ack set cybergrrl mail ack	

Finding out more about different automatic list handlers

Table 6.2 gives a list of email addresses for the three different automatic list handlers. You can send an email to the address and if you put the word **help** in the message part of the email, the list-processing package will send you a summary of its commands.

Table 6.2: Help information for automated lists

List Name	Email address	Message to send
LISTPROC	listproc@listproc.net	help
LISTSERV	listserv@uacsc2.albany.edu	send listserv memo
Majordomo	majordomo@csn.org	help

A worldwide bulletin board and discussion group: Usenet News

What is Usenet News ?

Usenet News (also known as Network News, Netnews or just Usenet) is the giant bulletin board and repository of thousands of discussion groups worldwide. If you're in need of a recipe for vegan lasagne, want to sell a mountain bike, need to know the cheapest hotel in Alice Springs, or perhaps you'd like to discuss the finer points of C++ garbage collection – there is bound to be a news group on it. The individual discussion groups are organized hierarchically and into topics. For instance, if a group is called rec.cooking.recipes, rec. is the main area for groups to do with recreational activities, cooking. is a subgroup of rec., and recipes is a subgroup of the cooking groups. There are currently more than 7000 thousand news groups and 2 million readers per day. Some groups get read literally by thousands of people per day; others have a relatively small audience. Apart from the large worldwide groups there also many local or even company-specific news groups.

These are the major categories into which Usenet News groups fall:

Group name	Topics the group covers
alt.	alternative topics, anything from art to very offensive stuff
comp.	computer related topics
news.	discussions relating to the Internet
rec.	recreation and hobbies
sci.	scientific discussions
soc.	cultural and social talk
talk.	an opportunity to put your views forward; can be very offensive.

Two of the most useful news groups are **news.announce.newusers** and **news.answers**. The first one is especially for people new to Usenet News and is a place were you can ask all the beginner's questions you may have. News.answer is the place were the FAQs (Frequently Asked Questions) for many technical and non-technical topics are posted. You can learn about anything from encryption to modem cables to how to program in python or breed Tonkinese cats. FAQs were one of my major sources of information for this book.

A word of warning. Unlike commercial on-line services, Usenet News is a true free-for-all. You may ask questions on any conceivable topic, but the answers you receive are in no way guaranteed to be correct. The answer might be spot-on or it may be pure fantasy. Some news groups are of course more reliable than others – there are even moderated news groups – but as a rule I am cautious about an answer that I have received via Usenet News.

How does Usenet News work?

Usenet News was developed in 1979 by students from Duke University and the University of Carolina to enable computers at both universities to exchange messages. The exchange was automatic and occurred at a prearranged time. This system used the UNIX-to-UNIX Copy protocol (UUCP) over ordinary phone-lines. Slowly as more UNIX computers at other locations were joined to this network, Usenet News developed. The Usenet News network was initially separate from the Internet. In 1986 the Network News Transfer Protocol (NNTP) was introduced to reach the wider Internet audience and link Usenet News to the Internet. Usenet News operates by storing and forwarding news groups, and it can take some days for a particular article to circulate around the world.

Usenet News is similar to email lists, but you don't automatically receive new postings to the news groups in your mailbox as you do on a mailing list. Instead Usenet News, like most other Internet services, uses a client-server arrangement to distribute news and enable users to read news. You use a news reader (the name for the client) to connect to a news server. The server that stores news articles is either a public server, or your ISP may store a selection of news groups on its computer. Most service providers keep news items for three days to two weeks. If you want to keep up-to-date with news, you must read it regularly.

There is a wide variety of news readers for all types of computers: e.g. WinTrumpet and Free Agent for Windows, Nuntius and Internews for Macintosh and Tin for UNIX. Some email programs such as Pine and Eudora also permit you to read news; so do most World Wide Web browsers. Addresses of some news readers are:

WinTrumpet for Windows
ftp://archie.au/micros/pc/oak/vendors/trumpet/wintrump/wtwsk10a.zip

Free Agent for Windows
http://www.forteinc.com/agent/freagent.htm

Nuntius for Macintosh
ftp://sunsite.anu.edu.au/pub/mac/comm/_Internet/nuntius-204.hqx

Internews
ftp://sunsite.anu.edu.au/pub/mac/info-mac/comm/_Internet/inter-news-101.hqx

Usenet News terminology

Usenet News has a number of specialized terms. For instance a **post** is a message that someone has posted to a news group. As others reply to the post, a **thread** or line of discussion evolves. Usually all posts within the same thread have the same subject line. If you want to change the thread of a discussion, you change the words on the subject line. A **cross-posting** is a posting that has been sent to several news groups. Before you answer, make sure your reply gets only sent to the relevant news groups by changing the To: field appropriately.

Reading news with a World Wide Web browser: Netscape Navigator 2.0

(See chapter 7 for more information on Web browsers.)
The software package Netscape Navigator 2.0 comes with an excellent news-reader. It offers too many options to describe in detail here. Make sure you explore all its different possibilities and don't be afraid to play. The description below will get you started. Many other graphical newsreaders work in a similar manner.

Getting ready to read Usenet News

To read Usenet News with Netscape Navigator 2.0 you need to tell Netscape Navigator the address of your news server. Select **Mail & News Preferences** from the **Options** menu. Click on the **Servers** tab. Type the name of the news server in the **News (NNTP) Server** field. Your ISP should tell you its preferred news server. Click on the **OK** button to close the window. You are ready to read news!

Subscribing and reading Usenet News groups

By default, you have access to all the news groups a Usenet News server carries. But most likely you won't want to wade through several thousands or even a few hundred news groups every time you read news. To receive only the news groups you are interested in, you need to subscribe to them:

1. To call up Usenet News from your Netscape Navigator browser select **Netscape News** from the **Windows** menu.
2. A new browser window will pop up:

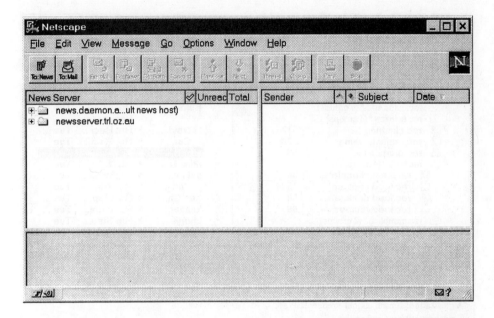

The Window is divided into three panes below the toolbar. The top left window displays the Usenet News server and the news groups you have subscribed to. The top right pane shows the article in a selected news group. The pane across the bottom of the window displays the article selected.

When you click on the line that contains the name of the server, the news groups that you have subscribed to appear. The first time you call up news, you will only see two or three groups that Netscape Navigator has automatically subscribed to. To subscribe to other news groups and have a look at the range of news groups available, select **Show all news groups** from the **Options** menu. Select **Show subscribed news groups** from the **Options** menu when you have finished selecting news groups and you want to see only the ones you have subscribed to. Subscribe to news groups by clicking on the group heading **rec.** – for instance – then on the subgroup like **rec.food** and finally click the box next to the group you want to subscribe to. To have a look at some articles discussed in a group, click on the group name. Netscape Navigator displays the subject lines of the news articles in the right pane for you. To read an article, click on the article. Articles that belong to a particular thread are slightly indented.

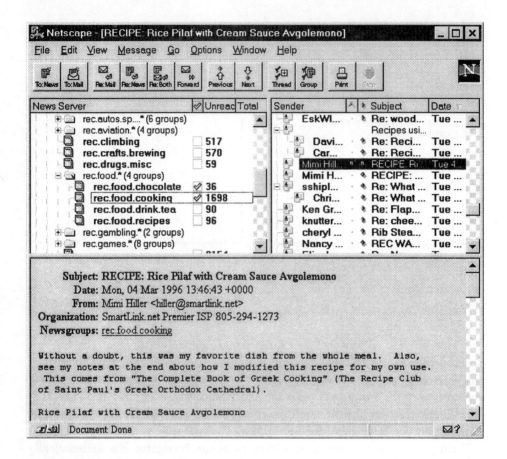

Responding to an article

To respond to an article press the **Re:News** button. A new window appears, which is similar to an email composition window. Netscape Navigator has already filled in all the relevant addressing information; all that remains is for you to type in your message. Press the **Send** button to post the article.

Writing a new article

If you want to send a new article to a particular news group press the **To:News** button (see chapter 5). A new window appears, which is similar to an email composition window. Fill in the address details and type your message. Press the **Send** button to post the article.

Posting an article using email

Not all service providers permit you to post articles to Usenet News. To get around this restriction you can email to certain addresses, who will then forward your posting to the appropriate news group. One such address is:

```
newsgroup@cs.utexas.edu
```

Replace any dots in the group name with dashes; for instance, alt.talk.ivftechnology becomes:

```
alt-talk-ivftechnology.
```

UseNet News Survival Hints
- Always direct your postings to the appropriate news group.
- Don't cross-post extensively.
- Unsubscribe from offensive news groups.

Internet Relay Chat: talking real-time with your sisters

What is Internet Relay Chat?

IRC is an Internet service that allows you to "talk" in real time with other people connected to the same "channel". IRC was developed in Finland by Jarko Oikarinen, who wanted to extend the UNIX talk program. The UNIX talk program allows two people to send text messages directly to each other's screens, rather than using email for this kind of communication.

IRC permits many users to send messages to each other simultaneously by selecting a channel. There are several thousands of these channels and the IRC protocol manages the communication and relay between all the channel participants. If you like meeting strangers and don't care if they are not really what they claim to be, joining an IRC channel could be for you. There are many different types of IRC channels, from very sleazy to spiritual. There are IRC channels devoted to discussing technical issues like C++ programming, channels for high-school students, and channels simply to hang out and waste time. If you have a topic that you would like discussed, you can create your own public or private channel. Private channels are great for discussing topics with a group of friends or organizing a real-time Internet-based meeting. IRC is a bit like a teleconferencing system where the IRC server acts as a central point for you to connect and to talk to others in real time. The only differences are that you use a keyboard instead of your voice, and it is a lot cheaper than a voice call.

The world of IRC

Like many other Internet services, IRC uses client-server architecture. You use a client on your computer to connect to one of the public servers, or Telnet to one of the public clients and connect from there to a server. If you have a dial-up IP connection you can use one of the graphical IRC clients. My favourite Windows-based IRC client is mIRC. The IRC server keeps track of users and channels, and makes sure that all the channels and private messages go to the correct place. Servers can be linked to form an IRC network and it doesn't matter which server on a particular network you connect to. Always try to connect to the server closest to you.

The FTP sites of some graphical IRC clients are:

homer (Mac)   ftp://sunsite.anu.edu.au/pub/mac/info-mac/comm/_Internet/home-094.hqx
ircle (Mac)   http://www.xs4all.nl/~ircle
WSIRC (PC)   ftp://papa.indstate.edu/winsock-l/winirc/wsirc20.exe
mIRC (PC)   http://www.ozemail.com.au/~mooremt/index.html

Before you try these, check what your ISP has available. Most ISPs have a range of clients for different Internet services available, ready for you to download.

There are two main IRC networks: EFnet and Undernet, and quite a number of smaller or local networks. EFnet is the older, larger and "main" IRC with about 5000 daily online users. While a number of new IRC networks have sprung up, it is still the most popular. Undernet is the main alternative to the EFnet. Considered by some to be more friendly, it is growing in size very rapidly and usually has about 1000 users online. You can obtain more information on IRC networks from the following addresses:

List of IRC nets
    http://uptown.turnpike.net/L/Larry14/irc.html
List of EFnet and Undernet servers
    EFnet/Undernet   http://uptown.turnpike.net/L/Larry14/servers.txt
    Undernet   http://servers.undernet.org/server-list.html
    EFnet   ftp://ftp.comco.com/pub/irc/server-list-current
EFnet information
    http://www.eyecandy.com/efnet.html
Undernet information
    http://www2.undernet.org:8080/~cs93jtl/Undernet.html
    http://www.undernet.org/

If you or your ISP don't have a local IRC client, you can use a public Telnet client (see chapter 9). A list of Undernet Telnet clients can be found at:

http://murc.undernet.org/undernet/telnet.html

Using IRC through a dial-up IP/graphical account: mIRC for Windows

If you have a dial-up IP/graphical account you can use a graphical IRC client like mIRC (go to http://www.ozemail.com.au/~mooremt/index.html for instructions on how to download and install it). It makes using IRC a lot easier. For instance each channel you join is displayed in a different window, which makes following conversations on different channels much easier. Once you have obtained mIRC from an FTP site it is fairly easy to install (just follow the instructions) and use. You may also want to retrieve an up-to-date list of IRC servers. Here is how to use mIRC for IRC:

1. Establish your dial-up IP Internet connection.

2. Double click on the **mIRC** icon.

3. A large empty window appears. Go to the **File** menu and select **setup**. This is what you see:

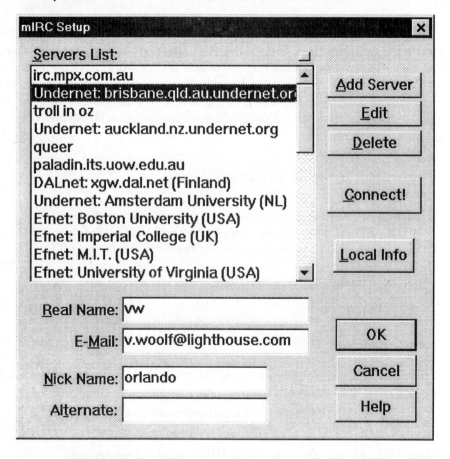

Fill in your personal details and select the server closest to you. Then press the **connect** button. There is a readymade list of servers on mIRC, but you can add your own favourite or closest server with the **Add Server** button.

4. Once you are connected to the server, the status window fills with information about the server. Now it's time to join a channel. But how do you find out which channel to join? Type /list and the server will send you a list of all

channels in use and the number of people using each at present. This can be a very long list. Type /list -MIN 5 to get a list of channels that have at least five participants. This will still produce a very long list of channels, so you might want to use a higher number. Channel names are identified by a # in front of the name, e.g. #england or #ircbar. When you have found a channel that sounds promising, type:

/join channelname

e.g.

/join #cybergrrl

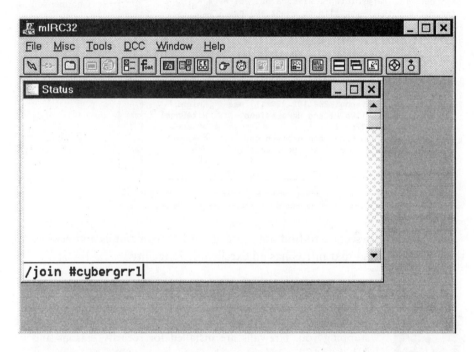

5. For each channel you join, a window will appear with two panes. One pane shows you what is said; the smaller pane on the right shows you the participants. Finally, there is a strip at the bottom where you can enter your own text or commands.

6. When you have had enough of a particular channel, type: /part in the channel window.

7. To end your IRC session type: /quit in the bar on the bottom of the status window.

8. Use the status window for general IRC commands, and the channel window for commands relating to a channel.

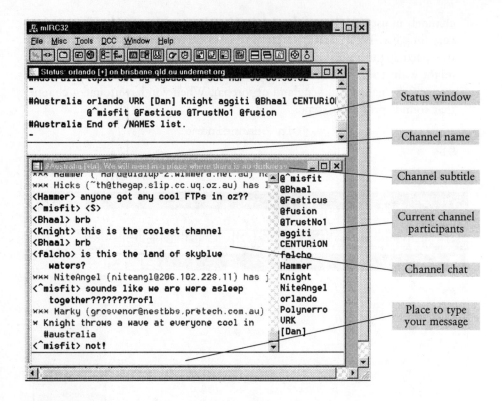

Read the next section to find out more about IRC commands and how to use them. You will find that mIRC has an excellent help facility.

If you have trouble connecting to an IRC server, a firewall may be stopping you. Firewalls are installed for security reasons and let only bona fide traffic through. Contact your ISP to check if you are behind a firewall and what you can do about it.

Using IRC with a dial-up shell/text account

If you connect to the Internet using a dial-up shell/text account, the first step is to connect to a server. Depending on your ISP, all you may have to do is type `irc` and the system will automatically connect you to the nearest server. If that doesn't work, you will have to use the Telnet service. Always connect to the server that is geographically closest to you. Here are the steps:

1. Assuming you need to connect to a server using **Telnet**, type:

    ```
    telnet addressOfServer
    ```

    e.g.
    ```
    telnet irc.mpx.com.au
    ```

2. Once you are connected to a server, you can join a channel (sometimes called a room) by typing:

    ```
    /join channelname
    ```

    e.g.
    ```
    /join #cybergrrl
    ```

    If you don't know which channel to join type:

    ```
    /list
    ```

    to get a list of all channels. This list can be very long. Type:

    ```
    /list -MIN 5
    ```

    to get a list of all channels with more than five users. You can put any number you like there, five still produces a fairly long list of channels.

IRC commands explained

General IRC commands are as follows:

Command	Action
/nick NickName	changes your nickname
/quit	exits your IRC session, (same as /bye, /signoff and /exit)
/help	prints help on the given command
/whois NickName	displays information about someone
/whowas NickName	displays information about someone who just left
/away	leaves a message saying you're not paying attention

Giving yourself a nickname

After you have connected to an IRC server and found a channel to join, the fun begins. One of the first things to do is give yourself a nickname. Most IRC users use nicknames rather than their username. When you first join a channel your nickname will be your username. To change to a nickname of your choice type:

```
/nick yourNickName
```

Communicating with other channel participants

Using slash (/) directly in front of some text indicates to the IRC server that you are sending a command, and anything following the slash will be evaluated accordingly. If you type some text without a slash in front, it will be sent to all other participants on the channel. So if your nickname is Virg and you type:

```
Hello it's me here.
```

All other channel participants will see:

```
<Virg> Hello it's me here.
```

Typing /me <text> is used to convey actions or emotions to others. If your nickname is Virg and you type:

```
/me waves to all beings
```

then all other participants of the channel you are on will see:

```
Virg waves to all beings
```

Finding out more about other channel participants

You can use the **/who** command to find out who else is on a channel. If you type /whois NickName the IRC server will display whatever is known about a particular nickname, usually the person's email address.

Creating new channels

You can create your own channel by typing /join #channelname, where #channelname is the name of a channel that does not yet exist. Channel names are usually identified by a # in front of the name, e.g. #oz or #lecafe.

Channel commands

Command	Action
/list	lists channels, number of users, topic
/names	shows the nicknames of the users on each channel
/join #channelname	sets your current channel, (same as CHANNEL)
/who #channelname	gives a listing of users
/invite NickName	sends an invitation to another user on another channel
/leave	leaves a channel, (same as PART)
/kick NickName	gets rid of someone on a channel
/topic	changes the topic of the channel
/me text	sends anything about you to a channel. This command is used to describe your actions, rather than what you are thinking.
/describe text	sends anything about you to a person or channel
/notify	warns you of people logging in or out of IRC
/ignore NickName	removes output from specific people off your screen
/summon username	invites someone who is not on IRC to join

Private conversation on IRC channels

Normally any text that you type into your computer while on IRC is redistributed to all people on a particular channel. However, it is possible to converse with another user privately on a public channel. Type

```
/query NickName channel
```

to request a private conversation with someone. To stop the private conversation, use

```
/query
```

Here are some commands that you will find useful for private conversations:

Command	Action
/msg NickName	sends a private message
/query NickName	starts a private conversation
/notice NickName	sends a private message surrounded by quotation marks, often used to send automated responses
/query	ends a private conversation

A channel just for you and your friends

I find IRC really exciting because I can have a private or even secret channel where my friends and I can converse about issues in real time. Meeting and talking with complete strangers does not interest me particularly. The advantages of using IRC rather than telephones are that IRC is usually a lot cheaper, you can talk to several people at the same time, and you can keep a record of your conversation. By default, all channels are public. This means that anyone can join the channel and see who is using it. If a channel is private, others can see that someone is using IRC, but not what channel the person is on. If you type the command /list or /names all you see is Prv: * next to their name. If you make your channel secret, only people on the secret channel know that you are chatting. You can easily change the channel's mode to private, secret or by invitation only by typing:

```
/mode #channel +modechar
```

However, you do need to have channel operator status for these commands to work. If you are the person who has created the channel, you automatically have channel operator status (an @ will appear next to your nickname). For instance to make the channel #womyn secret you would type:

```
/mode #womyn +s
```

You can also combine channel mode characters. For instance to set #womyn to private and secret you would type:

```
/mode #womyn +sp
```

Here are the steps to set up a private, secret and by-invitation-only channel:

1. Connect to an IRC server by using Telnet or a graphical IRC client.

2. Open up your own channel

    ```
    /join #mychannel
    ```

3. Make the channel private and by invitation only

    ```
    /mode #mychannel +isp
    ```

4. Summon people who are not already on IRC

    ```
    /summon username
    ```

    e.g.
    ```
    /summon virg@lighthouse.com.uk
    ```

    or invite people who are already on IRC
    ```
    /invite virg #mychannel
    ```

To change a channel mode, use **/mode #channelname + modechar**

Here is a list of mode characters and their meanings.

ModeChar	Effects on channels
i	channel is invite-only
l number	channel is limited, <number> users allowed max
m	channel is moderated, (only channel operators can talk)
n	external /MSGs to channel are not allowed
o NickName	makes <NickName> a channel operator
p	channel is private
s	channel is secret
t	topic limited, only channel operators may change it

Strange characters?

Many IRC users are non English speaking. If you see strange characters, such as }{|][\, appearing, it's likely that part or all of the message is in Swedish, Norwegian, Danish or German. The strange letters are a translation of part of the alphabet of these languages. IRC is supposed to display these characters in their correct form, but not all clients are able to display them properly. If your client does not display these characters properly, you'll have to make do with the table below and substitute the correct characters in your mind. A bit tedious, really.

These are the characters used to represent Nordic languages:

[, {	ä	"a" with two dots over it
], }	å	"a" with a small circle above it
\, |	ö, ø	"o" with two dots over it, or a dash ("/") through it
		Quotation marks (e.g. "[", {) = upper case (Ä)

IRC on the web

IRC is also available on the Web. It combines the attraction of real-time chat with the accessibility of using a Web browser and also allows people to add extra flavour to their text. This is achieved by having embedded HTML in the text or using picture icons to represent themselves. At present you still have to reload a page every 30 seconds to get updates from other users. However, I expect this requirement to disappear in the near future. Some IRC Web sites also enable you to select small cartoon characters to appear next to your name. Ultimately, I think you will be able to select a character and move it around in an imaginary three-dimensional world to meet and chat with others. Some of these systems are already experimentally available. You may need a state-of-the-art computer to participate in these "worlds". This area of IRC is changing rapidly, and it is best to get up-to-date information on what's available by searching for "webchat" with your favourite search engines.

Here are the URLs of some IRC sites:

> **Using the Web to do IRC**
> http://www.fiu.edu/~zyang01/wwwirc/
> http://chat.acmeweb.com/
>
> **Virtual (graphical) IRC Worlds**
> http://www.funcity.com/talk
> http://www.worlds.net/products/alphaworld/
> http://www.thepalace.com/
>
> **Information about Virtual Worlds**
> http://www.communities.com/habitat.html

Where to find out more about IRC ?

Here is a selection of starting points on the Web. These sites will lead you to information on IRC in general, the different IRC nets (EFnet, Undernet and others) and much more.

Try these pages on the Web:

General information
http://sunsite.unc.edu/dbarberi/chats.html/links/
http://mistral.enst.fr/~pioch/IRC/IRC.html
http://www.yahoo.com/Computers_and_Internet/Internet/Chatting/IRC
http://uptown.turnpike.net/L/Larry14/irc.html

List of dyke and dyke-friendly IRC channels
http://www.geocities.com/WestHollywood/1123/grrl.html

MUDs, MOOs, MUSHes:
role-playing and adventuring on the Net

```
Welcome to:
          _____..--========+*+==========---.._____
          _____  __,-='=====____   ===TrekMUSE=1.6===
          _____=====`=
          (._____I__) – _-=_/  `--------=+=--------'
          /  /__...--====='---+---_'
          "------'---.____ – _ = _.-'
                 `--------'
```

You head towards the Romulan Empire area. Rihannsu Star Empire Information Nexus. This is the recreational lounge on a Rihannsu Tracking Station in the remote planetary system Geillun III. A large, dark area greets your view. The surroundings are quiet, and the air is dank and chilly. As you get accustomed to the lighting, you notice that you are inside a bar. A gruff bartender tends the bar, near the side of which is located a recreational holographic emitter. About a dozen tables are scattered across the room occupied by a few patrons, speaking in hushed tones. Occupying the tables scattered around the bar, a few Rihannsu are seen enjoying their drinks. Though the bar is mostly dark, there is mild lighting around their tables illuminating them. You may "look" at them and try to entice them into a conversation.

Start up screen of TrekMuse (Telnet to grimy.cndir.org:1701)

This is an example of a welcoming screen on a Star Trek-based MUD.

What are MUDs?

MUDs are vivid text-based virtual environments, divided into rooms or areas that you can move around in. A MUD is a bit like reading a book, except you are the heroine so you can to some extent determine the direction of the story. Because you interact with other humans who are on-line at the same time as you, you not only feel as if you are really experiencing the story, but the presence of others adds an element of unpredictability and surprise to the storyline. MUDs (Multi-User Domains or Dungeons) started as role-playing adventure and fantasy games that involved solving puzzles, slaying monsters and saving fair maidens and handsome youth. However, today there are also numerous MUDs that are used solely for social or educational purposes. Some MUDs function as virtual schools, others as meeting places for teachers and scientists. You can also visit MUDs to practise French, Italian, German, Portuguese or Swedish.

Types of MUDs

MUDs are referred to by a number of names. The most common are:

MUD   Multi-User Dungeon, Multi-User Dimension or Multi-User Domain
MOO   Multi-User Dungeon, object oriented
MUSE   Multi-User Shared Environment
MUSH Multi-User Shared Hallucination.

The different types of MUDs have slight differences in the commands that perform specific actions. There is usually a help file or screen available for each particular site. Read the help file to get information on a particular environment and the commands in use. If you are still stuck after reading the help files, you could try asking other players for help. First type WHO to find out who else is playing, then type page person = message (replace "person" with the name of the player you want to contact and "message" with the text of your message) to contact another player.

A variety of MUDs

There are three types of MUDs: combat MUDs, social MUDs (usually known as MOOs) and role-play MUDs (usually known as MUSHes). Popular themes for combat MUDs include fantasy and science-fiction worlds. Combat MUDs support combat between players and computer-controlled monsters. As you slay more and more monsters you accumulate experience, advance to new levels and acquire new abilities. Popular themes for non-combat-oriented MUDs include Anne McCaffrey's book *Dragon Riders of Pern*, *Star Trek* and medieval chivalry, where ladies are bold and knights too stupid to wear soft clothing, preferring armour instead.

Role-play MUDs involve little or no combat and have as their central goal the development of the story. Many more women are involved in role-play MUDs than in combat MUDs. In these worlds you make a life for your imaginary character, interact with other imaginary characters, and become part of a living book whose theme and storyline are determined by consensus. You create a character much as an author or actor does. The story can include anything players can imagine and agree upon, including sex and played-out scenes. However almost all MUSHes require that players be allowed to say "I don't want this particular action to be part of my story" and that you can't get hurt unless you agree. On MUDs and MUSHes where wars and killings are part of the environment, a clear warning is usually given on the starting screen. When participating in these environments, it is important to stay within the set theme. This gives all players the opportunity to play the story they want to play and gives you the security that others who are playing bit parts are acting out roles that fit into the agreed scene.

Social MUDs are just that: you meet people, you explore the world provided by the MUD, and you can even extend the MUD world. Well-known social MUDs are LambdaMoo and MicroMuse. MicroMuse is a MUD that provides adventure, puzzles, cultural, recreational and educational content for students of all ages. Young players can hone their literacy skills, adolescents can learn about social and interpersonal interactions, and college students can learn about computing by creating their own contributions to microbes. Another interesting MUD is the Cyberia Writing Center Consultation Project. In this virtual environment students can present and discuss their writing with professional writers and university students. MUDs are also used by virtual universities to enable students to meet each other. Three-dimensional/graphical MUDs are also starting to appear. Rather than just interacting through text, participants are also able to select graphical characters and can move in a graphical three-dimensional world. As you can imagine, the possibilities are quite astounding.

Sherry Turkle in her book *Life on the Screen: Identity in the Age of the Internet*, explains that using computers we are able to "*project ourselves into our own dramas, dramas in which we are producer, director, and star*". The conceptualization of computers has moved from giant calculator to an instrument of simulation, navigation and interaction. While it is easy to dismiss MUDs as playgrounds for adolescent males, they are also the beginnings of a new type of virtual community and a new form of collaboratively written literature. According to Sherry Turkle, "*MUD players are the creators as well as the consumers of media content . . . a MUD has much in common with scriptwriting, performance art and street theater . . . The anonymity of MUDs gives people the chance to express multiple and often unexplored aspects of the self to play with their identity and try out new ones.*"

Many people enjoy playing computer games, even feminists! MUDs are played on your computer via the Internet. They are not just games, although they can be used for recreational purposes. They are text-based theatre involving real people in real time. MUDs are becoming increasingly popular with adults as well as children. You might think adults should have grown out of role-playing games, but most of us enjoy the experience of escapism when we go to the live theatre or watch movies – perhaps even imagining ourselves in the role of the heroine. MUDs allow you to participate in the action and help determine the outcome of a scene. You are no longer just a spectator in another person's creation.

How to connect to a MUD

Most MUDs can be reached by using the Telnet command (see chapter 9). Some MUDs have Web pages that you can visit first to get a "feel" for the environment.

Some MUDs to visit

There are hundreds of MUDs on the Internet, and they frequently move. Rather than giving addresses for specific MUDs, we suggest you visit the following sites for up-to-date information:

> http://www.lysator.liu.se:7500/mud/main.html
> http://www.ccs.neu.edu/django/docs/cncmast.html
> http://cis.upenn/~lwl/~mudinfo
> gopher://spinaltap.micro.umn.edu/11/fun/Games/MUDs/Links/

Remember you may have to visit a few different MUDs till you find one in which you feel comfortable.

How to participate in a MUD

Many different programs are used to create MUDs and the commands used differ depending on the type of program used. I have not included a complete summary of commands. The best thing is to visit different MUDs and explore their possibilities. Here is how you connect to a MUD and get started:

1. Connect to the MUD of your choice by using either a graphical Telnet client (if you have a dial-up IP/graphical account), by using TinyFugue (a specialized Telnet client for MUDs), or by typing at the operating prompt (dial-up shell/text account):

   ```
   telnet mudaddress
   ```

   e.g.
   ```
   telnet moo.du.org:8888
   ```

2. Once you are connected, simply follow the instructions given by the particular MUD. Typing `help` will usually get you more information. `Quit` usually ends a MUD session, or use the **disconnect** button or menu option if you are using a graphical Telnet client.

Visiting a MUD can be very time-consuming. Hours fly by and hopefully you will be having fun. Be prepared to explore and ask questions. The game's administrators are usually happy to help you, and there are often players whose sole job is helping new players to feel comfortable.

Choosing a character

On a MUD there are players/participants and system administrators. System administrators are known under a variety of colourful names: gods, janitors, wizards, elders. When you first log onto a MUD you choose a name, a character and a gender. For instance on some combat MUDs you can choose between bards, druids, fighters, pages, monks, priestesses and thieves. Each type of character comes with certain abilities, strengths and weaknesses. On social MUDs you choose a name and a gender. You can also create a description of yourself that other players can look up, such as:

> *Sappho is a small, dark-haired woman, with beautiful green eyes. A smile is always playing on her lips.*

When you visit a MUD for the first time and you just want to have a look around, you may be assigned a guest name, such as SilverGuest. When you have decided to become a regular visitor, you register and choose a permanent name.

Exploring the virtual world

Once you have selected a character, you are ready to explore the virtual world by typing messages at the prompt. You can move around the MUD by typing a direction, such as down, east, west. Most MUDs respond to abbreviations such as s for south, n for north. Type look or l to see what the place or room you are located in is like. You can also use this command to examine objects.

If there are other players around you can communicate with them by using say or ". The command say yourMessage broadcasts your message to all the players in a particular area, room or place; that is, it appears on their screens. For example, if my nickname is Gertie and I type:

        "Virg how is Orlando?

Virg and everyone else will see:

        Gertie says: How is Orlando?

If you desire a private conversation use page, as in:

        page playerName = message

For instance to send a private message to Virg I would type:

        page Virg = Hear the latest about Orlando?

To express an emotion like laughing or rolling on the floor use emote (for combat MUDs), pose (MUCKs, MUSHes) or act (MOOs). For example, I type:

        emote smiles Virg

Virg (and everyone else present) sees:

```
Gertie smiles at Virg
```

Combat MUDs and some MOOs also have a long list of canned emotions. For instance if you type:

```
waggle Thatcher
```

everyone will see:

```
Gertie waggles her finger sternly at Thatcher.
```

TinyFugue (tf): a text-based Telnet client for MUDs

TinyFugue is a specialized text-only Telnet client for accessing MUDs. It provides a text-based environment in which aliases, scripts, session parameters, and other facilities can be programmed and offers greater flexibility and power than using ordinary text-based Telnet. TinyFugue has an extensive on-line help system, but there is little external documentation available. If you only have a dial-up shell/text-based account and you think you will be doing a lot of MUDing visit the unofficial TinyFugue Web page at **http://fly.ccs.yorku.ca/mush/tf.html**.

It is possible for people to become immersed in MUDs and other computer-mediated communications while at the same time being unable to function normally in the real world. Some people become addicted to MUDs or IRCs, and spend days and nights chained to their computers. Often young people who feel uncomfortable in social gatherings find friendships and interactions with other people less threatening when they are disguised within a role in a MUD. Women too can experience the world as frightening and alienating. However, finding refuge within a MUD or on IRC can ultimately increase a person's feelings of isolation. If you know of someone, whether child or adult, who seems more comfortable in computer-mediated communication than in real-life situations, speak to them about it, and offer your help.

Chapter 7

Browsing for information: the World Wide Web and Gopher

A magic carpet of your own: the World Wide Web

The World Wide Web is the most exciting and powerful Internet tool for retrieving and distributing information. Its appearance has, more than anything else, catapulted the Internet into the attention of the media and thereby the general public. While email, Usenet News groups and other Internet services are very popular and useful, the Web is like a magic carpet that can take you around the world. If you have a powerful enough computer, you have at your fingertips access to coloured photographs, graphics, sound and video. If you have a basic computer, you still have access to all the text with the added advantage that you'll retrieve information more quickly.

The most exciting aspect of the Web is that, if you wish, you can participate by creating your very own site on the Web. This site is known as a Web or home page and it is entirely up to you how it looks and sounds. It's a place where you can be as innovative and truly imaginative as you like – you are limited only by your creative ability and knowledge of computer software. On the Web anyone can be an author. You won't necessarily have a huge audience, but the potential is enormous: the Web already has a huge following and every day more and more people become devotees. All around the world, from the Shetland Islands to Nicaragua, people are putting up Web pages. They cover a range of interests as diverse as we are ourselves. If you know how to find your way around the Web – and I'm going to help you with that in just a moment – the world is at the click of your mouse!

The Internet used to be a place of software, obscure command sequences, and esoteric discussions on compilers, operating systems and computer code. The technology of the World Wide Web has made large parts of the Internet accessible and easy to use. More importantly, it has made being an author – being able to broadcast your particular message – almost as easy as word-processing. While mailing lists have long been tools for building communities, the Web enabled information dissemination on an unprecedented scale. The number of Web pages devoted to issues relevant to women has simply snowballed.

How does the World Wide Web work?

The Web functions by connecting Web pages together, via computers, using links. On a Web page you will easily find the parts that are linked to other computers because they are underlined or highlighted in a different shade or colour. The highlighted part usually consists of one word or a short sentence. Hidden behind this is the address of another Web page (called a Universal Resource Locator or URL). If you click on the link, your computer will take you to the Web page indicated by the hidden address. A Web page itself may be a list of highlighted words or sentences, in effect operating like a table of contents, which lead you on to the sites where more information can be found. Other Web pages contain a lot of information, pictures and/or sound with one or two highlighted or linked parts. The way an individual Web page looks and functions depends entirely on the person who creates it. To be part of the Web, all Web pages must be linked in some way to each other.

The function that links pages together is called Hypertext. Hypertext connects text or images together by embedding links or hotspots into the text or image, which you then see highlighted. Clicking on a highlighted link with your mouse (or using arrow keys) takes you to a new piece of text or image. The new text may be located in a computer anywhere in the world. Each hypertext Web page exists quite independent of any other page, but is connected to all other pages through hypertext links.

It's easy to see how people spend hours on the Web, as each page reveals a new little tidbit (the highlighted link). Before you know it, you've been led down a path you never intended to travel. When you are intent on finding information of particular interest, you may find the Web irritating. Sometimes highlighted links can be misleading because they just lead you on to more links, with no actual solid information on your subject to be found. However, there is so much of interest on the Web that minor irritations are soon forgotten.

Web browsers (or clients) are software programs that reside on your computer. Browsers allow you, with a simple click, to establish a connection to a remote machine, retrieve a variety of objects such as files, pictures and sound, and then view these objects on your screen or listen to them. You can use Web browsers to access many other Internet tools such as FTP, Gopher, Usenet News and email, with the ease of simply pointing and clicking with your mouse.

How the World Wide Web operates: HTML and HTTP

To use the World Wide Web you need a client or browser to manage the connection to Web servers and display the pages retrieved. Probably the most common browser in use today is Netscape Naigator; other well-known ones are Lynx (text-only) and Microsoft Internet Explorer. Web servers are computers that store Web pages. The language or protocol that these browsers use to connect to Web servers is called or hyper text transfer protocol or HTTP. It is a simple protocol that knows only four activities: making a connection, requesting an action, responding to an action, and closing the connection.

Web documents or pages are written in hyper text mark-up language or HTML. HTML is placed within the document in < > and tells your browser how to display items such as links, lists, headings, titles, images, forms, maps and sound.

Web page or home page?

A Web page usually refers to a single page of hypertext. In contrast, a home page is the entry point to a local Web space. When people refer to their "home page", they mean their main Web page.

All about URLs

The Uniform Resource Locator or URL (pronounced *earl* or *you-aar-elle*) is the means of identifying where exactly a resource (such as a Web page) is located within the information space of the Internet. It is the URL that tells the browser which computer to connect to and where on the computer the Web page is. The general format of an URL is:

protocol://host:port/path

The protocol specifies how the information is to be retrieved, e.g. HTTP, FTP, Gopher or Usenet News. The host is the address of the computer, on which the resource resides. A port or communications channel number may be specified, if the resource is not located on the default port. The path tells us in which directory the Web page resides and what its name is. Web pages usually end with .html or .htm (only for PCs), if created on a Windows machine. Let's look at an example:

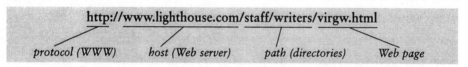

http://www.lighthouse.com/staff/writers/virgw.html

protocol (WWW)   *host (Web server)*   *path (directories)*   *Web page*

Sometimes there is a 3- or 4-digit number directly after the host address, e.g. www.lighthouse.com:8888. These are called port numbers and identify the location of a particular program on the host computer. Port numbers are often used to identify IRC or MUD servers.

Being able to decipher URLs can be very useful. Someone might give you an URL and when you try to connect to the resource you get an error message. If you are sure that the Web page exists, you might go further up the directory structure to see if you can find the page by entering higher up in the Web space. Or you may know that Virginia works for lighthouse.com and you think she might have a Web page. Because many Web pages have an address that starts with www, you could try www.lighthouse.com and see if this will connect you to the Lighthouse company. From there you might be able to delve into the company's Web space and see if Virginia has her own Web page.

A carefully examined URL can tell you many things. It will tell you what protocol will be used to connect to the remote computer and hence what sort of resources you can expect to retrieve. It tells you the name of the host computer and possibly where it is located. It is usually best to connect to the computer which is geographically closest to you.

Internet tools and their generic URLs		
	Generic address	Example
Web page	http://webAddress	http://www.lighthouse.com
Gopher	gopher://gopherAddress	gopher://gopher.lighthouse:4444
Ftp	ftp://ftpAddress	ftp://ftp.lighthouse.com
Usenet News	news:newsgroupName	news:rec.lighthouse

The last part of an URL can tell you something about the resource. Here are some common URL endings and what they mean:

Ending	Type of file
.html	hypertext file
.htm	hypertext file created on a PC
?string	the URL points to a query
#anchor	the URL points to a specific place in the document
.ps	postscript file
.txt	text file
.tex	TeX or LaTex file, a typesetting language
.au	sound file
.mov	movie file
.gif	image file
.jpeg	image file
.wrl	VRML file

Browsers

The browser is the software that allows you to access and browse the World Wide Web. A good browser not only able displays Web pages, but also allows you to use other Internet tools such as Gopher and FTP. The most widely used graphical browser is Netscape Navigator. Others are MacWeb, Microsoft Internet Explorer, and Slipknot for Windows. If you are still using a 286 PC or have access only to a dial-up shell/text account, don't despair. There are a number of text-based browsers that, while not capable of displaying fancy graphics, will do the job of displaying the text very adequately. You still have most of the functionality that you get in Netscape (bookmarks, saving files etc.), and being text-only it will be a lot faster. The most commonly available text-based browser is Lynx.

- Browsers communicate with remote machines over long distances. **Expect problems.** It can take time to connect to the remote machine and can take even longer to download a Web page.

- **URLs are notoriously easy to get wrong.** If you get an error message when you are trying to connect to a particular page, first check for spelling mistakes or whether something is missing from the URL. Be inventive and try to connect to the remote host by using only parts of the URL, like the protocol/host part only.

- **If you can't get a connection, try again later.** Many Web servers are run as a public service and may not always be available.

Bookmarks/ Favourites/Hotlist

An important part of each browser is the hotlist or bookmarks file (also called favourites) which are places were you can record your favourite URLs. When you wish to revisit these URLs you can simply open your hotlist or bookmarks file and click on the address and the browser will connect you. Remember to save your hotlist to another file occasionally, so it can not get lost.

The history list

The history list records the links visited in the current session. The browser does not remember links between sessions: you can use the bookmark for this purpose. Because of its non-hierarchical nature, the history list has a feature that may initially cause confusion and is sometimes a little annoying. Depending on how you traverse the Web space, some links are nipped and whole branches may disappear from the history list. Here is an example: I first visit a page on women poets; on this page I find a link to Gertrude Stein, which I visit. Gertrude Stein's page mentions the Alice B. Toklas cookbook and I can't resist and follow the link to the cookbook. If I have a look at my history list, it will contain women poets, Gertrude Stein and Alice B. Toklas' Cookbook. I now go back to the page on women poets and follow a link that leads me to Sappho. If I now look at my history page I will notice that the Alice B. Toklas Cookbook page has disappeared! This is because the link has been nipped. The important thing to remember is: if you really like a page, put it in your bookmark.

Graphical Web browsers for dial-up IP/graphical accounts: Netscape Navigator 2.0

The Netscape Navigator 2.0 screen

Web browsers are becoming the only piece of software that you need to use many Internet services. Netscape Navigator is a front-runner in this development. Here are the main features of a Netscape screen:

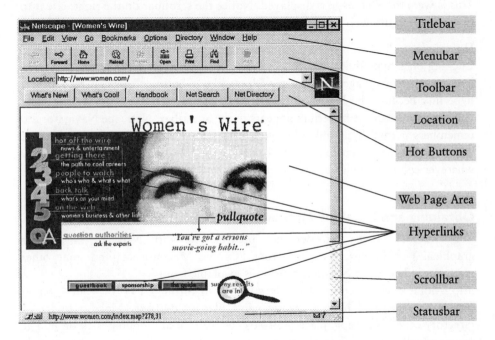

Titlebar
Here you can see the title of the document currently viewed. If you add the page to your bookmark list, the title gets saved.

Menubar
The menubar contains all the pull down basic browser commands.

Toolbar
Commonly used commands turned into icons. Just click and you're away.

Location
This is the place were you enter the addres or URL of the page you want to visit. You can click on the down arrow to access your **history file**. Netscape Navigator 2.0 remembers your history between sessions.

Hot Buttons

The hot buttons work similarly to the tollbar icons, except that they take you to particular Web sites that Netscape Navigator 2.0 deems of interest to its customers. **Net Search** and **Net Directory** are two especially useful hot buttons. Net Search takes you to a list of search engines and Net Directory takes you to a list of subject-based directories. If you are looking for new sites that you hope will be interesting, press the **What's Cool** or **What's New** button.

Web page

This is were the Web page is displayed. Notice the **scrollbar** on the right. Use it to move through the Web page.

Hyperlinks

Clicking on a hyperlink takes you to a new Web page. Hyperlinks can be underlined text or an image, or they may look like a button. You can recognize a hyperlink because the Netscape Navigator 2.0 cursor changes into a little hand and the address of the hyperlink appears in the **Statusbar**. Netscape Navigator 2.0 remembers textual hyperlinks that you have visited during a session, no matter which pages they occurred on, and change their colour from blue to red (or whatever colour you chose when you customized your browser).

Obtaining and installing Netscape Navigator 2.0

Your Internet service provider may provide you with Netscape or another graphical Web browser. Netscape runs PCs and Macintoshes (and some other platforms). The latest Netscape version is available from **http://home.netscape.com/**. The file you obtain through FTP or your Internet service provider will have a cryptic name like n32d40.exe. Make a folder or directory called Netscape, place the Netscape file in it and double click on it. The program will now take you through a set-up process.

Using Netscape Navigator 2.0 for the first time

Before dialling your ISP, double click on the Netscape icon. Select **Network Preferences** from the **Options** menu. Click on **Proxies**. Proxies are programs that manage Internet access through a firewall. A firewall places a protective barrier between the wider Internet and the internal network and provides protection from unwelcome intruders. Proxies also speed up your access to popular Web pages as they keep a copy of these pages. Your ISP should provide you with information on the proxy settings. If in doubt, click on **No Proxies** then press **OK** to close the window.

Navigating the World Wide Web with Netscape Navigator 2.0

To use Netscape Navigator 2.0 follow these steps:

1. Connect to your ISP.
2. Double click on the **Netscape Navigator 2.0** icon. Netscape will fire up.
3. To visit a Web page, type the URL into the **Location** field and press return. Netscape will now retrieve the page for you. This may take a while, depending on the speed of your computer and modem, the size of Internet connection, and the popularity of Web page. Be patient.
4. Use the **Forward** and **Back** icons on the toolbar to move quickly between Web pages that you've already visited. Use **Reload** to update the page you are currently viewing. The **Open** button pops up a dialog box which allows you to type in a new Web page address. This functions the same way as the Location field.

Customizing Netscape Navigator 2.0

Customize colour, fonts, helper applications and more by selecting **General Preferences** from the **Options** menu. The **Options** menu is also the place to set Network, Security, Mail and News Preferences. You can also decide whether you want the **Toolbar**, the **Hot buttons** and the **Location** bar displayed.

Bookmarks in Netscape Navigator 2.0

Bookmarks offer a permanent shortcut to your favourite pages. To add a Web page to your bookmark list, select **Add Bookmark** from the **Bookmarks** menu.

If you are like me you'll soon have too many bookmarks to view convieniently in the allotted space. If you are using a PC, this is how you organize your bookmarks into folders:

1. Choose **Go Bookmarks** from the **Bookmarks** menu. The **Netscape Bookmarks** window will appear.
2. Choose **Insert Folder** from the **Item** menu. Type a name for the new folder, a name in the dialog box, then close the dialog by clicking on **OK**. You can now put bookmarks into the new folder by first clicking and then dragging (keep the mouse button pressed down and move the mouse) the highlighted bookmark into the new folder.

Plug-ins and Helper applications

Plug-ins extend your browser capabilites (they may add animation or sound) and are fully integrated into your browser. For instance, Shockwave is used in Web pages to give the page a multimedia appearance. You can see these pages in their full glory only if you have the Shockwave plug-in installed. If you visit a site that requires a plug-in, it will probably also have the plug-in software there for you to download. Simply follow the instructions, and if all goes well you'll experience the added "multimedia" features. Once the plug-in is installed, it springs into action automatically when it is needed.

Helper applications are programs that are linked to your Web browser to extend its abilities, but they are separate. They are a little more clumsy than plug-ins. If a helper is needed and you have it installed, it will pop up a window and ask you if you want to proceed. If you agree, it will go ahead and, depending on the helper application, you will be able to listen to sounds, play movies, automatically decompress downloaded applications, and get a better display of images. Most plug-ins and helper applications can be obtained free or as shareware. They reside on the hard disk of your computer and are loaded when the browser needs them. For a complete list of helper applications and plug-ins have a look at **http://www.browserwatch.com/plug-in.html**

Learning more about Netscape Navigator 2.0

Select **Handbook** from the **Help** menu to learn more about Netscape 2.0. This will connect you to **http://home.netscape.com/eng/mozilla/2.0/handbook/**. The handbook contains a tutorial and a reference section. Here you can look up onscreen fundamentals, all about bookmarks and much more. There is also an alphabetical index that will take you straight to a particular topic. The **Help** menu also contains other useful items, such as frequently asked questions and information on software upgrades and security.

Text-based Web browsers: Lynx

Lynx is a fully fledged text-based Web browser that allows you to access the Web by using the cursor keys, to move around a Web page, and to select links. It runs under DOS, UNIX and VMS. You can see if your ISP already has a Lynx client running by typing lynx or www at the operating system's prompt. If your ISP provides a menuing system the word World Wide Web or Lynx will appear in your menu option.

Obtaining Lynx

You can get all the files that you need to run Lynx by anonymous FTP from:

```
ftp://ftp2.cc.ukans.edu/pub/WWW/lynx
```

Running Lynx

Whether you are using a public client or a client on your ISP's computer, you start Lynx by typing:

```
lynx URL
```

for example, if you want to visit the Australian magazine *geekgirl* you type:

```
lynx http://www.geekgirl.com.au/
```

Leaving Lynx

When you have surfed to your satisfaction, you can leave lynx by typing:

q then confirm with `y`

or

Q then type

`cntrl d`

You will not be prompted to confirm your decision to leave Lynx.

Navigating the World Wide Web with Lynx

To navigate around a document while viewing it with Lynx, use the **arrow keys.** The links will usually appear as bold text, which changes to reverse video (black text on a white background reverses to white text on a black background) when selected. You select a link by moving over it with your cursor key and then pressing the **Enter** key.

The Lynx history list

The history list, a list of locations you have visited during the current session, can be accessed by using the **backspace** or **delete** key. Once inside the history list, typing m takes you to the beginning of the list.

Bookmarks in Lynx

Lynx allows you to create two types of bookmarks. You can save either the whole page or just its location. Before you can save anything to the bookmark file you need to create a file called **bookmark_home**, while not in Lynx. Then when you are in Lynx and you want to save a Web page, type: a

You will be prompted with

```
save D)ocument or L)ink to bookmarkfile or C)ancel? (d,l,c):
```

Type in the letter of your choice, depending on whether you wish to save the document (D), the link or URL (L), or to cancel the action (C).

You can look at your book mark file by typing: v

Moving around the Web from within Lynx

If you are already in Lynx and you wish to go to a new URL, type: g

Lynx then asks you to type in the new location.

Customizing Lynx

Lynx can be set up in a variety of ways. Type o when you are inside Lynx to get the **Options** menu. Select the appropriate letter to choose an option from the **Options** menu. For instance, if you want to put in your personal email address, type P. You are then prompted to type in your email address. Press the **return** key to save this new setting, then R to return to Lynx.

Lynx commands

Here are some useful commands for Lynx:

up arrow	moves back a link
down arrow	moves forward a link
right arrow	follows a link
left arrow	returns to previous link
space bar	moves to the next page in the document
-	moves to the previous page in the document
/	searches for string on current page
\	toggles to view HTML format
=	views details (URL, size, owner etc.) of current page
backspace or delete	accesses the history list
h	accesses on-line help
a	creates a bookmark for current page
c	sends a comment to owner of current page
d	downloads the current page
e	edits the current page (if local and if you are the owner)
g	goes to a URL

i	accesses a Web index
m	returns to first page you visited during current session
n	searches a non-indexed document for key words
o	accesses the options menu
p	prints, mails or saves a file
q	leaves Lynx with confirmation
Q	leaves Lynx without confirmation
r	removes a bookmark
u	returns to previous document
v	accesses the bookmark
z	abandons the current transfer process

Creating your own Web page

After you have surfed the Web for a while, you may feel the urge to create your own Web page. The Web is one of the easiest ways of reaching an audience of millions, and creating a simple personal Web page is not difficult. Reaching your audience is a two-step process: first you must create your Web page, then you place the Web page on your ISP's Web server. This function is called Web page hosting. Web servers are software programs that reside on computers that are permanently connected to the Internet. The Web server software is capable of responding to requests by Web browsers for particular Web pages. Commercial Web page hosting can be very expensive, and it pays to look around for the best deal. However, many ISPs give non-commercial customers free space on their Web server. Some even set up Web page templates which make it easy for their customers to create personal Web pages. But it is a lot more fun to create your own Web page from scratch, and you can be assured that it will reflect your individuality.

HTML (Hypertext Mark-up Language) is used to add various attributes to plain text files, which can then be published on the World Wide Web. HTML can be used to display images, text, activate sound and video, allow user interaction and create hypertext links in a Web page. HTML is not primarily concerned with the appearance and format of a document, but is a method to add structure to the document. In paper publishing, the author creates the content and the designer decides what it looks like. On the World Wide Web, control over a document's appearance is partly given over to the user. Users can customize their browser and hence the appearance of documents according to their taste. Different browsers have slightly divergent features. HTML is less concerned with how a document looks, but ensures that the document is portable and readable independent of the browser and hardware platform used.

Internet Career Opportunities : Web Design

Sonia De Launey "Electric Prisms," 1914 (detail)

Georgia O'Keeffe "Jimson Weed," 1932 (detail)

Judy Chicago "Virginia Woolf," Triptych 1973 (detail)

Ada Spider "She 1," 1996

HTML editors

The simplest way to create a Web page is to use a word-processor to generate the text, and then add HTML tags in the appropriate places. If you want to create a large Web site with many intertwined pages, this can be a lengthy and tedious process. HTML editors such as HotDog Pro, HoTMetaL Pro, HTML Assistant, Incontext Spider, NaviPress, FrontPage, Netscape Gold and PageMill (to name a few), can make creating Web pages easier and faster. New HTML editors are available on the Internet almost daily and the latest releases of popular word-processing packages such as WordPerfect (WordPerfect Internet Publisher) and Word (MS Internet Assistant) also include rudimentary facilities for creating Web pages. Which product to choose depends on your needs and how much you want to pay. Many of the HTML editors can be downloaded directly from the Internet on a trial basis. If you are serious about developing a Web page you should download two or three different packages and compare their features and ease of use.

When evaluating a package, you need to consider how the HTML editor allows you to interact with the HTML language constructs, and whether the program checks for valid HTML. Some editors use plain text style (you see the HTML tags), others are WYSIWYG graphical editors (what you see is what you get, or at least an approximation). Many HTML editors also provide you with easy-to-follow Web page templates, facilities to view your Web page in a Web browser at the press of a button, and the ability to upload your finished Web pages to a Web server. For reviews of different HTML editors have a look at the following Web sites:

> **Stroud's CWS Apps list (PC)**
> http://cwsapps.tower.com.au/
> http://www.stroud.com/
>
> **Macintosh WWW Resource Directory**
> http://www.comvista.com/net/www/htmleditor.html

Independent of which HTML editor you choose, it is useful to have a rudimentary knowledge of HTML, especially if you want to be experimental with your page.

The mysteries of HTML

HTML is based on the concept of tags to designate information about the format and style of a Web page. All tags are contained within brackets and are not case-sensitive (it does not matter whether you use upper or lower case). An example of a bracketed tag is <i>, which creates italicised text.

Most HTML commands consist of two tags that surround some text, also known as a container. The opening tag marks the beginning of a formatted item, while the closing tag signals the end of a formatted feature. A closing tag looks exactly like the opening tag, except the designator is preceded by a slash, e.g. <title> This is a title </title>. Some HTML commands consist of only a single tag, such as the line break and the horizontal ruler command.

Unlike a word-processing package, white spaces and blank lines are totally ignored in an HTML document. If you want to add a blank line or some white space, you need to give the appropriate command. You can use the <br> tag to insert a line break or the <pre> tag pair to insert a number of empty lines or white space.

Here is the minimum document skeleton that every HTML marked-up document adheres to (I have indented it to make the different parts more obvious):

```
<html>
      <head>
            <title> This is a title  </title>
      </head>
      <body>
            <address> myaddress@isp.com.au </address>
      </body
</html>
```

All HTML documents are surrounded by the tag pair **<html> </html>**. This tells the browser that this document is marked up in HTML. The document is in two parts: the head and the body. The tag pair **<head> </head>** encloses the material contained in the head, usually the title of the document. The title, which is contained in the tag pair (**<title> </title>**), appears in the window header of the browser and is the text saved in hotlists. It is important to select a title that is descriptive of the page. Additionally some of the Web index services use the title to classify Web pages. The body tag pair **<body> </body>** encloses the main part of a Web page. Besides the Web page text, it is important to include an address at which readers of the page can contact the author. The address tag pair **<address> </address>** is used for this purpose.

Let's explore other HTML tags by building a home page for the Coalition Against Trafficking in Women.

The basic page

We start with the basic html page (you need at least these elements to create a Web page) and fill in the title of the page and the email address:

```
<html>
<head> <title> Coalition Against Trafficking in Women  </title>
</head>
<body>
<address> catw@daemon.apana.org.au </address>
</body>
</html>
```

Headings

Now we need to add some text and structure to the body of the page. HTML recognizes up to six structural levels: headings, subheadings, sub-subheadings etc. The tag pair for headings is **<hN> </hN>**, where N represents a number from one to six. Each heading level is given a distinctive style, with h1 being the largest. For your first page, it is probably easiest to use heading levels to reflect the organization of your document; later, you can be more adventurous. Here are the headings for the Coalition Web page:

> <h1> Coalition Against Trafficking in Women </h1>
> <h5> Category II consultative status with the United Nations Economic and Social Council </h5>
> <h4> What is the coalition ?</h4>

Paragraphs and line breaks

Now we need to add some text to each of these headings. The tag pair for ordinary paragraphs is **<p> </p>**. The effect of the paragraph tag is to add a single line break. If you want to add extra line breaks, use the **
** tag. The line break tag does not have a closing tag. Alternatively you can use the <pre> tag pair to insert a number of empty lines. Here is the first paragraph of the our Web page:

> <body>
> <h1> Coalition Against Trafficking in Women </h1>
> <h5> Category II consultative status with the United Nations Economic and Social Council </h5>
> <h3> What is the coalition? </h3>
> <p> The Coalition Against Trafficking in Women (Australia) is a feminist non-governmental organization (NGO) which promotes women's human rights. We work within an international coalition to combat sexual exploitation in all its forms, especially prostitution and trafficking in women. We believe it is a fundamental human right to be free of sexual exploitation in all its forms.
> </p>
> </body>

Lists

HTML recognizes a number of different lists, with ordered and unordered lists being the most useful. The unordered list tag pair (<ul> </ul>) uses bullets to mark each item, while the <ol> </ol> tag pair creates an ordered list. When you create an ordered list, the browser inserts the correct number consecutively in front of each list item. You will also need to precede each list item with the tag pair <li> </li>. Here is the unordered list I have created for the Coalition Web page:

```
<p>   <h4> We work with: </h4>
      <ul>
            <li> national and international policy makers, </li>
            <li> women's rights and human rights advocates, </li>
            <li> and the United Nations </li>
      </ul>
</p>
```

Notice how I have nested the unordered list within the paragraph and made "we work with" into a small heading.

Viewing the newly created Web page

If you created your Web page with a word-processor and you want to see what the page looks like displayed in a Web browser, you need to do the following:

1. Save the file as a text file and give it the extension html or htm (PCs). For instance I saved the Coalition's Web page as "catw.htm".

2. Open the Web browser of your choice. I used Netscape Navigator 2.0. You don't have to be connected to the Internet to open your Web browser.

3. Select **Open File** from the **File menu**. The Open Window appears. Select the directory and the file, then press **Open**. The Web browser will now load the HTML file you want to view. Here is what the Coalition's Web page looks like so far:

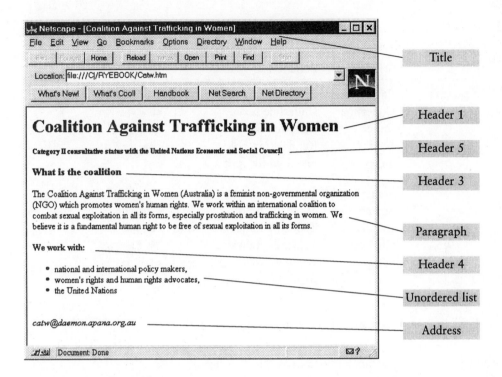

Playing with text

The tags discussed so far give you control over the structure and format of your Web page, but often you will want to have more control over how the text appears. Two useful tags for the control of the appearance of chunks of text are the preformatted text tag pair (**<pre> </pre>**) and the block quote tag pair (**<blockquote> </blockquote>**). When you enclose text with the **<pre>** tag, all carriage returns and spaces between words are maintained and a constant width text font is used. In comparison, the effect of using the **<blockquote>** is to preserve the original formatting of text.

HTML has a number of character style tags that allow you to control the appearance of the text itself. You can specify whether text should be in italics, underlined or displayed in bold, right down to a single character. There are two ways of specifying text appearance: physical or logical tags. Physical character tags use explicit typographical characteristics (italics, bold, underline, teletype), while logical character tags refer to the function of some pieces of text and permit each browser to interpret how to display a particular characteristic. For instance the logical character tag **<citation>** can be interpreted as text in italics or bold. Table 7.1 gives a list of the most important physical and logical tags.

Table 7.1 HTML tags for character styles

Style	Function	Tag
Physical Styles		
Underline	Underline text	<u>
Italics	Italicize text	<I>
Bold	Render text bold	<b>
Teletype	Fixed width font	<tt>
Some Logical Styles		
Strong	Typically bold	<strong>
Emphasis	Typically italics	<em>
Citation	Typically italics	<cite>
Sample	For computer messages, fixed-width font	<samp>

For instance, I have included the following lines in the Coalition's HTML file:

```
<strong> Write to us at: </strong>
<address> catw@daemon.apana.org.au </address>
```

The **<strong>** tag pair makes the enclosed text appear in bold letters.

A horizontal line is a nice way to break up distinct pieces of text. The tag to create a horizontal rule is **<hr>**. This tag has a number of optional specifications:

<hr width = X%   align = Y   size = Z>

X represents the percentage of page width that the line will take up.
Y represents the position centre, left or right.
Z represents the thickness of the line. For example:

```
<h1> Coalition Against Trafficking in Women </h1>
<h5> Category II consultative status with the United Nations Economic
      and Social Council </h5>
<hr width = 95% align = left>
```

Creating Links

The most important feature, and what makes Web pages unique, is the ability to link geographically separated Web pages together. The format for embedding a hypertext link within a Web page is:

<a href = "URL"> text of link </a>

The URL (Universal Resource Locator) is the address of the Web page and describes exactly where a particular Web page is located on the Internet. The only thing visible on the page itself is the text of the link. Depending on how a Web browser is set up, the text of a link will be either in a different colour or underlined. Many browsers reveal the address of the link when you move your mouse over the link. As an example of a link, I have changed the unordered list that I created for the Coalition's Web page to include some links to other Web pages:

```
<p>  <h4> We work with: </h4>
<ul>
<li>  national and international policy makers, </li>
<li>
<a href = "http://www.igc.apc.org/womensnet/dworkin/"> women's rights </a>
     and human rights advocates, </li>
<li> and
<a href = "http://www.undcp.or.at/unlinks.html"> the United Nations </a></li>
</ul>
</p>
```

You can create a link to anywhere on the Internet, including a link to specific sections in your own Web page. You can also create a link to other Web pages residing in the same directory as the Web page containing the link. In this case you need only specify the file name of the Web page, rather than the whole URL. For instance, if I want to link catw2.htm to the word *prostitution* in catw1.htm and if both Web pages are in the same directory, the command looks like this:

<a href = "catw2.htm" > prostitution </a>

Images

Images and graphics can liven up Web pages and convey textual messages in another form. The most commonly used image formats are JPEG and GIF images. Images can be displayed either as inline images or external images. Inline images allow you to display graphics alongside other elements on a page and they are loaded at the same time as the Web page. External images appear in a separate viewing window and require special helper applications.

The HTML tag for including inline images in a Web page is:

<img src = "image.gif" >

There are three optional attributes that you can include in this command: an aligment indication (**align =**), an alternative text indication (**alt = text**) and an image map indication (**ismap =**). The alignment indication lets you specify how the image should be aligned in relation to adjacent text. The possible alignment options are top, middle or bottom. For instance **align = top** aligns the image with the top of the adjacent text. The alternative text indicator can be used to display some text instead of the image. This is useful for browsers that are text-only or where the image loading function is disabled. The image map attribute tells the Web browser to jump to a different location when the user clicks on the link. This can be used to "sensitise" different parts of maps and link these "hotspots" to new Web pages. This is an advanced feature of HTML and I will not go into further detail.

Images can also be used as hotlinks to other Web pages if you include the appropriate linking tags. This is how I have integrated an image into the Coalition's Web page:

```
<h4> More information on: </h4>
<img src = "world.gif" align=center alt ="Global trafficking in women">
<a href=traffic.html"> click here </a>
<br>
```

Notice that I have used the **alt** tag to make sure people with text browsers can still use the Web page. I could have made the image itself into a hotlink, by placing the reference to the image inside the **<a> </a>** tag pair:

<a href=traffic.html"> <img src ="world.gif" alt ="Global trafficking in women"> </a>

If you use an image as a hotlink, many browsers place a border around it. You can avoid this "boxed in" look by specifying border=0 within the <img> tag.

Now it's time to have a final look at the Coalition Web page as viewed through Netscape Navigator 2.0 and the raw HTML text. Here is the HTML text:

```
<html>
<head> <title> Coalition Against Trafficking in Women </title>
</head>
<body>
<h1> Coalition Against Trafficking in Women </h1>
<h5> Category II consultative status with the United Nations Economic and Social
      Council</h5>
<hr width= 95% align = left >
<h3> What is the Coalition? </h3>
<p> The Coalition Against Trafficking in Women (Australia) is a feminist non-
governmental organization (NGO) which promotes women's human rights. We work
within an international coalition to combat sexual exploitation in all its forms,
especially
<a href = "catw2.htm" > prostitution </a>
and trafficking in women. We believe it is a fundamental human right to be free of
sexual exploitation in all its forms.</p>
<p> <h4> We work with: </h4>
<ul>
<li> national and international policy makers, </li>
<li> <a href = "http://www.igc.apc.org/womensnet/dworkin/"> women's rights </a>
      and human rights advocates, </li>
<li> and <a href = "http://www.undcp.or.at/unlinks.html">the United Nations
      </a></li>
</ul>
</p>
<p> <h4> More information on: </h4></p>
<h4> More information on: </h4>
<img src = "world.gif" align=center alt ="Global trafficking in women">
      <a href=traffic.html"> click here </a>
<br>
<strong> Write to us at: </strong> <address> catw@daemon.apana.org.au </address>
      </body>
      </html>
```

And here is the finished Web page:

Coalition Against Trafficking in Women

Category II consultative status with the United Nations Economic and Social Council

---

What is the Coalition ?

The Coalition Against Trafficking in Women (Australia) is a feminist non-governmental organization (NGO) which promotes women's human rights. We work within an international coalition to combat sexual exploitation in all its forms, especially prostitution and trafficking in women. We believe it is a fundamental human right to be free of sexual exploitation in all its forms.

We work with:

- national and international policy makers,
- women's rights and human rights advocates,
- and the United Nations

More information on:

click here

Global Trafficking
in Women

Learning more about HTML

You now have enough knowledge of HTML to get started. Of course, there is much more to learn and experiment with. The Internet itself is a good source of information on HTML and Web publishing. Here are some Internet sites that will start you off on your Web publishing journey:

> http://www.w3.org/pub/WWW/MarkUp/MarkUp.html
> http://www.sirius.com/~tim/html.htm
> http://pobox.com/~gerald/guild/style.html
> http://union.ncsa.uiuc.edu/HyperNews/get/www/html/guides.html
> http://www.stars.com

There are literally hundreds of sites filled with advice on how to write HTML, and ready-made graphics and icons are also available through the Internet. Another good way of learning about HTML is to look at other people's code. Most Web browsers allow you to look at the HTML source code. Using Netscape Navigator 2.0 this is what you do to see the HTML code that creates a Web page:

1. Connect to your Internet service provider and open up Netscape.
2. Connect to a Web page of your choice.
3. Select **Document Source** from the View menu. Netscape will open another window to display the document you are currently viewing, in HTML.

The multimedia Web: animation, sound and video

Web publishing is becoming more and more sophisticated. Recent developments now allow you to incorporate sound, video, animation and virtual reality concepts into your Web page. Leading-edge Web applications integrate conventional computer applications, such as databases and financial analysis programs, into interactive Web environments. You can listen to Internet-based radio stations, download short video clips, or play interactive Web-based games. To access these capabilities as a user, you need to download the appropriate helper or plug-in. These are usually free. Additionally, you may require the latest version of Netscape Navigator or one of the other leading browsers. Some of these advanced Web capabilities will run only under Windows 95, NT or Sun Solaris.

Here are the addresses for the front-runners in audio and video over the Web:

Audio-on Demand	http://www.realaudio.com
Video-on Demand	http://www.vdolive.com

Three of the hottest Web development tools in recent times are Java, Shockwave and VRML.

Java

This programming language can deliver small programs (applets) to your Web browser. These applets can then run on your computer like other applications such as word-processing packages or spreadsheets. Java can be used to animate and update Web pages and deliver interactivity and games to your computer. Java has caused so much excitement in the Internet community because it is multi-threaded (more than one thing can happen at a time) and it is very portable between different operating systems. The latter means you need to write only one version of your Java program, which will then run on any type of computer.

The advent of Java and the ubiquity of the Internet make it possible to build Internet appliances, otherwise known as Network computers. These computers are cut-down versions of today's PCs. The Network computer will have no hard disk, limited memory, and no software. All you will have to do is to turn this appliance on and you will be connected to the Internet. The network will supply all the software you need, and you will pay every time you use it. The idea behind the Network computer is that today's PCs are too expensive and complicated for the mass market. Proponents of Network computers claim they will be as easy to use as a telephone and save businesses millions of dollars in computer maintenance costs. Whether this dream will come true remains to be seen.

Shockwave

This application allows Macromedia Director files to be seen on Web pages. Director is one of the major multimedia authoring tools and is widely used in advertising. Unlike other Web-based animation packages, Director files bring a sophisticated multimedia feel to the Web by integrating page navigation, sound and video into one file. Undoubtedly much of the excitement about Shockwave stems from the fact a lot of people already have Macromedia Director skills. This skill can now be utilized to create Web pages.

VRML (Virtual Reality Markup Language) allows you to create 3D spaces and objects on the Internet (VRML files have the **.wrl** extension). VRML is similar to HTML, but where HTML is based around text, sound and 2D images, using VRML you can create virtual space and hyperlinks within a scene. 3D representation of cyberspace is still very much in its infancy, and standard ways of navigating the space and interacting with it have yet to be developed, but there are many potential and exciting applications. Personally, I find the development of 3D social spaces (graphical MUDs and IRC) the most interesting. At present, social spaces are represented almost entirely in text (a few graphical 2D environments have started to appear), and much is left to your imagination. Using VRML richer, more intuitive worlds could be created. 3D worlds have already started to appear in computer games, but playing these games is still very much a solitary pursuit. With the development of VRML environments we will be able to play and meet in a more visual cyberspace.

More information on Java, Shockwave and VRML can be found at these sites:

Java	http://java.sun.com/index.html
Shockwave	http://www.macromedia.com/
VRML	http://www.sdsc.edu/vrml/

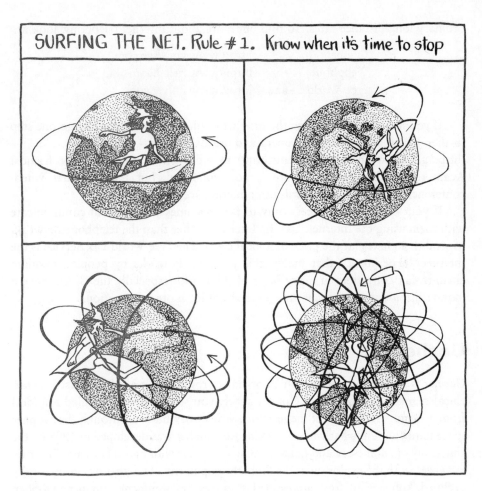

Phone, video and fax via the Internet

Another application that you might want to explore is Internet-based telephony. If your computer has a sound card and speakers, all you need is a microphone and one of the many Internet phone packages to allow you to use your computer as a phone. You can now use your computer and the Internet to connect to anyone in the world who has the same set-up. Some of the Internet phone packages also permit you to share a whiteboard and to conduct conference calls (for example cooltalk which comes with Netscape 3.0). There are experiments under way that will allow you to use the the Internet to "ring" people with ordinary phones (Free World Phone project) and to use the Internet rather than the telephone network as the transport mechanism for phone calls. The voice quality of such calls is not comparable to that of the telephone network, but it's usually a lot cheaper than ordinary long-distance rates. To find out more about Internet telephony, look at:

Iphone	http://www.vocaltec.com
Webphone	http://www.itelco.com
Free World Phone	http://www.pulver.com

If you like the idea of using the Internet to phone friends, you can go one step further. Install a small digital camera and use CU-SeeMe (http://goliath.wpine.com/cu-seeme.html) to videoconference with your friends! Again the quality of the picture is not wonderful, but I expect that video-conferencing via the Internet will be commonplace in a few years.

If your friends have access only to fax machines you can still communicate with them using the Internet. Use the Internet, rather than the telephone network, to send them faxes (at the price of a local call!). The Free World Fax Service is the Internet "experiment" that makes this possible. It works by people providing email-to-fax converters in many parts of the world (especially the USA). Have a look at http://www-usa.tpc.int/tpc_home.html for more information.

Gopher

Gopher is an Internet service which organizes resources in a subject-based hierar-chical manner. To navigate a Gopher space, you select one item (called a folder) from a menu. As you select menu items, you slowly burrow through the Gopher space until you find what you are looking for. Gopher was developed in 1991 by the University of Minnesota and quickly became popular with universities and libraries. However, with the explosion of the Web, the popularity of Gopher has dramatically declined. You can still find interesting bits and pieces of information using Gopher, but information is often out of date or might have shifted to a Web site. I suspect Gopher will eventually become nothing more than a historical curiosity.

There is one important difference between the Web and Gopher: a Web document can contain links to many other Web documents; in Gopher, only a folder or menu item can contain links. One of the advantages of Gopher is that you don't need to know where the address of the resource is kept.

You can think of Gopher menus as tables of contents. You follow the menu structure by selecting an option from the menu, using your cursor key or mouse to move around, or by entering the number preceding the menu selection. Gopher is at its most useful when you are searching through libraries or looking for a telephone number or other information about educational institutions.

Gopher clients

Like many other Internet tools, Gopher uses a client-server architecture. You can either telnet to a public client, use one of the common Gopher clients such as Hgopher(PC), Turbo Gopher for Macintosh, or WinGopher, or use your Web browser. A Gopher client needs to be able to perform the basic task of displaying a hierarchical menu of documents and fetching and displaying the selected document. Depending on the capabilities of your client, display of the documents will vary.

To find out if your service provider has a Gopher client installed, type gopher at the prompt or scan your file manager for the name of one of the common client programs. By far the easiest way to use Gopher is by using your Web browser as a client.

Using Gopher with a Web browser

You can telnet to a public Gopher server or use your Web browser to handle the connection for you. In the sample session below I have used my Web browser (Netscape Navigator 2.0) to connect to the public Gopher server at the University of Minnesota. Note how the URL starts with the word gopher, rather than the usual http. Using your Web browser also means you don't have to worry about the login.

If you click on any of the titles below each heading you will be taken to the next Gopher area. Continue selecting menu items by clicking on them till you arrive at your destination. You can use all the usual Web browser commands to mark favourite pages, save text, send pages by email to other people, and so on.

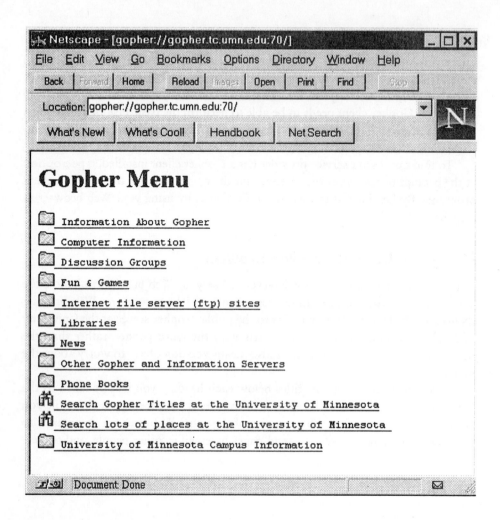

Using Gopher through a dial-up shell/text account

If you use a dial-up shell/text account, use your text-only browser (e.g. Lynx) to access Gopher services. Note that a Gopher URL starts with the word gopher, rather than the usual http. Using your Web browser also means you don't have to worry about the login.

Finding out more about Gophers

Some general purpose Gophers can be found at:
Australian National University   gopher://info.anu.edu.au/
Cornell University Law School, USA   gopher://fatty.law.cornell.edu/
University of Maryland, USA   gopher://info.umd.edu/

For a searchable list of worldwide Gophers connect to:
gopher://main.morris.org:70/11gopher_root%3a%5b_servers%5d

To find more information on Gopher, try:
gopher://gopher.tc.umn.edu:70
Select from the menu: info about gopher folder

Chapter 8

Searching for information and bringing it home

Searching for information on the World Wide Web

You can access millions of Web pages through the World Wide Web. Once you have a starting address, you will soon find yourself following well-worn roads, unexpected side alleys and often venturing into completely new territory. If you don't have an address already for the subject that interests you, don't despair. The World Wide Web has a number of different services that you can use to find information:

- subject-based guides such as Yahoo, Cool site of the day etc.
- search engines that use automatically built indices of Internet information such as Lycos, Infoseek etc.
- specialist sites, that point to and keep people up-to-date on information in a particular topic;
- Usenet News databases that archive and track past postings;
- FTP indexes that track which files are available at the various FTP sites.

Search engines also provide subject-oriented indices. How do all the various guides and indices find out about new Web sites? There are programs that collect Web page information by automatically traversing the World Wide Web. These programs are known as spiders, robots or worms. They work by contacting a particular Web site and collecting all the pages contained in it. The pages are then analysed and indexed, and any links contained in the pages are followed. Apart from automatic programs that scour the Web for new sites, authors of Web pages can also inform the various indices about their Web page.

Subject-oriented Web guides

Subject-oriented Web guides are usually compiled by an editorial team, which looks at different Web pages and then puts them under the appropriate subject headings. These guides are ideal for browsing. If you are interested in a fairly general topic, such as women and technology, a subject-oriented guide like Yahoo can be a good first point of call to see what's there. Once you have at least one address, it's easy to find more information, as most Web pages have links to other pages.

Here are the URLs for a small selection of subject-oriented Web guides.

Web Guide	URL
Einet	http://www.einet.net/galaxy.html
GNN's Whole Internet Catalog	http://www-e1c.gnn.com/gnn/wic/index.html
Internet Web Text	http://www.december.com/web/text/index.html
Subject Oriented Clearinghouse	http://www.lib.umich.edu/chhome.html
Yahoo	http://www.yahoo.com
Yanoff's list	http://www.spectracom.com/islist/
WWW Virtual Library	http://www.w3.org/pub/DataSources/bySubject/Overview.html

Search engines

The best place to start any search on the World Wide Web is to use one of the many Internet search engines. If you use Netscape Navigator, all you need to do is press the **Net Search** button and you are automatically taken to a list of search engines. Select the engine of your choice with the click of a mouse button. Each search engine uses a different mechanism for indexing and finding information, but all search engines will ask you to specify a topic to search for. Most use a specialized language to allow you to restrict the search using special words or symbols. For instance using a plus sign (+) tells InfoSeek that the pages it searches must contain both words on either side of the plus sign. You can also specify whether you want to search Web sites, Usenet News groups or both. In my experience Alta Vista and Lycos are the most extensive search engines, but others are worth a try if the first two don't come up with an answer. New search engines pop up frequently, and each one claims to be the best. You have to try them out and judge for yourself. Most search engines have a heavy emphasis on US information, and you might want to consider searching a country-specific search engine such as Web Wombat for Australian sites. At the moment, use of most search engines is still free, but I expect at least some of them will start charging for searches.

Here are the URLs for some popular search engines:

Search Engine	URL
InfoSeek	http://www.infoseek.com
Lycos	http://www.lycos.com
Excite	http://www.excite.com
Alta Vista	http://altavista.digital.com
Web Crawler	http://www.webcrawler.com
Web Wombat	http://www.intercom.com.au/wombat

Here is an example using Lycos to search for information on menstruation. Because I was using only one word in my search, I didn't use the **enhance your search** option, which lets you specify how to connect the words (*and, or*) and the type of search you want.

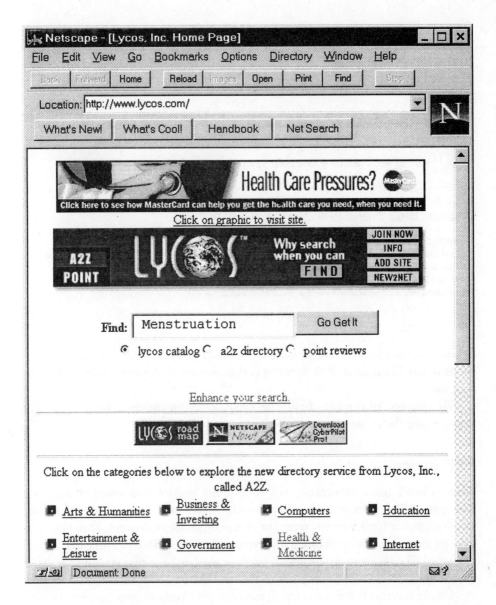

Here is some of the information Lycos returned:

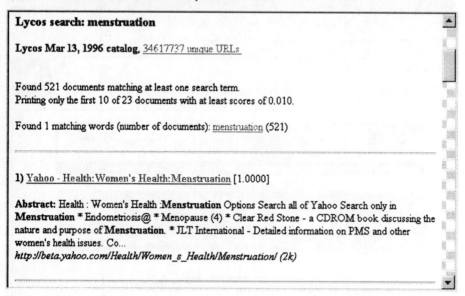

Lycos search: menstruation

Lycos Mar 13, 1996 catalog, 34617737 unique URLs

Found 521 documents matching at least one search term.
Printing only the first 10 of 23 documents with at least scores of 0.010.

Found 1 matching words (number of documents): menstruation (521)

1) Yahoo - Health:Women's Health:Menstruation [1.0000]

Abstract: Health : Women's Health :**Menstruation** Options Search all of Yahoo Search only in **Menstruation** * Endometriosis@ * Menopause (4) * Clear Red Stone - a CDROM book discussing the nature and purpose of **Menstruation**. * JLT International - Detailed information on PMS and other women's health issues. Co...
http://beta.yahoo.com/Health/Women_s_Health/Menstruation/ (2k)

Notice that the Lycos contained more than 3 million unique URLs in March 1996. Lycos found 521 unique Web documents that contained the word *menstruation* at least once.

To visit one of the sites found by Lycos, click on the underlined title; your browser will then take you to the Web page in question.

FTP indices

There is much more information on the Internet besides that which is found on Web pages. This information is kept in files. Files may contain text (like your word-processor files), images, sound or executable code (software). Many of these files are kept in special sites called anonymous FTP sites, which anyone can access. The word FTP (file transfer protocol) refers to the language that is used to transfer the information from one computer to the next. More about this later.

On the Internet there is no central repository: nobody assigns numbers to each new resource or keeps track of where the latest version of the resource is located. You simply have to go and look for it yourself. Working out which FTP site has the information you want can be very difficult. Traditionally a tool called archie was used to search the database of files that you could FTP. Archie works by regularly collecting the names of files stored at FTP sites worldwide and adding them to a searchable database. There is also a World Wide Web interface to archie, called archieplex, which makes interacting with archie a lot easier. There are also a few other FTP indices on the World Wide Web that can make finding that elusive file easier, especially if you are looking for software.

Here are the URLs for some FTP indices:

Index	URL
Archieplex	http://pubweb.nexor.co.uk/public/archie/servers.html
Snoopie	http://www.snoopie.com
Virtual Shareware.com	http://www.shareware.com/
Winsite	http://www.winsite.com
Info Mac HyperArchive	http://hyperarchive.lcs.mit.edu/HyperArchive.html

The Usenet News database

Usenet News is like a large posting board which you can send messages to and read messages others have posted. You can access messages posted by using a News reader (chapter 6 describes Usenet News in detail). Usenet News is organized into specialist groups that cover every imaginable topic. These groups announce Internet happenings such as an on-line concert with k.d. lang, a specialist chat channel for women entomologists, a new mailing list for Virginia Woolf fans, or the latest release of the Netscape Navigator. Some of the Internet search engines archive a month's worth of Usenet News and you can search these archives to check if they contain the topic of your choice. You can also use these databases to find out if there is a news group that covers the topic you are interested in. Lycos keeps News for a month, Excite for two weeks and Deja News (**http://www.dejanews.com/**) keeps News longer, but does not keep the alt., soc. or rec. Usenet News groups.

Using Veronica to search Gophers

Working your way through the many Gopher menus to find what you want soon becomes boring and tiresome. Veronica (<u>v</u>ery <u>e</u>asy <u>r</u>odent-<u>o</u>riented <u>N</u>etwide <u>I</u>ndex to <u>C</u>omputerized <u>A</u>rchives) comes to the rescue. Veronica pops up as a menu choice on many Gophers and is easy to use. Just follow the Veronica menus until you are presented with a text box into which you can type keywords to search for. Veronica will return all the documents or menu items it finds that match a particular set of keywords. I have not explained Veronica in any detail, because Gopher is a tool that is increasingly becoming a historical curiosity. If you really need to use Veronica, have a look at the FAQ about Gopher at:

ftp://rtfm.mit.edu/pub/usenet/news.answers/gopher-faq

Bringing information home with FTP

Information on the Internet is kept in the form of files. The word *file* is derived from the idea associated with filing cabinets and the files that are kept in them. Computer files contain information in electronic form and can be all manner of things – software programs, images, text, sound, whole books, or just a sentence. Much of the information available on the Internet is kept in special repositories called FTP sites. Some of these sites are anonymous FTP sites, which means you don't need a special password. The convention is to use the word **anonymous** as your login word and **your email address** as your password. FTP sites can be contacted using an Internet tool called FTP or file transfer protocol. This protocol enables you to collect a file from a particular site and bring it to your home computer.

You may come across FTP addresses in a variety of places, but the two most likely are from computer magazines and the results of an Internet search. Many ISPs also operate FTP sites to make a variety of software available to their customers.

FTP sites usually have two types of files available: articles and software. The software is either public-domain software, shareware or freeware. Public domain software and freeware can be used without having to pay anyone for it, but in freeware the author retains the copyright on the software. Shareware is software that you can use for a trial period; after that you are expected to pay the author a fee (usually small).

If you have a dial-up IP/graphical Internet account you can use your Web browser to connect to an FTP site or use a self-contained graphical program like fetch. If you use a dial-up shell/text account you can use FTP in text-mode from the operating prompt. Using your Web browser is by far the easiest option, as you do not need to remember any of the FTP commands. Here are two example sessions, first using your Web browser, then using FTP with a dial-up shell/text account.

Using FTP through a dialup IP/graphical account: Netscape Navigator 2.0

1. Connect to your ISP, then double click on the **Netscape Navigator** icon.
2. Enter the FTP address into the location field and press enter. Or choose **Open Location** from the **File** menu, enter the address into the dialog box and press **open**. Netscape will now contact the FTP server for you, then take you straight to the directory you have specified.
3. Move around the hierarchical directory tree, by clicking on the directory name, until you locate the file you want to transfer.
4. Next to the file name you will see information on the file size, the date it was placed in the directory, and the file type. When you are ready to FTP a file,

click on the file. A window will pop up that will ask you to specify where to save the file and under which name. Click **OK** when you have decided on the file name and location. The **Saving Location** window will now pop up (sometimes it hides under the browser). This window keeps you informed about the progress of the transfer. If you want to stop the transfer at any time, simply click the cancel button.

Using FTP through a dial-up shell/text account

Connecting to the FTP server

Using a graphical Web browser or one of the graphical FTP programs is the easiest and most convenient way of using FTP. But using FTP directly is also quite straight forward, if a little more longwinded.

Connect to your ISP and, if you are in a menu, look for an option which indicates file transfer, select this menu option and follow the instructions. Otherwise change to the operating prompt and connect to the remote computer by typing:

```
ftp <address>
```

For instance:

```
ftp ftp.wave.com.au
```

After some time the machine will reply with a message and ask you to login:

```
connected to ftp.wave.com.au
220 wave company ftp server
Name(ftp.wave.com.au): anonymous
331 Guest login ok, send email address as password
```

If the FTP server is anonymous you login as anonymous and use your email address as password.

Bringing a file home

1. After you have logged-on to the server, you need to go to the directory that the file resides in. To change from one level of a directory to the next level down, type `cd`
    To see what is contained in a directory type `ls` or `dir`.
    To go up one level in the directory structure type `cd ..`
    If you know exactly where the file resides, type `cd directoryname`
    For instance: `cd pub\woolf\texts`

2. Files come in a variety of formats. The basic division is whether a file is in text or binary format. Software or compressed text files are usually in binary format. Text format is the default. You need to tell FTP whether a file is binary or text. It is safest to always set the format to binary, irrespective of the format. Type `binary`

   FTP will reply: `200 Type set to I`

3. Now you can bring the file to your ISP's computer by typing `get filename`

4. When you are finished bringing the file to your ISP's computer, type `quit` to leave FTP.

5. If you want to bring the file from your ISP's computer to your home computer, you need to use a communications package. It will provide you with either **xmodem, ymodem, zmodem** or **kermit**. These are the names of different file transfer protocols that manage the uploading and downloading from your computer to your ISP (or any other computer that you can reach by modem) and vice versa. Which file transfer protocol to use depends on which protocol your ISP supports. Consult your communications package online help or manual for the actual commands, as they vary from package to package. The communications software I use (**Comit for Windows**) has an easy-to-use menu system that guides you through sending and receiving files.

Sending a file to an FTP server

FTP can be used not only to retrieve files, but also to place files on a remote computer. Submissions to anonymous FTP servers are usually placed into a special directory called **/incoming**. You may also want to send an email message to the administrator of the FTP site telling her of your submission. It is also becoming increasingly common to submit papers for conferences via FTP. In this case you may be given a special login name and password. If you have accounts on two different computers on the Internet, then FTP makes it easy to transfer the files between these accounts.

Here is how to upload a file to an FTP site:

1. Connect to your ISP and look for an option which indicates file transfer, select this menu option and follow the instructions. Otherwise change to the operating prompt and connect to the remote computer you want to place your files on by typing:

   `ftp address`

   For instance: `ftp ftp.lighthouse.com.uk`

2. Switch to the appropriate directory, such as incoming, by typing:

   `cd incoming`

3. Transfer your file by typing:

    put orlando.txt

4. When the transfer has been completed, type quit to finish the FTP process.

This is what you see on your computer:

```
Connected to ftp.lighthouse.com
220- Welcome to the ftp service of Lighthouse Inc.
Name (ftp.lighthouse.com:rww) anonymous
331-Guest login ok, send email address as password.
Password: v.woolf@lighthouse.com.gb
331-Guest login ok, access restrictions apply.
ftp> cd incoming
ftp> put orlando.txt
200- Port command successful
150-Opening ASCII mode data connection for pub/incoming(3434
bytes)
226-Transfer complete
local: orlando.txt remote: orlando.txt 323453 bytes send in 54.04
seconds (14.03 Kbytes/s)
ftp>quit
221-Goodbye
```

Table 8.1 Major anonymous ftp archives

FTP address	Name of Institution	What the archive contains
ftp://wuarchive.wust1.edu	Washington University, St Louis	MsDOS & Macintosh tools
ftp://mac.archive.umich.edu	University of Michigan	Macintosh tools
ftp://oak.oakland.edu	Oakland University	Macintosh & PC tools, mirrors some other sites
ftp://sumex.stanford.edu	Stanford University	Macintosh tools
ftp://nic.funet.fi	Finnish University Network	Variety of tools, esp. images
ftp://archie.au	Australian Academic & Research Network	Mirrors of various other sites

Summary of FTP commands for dial-up shell/text accounts

ascii	ASCII file format (ASCII stands for text)
binary	binary file format
bye	ends an ftp session
cd directoryname	changes directory on remote computer
dir	list content of current directory
mdir	list content of all directories
help	list major ftp commands
get filename	bring a file to home computer
mget filename	brings all specified files to home computer
put filename	send a file to the remote computer
pwd	prints the name of the current directory
status	checks the filetype and other features
hash	monitors downloading
lcd	change directory to the local drive

Using email to obtain files (ftpmail)

Not everyone has direct access to all Internet facilities. A large number of countries still have only email access, but you can use email to utilize most Internet facilities.

Finding an FTP site by email

First you need to find the ftpmail site you want to use by email. Here is a list of sites:

FTP mail servers	
Address	Location
ftpmail@cs.uow.edu.au	Australia
ftpmail@grasp.insa-lyon.fr	France
ftpmail@ftp.uni-stuttgart.de	Germany
ftpmail@ftp.sunet.se	Sweden
ftpmail@doc.ic.ac.uk	Great Britain
ftpmail@ieunet.ie	Italy
ftpmail@archie.inesc.pt	Portugal
ftpmail@census.gov	USA
ftpmail@decwrl.dec.com	USA
ftpmail@ftp.Dartmouth.EDU	USA
ftpmail@sunsite.unc.edu	USA
ftpmail@ftp.SHSU.edu	USA

Many ftpmail servers are of an experimental nature and may have disappeared by the time you contact them. To get an updated list, point your Web browser to either of these Web addresses:

http://www.tex.ac.uk/tex-archive/archive-tools/ftpmail/ftpmail-servers.html
http://rtfm.mit.edu/pub/usenet/news.answers/ftp-list/sitelist

Alternatively you can get a list of sites by sending email to:
mail-server@rtfm.mit.edu

Send the message:
send usenet/news.answers/ftp-list/sitelist/part1

Note: Because the list has 18 parts you need to type this line 18 times, changing the number from 1 to 18, as you go.

Getting files home using ftpmail

After you have located the nearest ftpmail server, you need to send a sequence of messages to the ftpmail server of your choice. The first message to send is:

```
open nameofsite
dir
quit
```

The server will reply to you with a list of files stored in the root directory. In your next message to the server, you start to navigate the directory of your choice and obtain a listing of the files by sending:

```
open filename
chdir pub
ls
quit
```

Finally you retrieve the file you desire

```
open nameofsite
chdir pub
binary
get orlando.txt
quit
```

As you can see, if you don't know the exact location of a file on a server, retrieving a file by ftpmail can require a few messages. Receiving a reply from an ftpmail server can take anything from a few minutes to a few days, depending on how busy the server is. Large files may be split into several smaller ones, and you may have to reassemble them using a word-processor.

If you want to find out more, a list of frequently asked questions can be obtained from:

mail-server@rtfm.mit.edu :

Send the message:

send usenet/news.answers/ftp-list/faq

FTP Netiquette

When you are using an FTP site there are a few things to remember:

- **FTP is a service, not a right.** If possible, please make sure you are connecting to FTP sites out of working hours (local time) to minimize the load on the remote computer. Always use the FTP server closest to you.

- **Software on an FTP site may not be the most up-to-date.** It is up to you to ensure that you find the latest version of a particular software. You can keep up with the latest software versions and where to find them by subscribing to relevant email lists or Usenet News groups.

- **Only download software from well-known sites and always scan it for virus attacks.**

- **Be careful that you don't overwrite existing files when you download files.** Sometimes the transfer of a file may not work completely and if you overwrite an existing copy of a file, you may end up with nothing. Always download files into a temporary directory.

- **Use ftpmail only when necessary.**

a<virus>from.the.Net has.down-
loaded_into.my.system :-(so.don't.
expect.me@com.2day~i'm.a bit :-/

Viruses from the Internet?

We all occasionally contract the flu, a sore throat and other minor diseases, ailments which are sometimes caused by viruses. Undoubtedly you have also heard that it is possible for computers to be invaded by a virus. But is it possible for a computer to acquire a virus through the Internet? The bad news is that yes, it is possible. It is something you need to be aware of, but you can take precautions.

What is a virus?

A computer virus is a program that was designed to replicate itself. Some computer viruses just duplicate themselves, taking up increasing amounts of space on your hard disk and eventually bringing you computer to a grinding halt. Other viruses are more destructive and actively destroy files on your hard disk. Like biological viruses, computer viruses need a host to infect and a medium that can spread the infection. The host may be an executable program (program virus) or the virus may take over the whole system when you first turn it on (boot virus) by interfering with information that is needed to start the computer properly. A program virus can be contained only in files with names ending in .com, .exe, .sys, .ovl, .drv or .bin. On Macintosh computers this also includes system files, INITs and control panels. A boot virus invades the boot and master boot records. These records hold information that the computer requires to start correctly. Boot viruses enter a computer when you start (boot) your computer from a floppy diskette which contains the virus. They attach themselves to small areas on your hard disk and interfere with the correct running of the computer. Program viruses spread when you run the infected program file. The medium for spreading computer virus infection is most commonly a floppy diskette. Boot viruses can be spread only in this way. However, it is possible to download infected programs from the Internet.

There have also been reports of special kinds of program viruses called macro viruses. These viruses are associated with software packages such as word processors or spreadsheets that permit users to create a single command (a macro) out of a series of commands. Macros can make everyday tasks faster and easier. It is not clear how common these viruses are, but apparently Microsoft Word 6.0 documents can be carriers. Macro viruses spread because people attach word-processed documents to their email: they become activated when the attached document is converted into a readable file.

How do I protect myself from a virus?

There are some indications that the prevalence of viruses is exaggerated, but it pays to be cautious. Here are some simple rules that will protect you from most viruses:

- Obtain some virus-scanning software, install it and use it. If you upgrade from Windows 3.1 to Windows 95, make sure you upgrade your virus-scanning software as well.
- Never start your computer from a floppy diskette.
- Scan all new software, irrespective of its origin (floppy diskette, CD-ROM or the Internet).
- Scan any attachments before you read them.

File formats

Files come in different formats. Text, executable code, images and sound are all represented internally in a different way. These files can then be compressed and archived to make transport easier and more efficient. Files may also be encoded to make sure they don't get corrupted during network transmission. Usually it is not necessary to encode files for FTP transmission, because the binary format protects them, but you may still come across the occasional encoded file. You can tell which layers of packaging have been applied to a particular file by its extensions. The file extension is the three-letter mnemonic found at the end of a filename, usually separated by a dot, e.g. orlando.txt. If several layers of packaging have been applied you may see something like this: orlando.text.tar.Z.

Compressed and archived files

Compressing files saves disk space and makes their retrieval substantially faster. The file extension can tell you which utility was used to compress and hence decompress a file. There are quite a number of de/compression utilities, but luckily they can all be FTPed.

The most common utility for PCs is Pkunzip and for Macintosh the Stuffit program. On UNIX systems the most common utilities are the Compress, Zip, and the Gzip programs. There are many other compression formats, including ARC, ARJ, LHA, SQX, and ZOO. Utilities to deal with these formats can be retrieved from the major FTP sites.

Compressing your file does not delete the original file, but makes a compressed copy, leaving the original file untouched. Compressing a file is useful when you want to make a back-up of the file and store it on a floppy disk.

Archiving programs provides a means of putting many files into a single archive file. This is useful for making back-up copies of files, or for packaging a set of files to move them to another system. Tar and shar are two commonly used UNIX archiving programs.

Often compression and archiving are used in combination. You might see something like this:

orlando1.tar.Z or orlando.sit.hqx

Orlando1.tar.Z was compressed using the UNIX utility Compress and archived using tar. Orlando.sit.hqx was compressed using the Stuffit utility and then encoded using BinHex for Macintoshes. As you can see, the file extensions can tell you which computer platform a particular file was intended for. When you want to restore these files to their original state approach them from right to left, e.g. deal first with the extension furthest to the right.

Tables 8.2 and 8.3 list some utilities for compressing and archiving files.

Table 8.2 Compression utilities

File extension	Name of utility	Command to unzip file
.zip	Pkunzip	pkunzip filename.zip
.z	Uncompress	decompress filename. Z
.gz	GNU zip	gunzip filename.gz
.sit	Stuffit for Mac	use Stuffit Expander to decompress the file

Table 8.3 Archiving utilities

File extension	Command for utility	Effect of command
.tar	tar -xf	decodes & extracts archive
	filename tar -tf	lists content
.shar	unshar filename	decodes & extracts
	shar filename	encodes & archives
.sea	Download as MacBinary,	Macintosh Self Extracting
	and launch it	archive

Table 8.4 Encoding schemes for attachments

File extension	Name of utility	Effect of utility
.uu	uuencode	Uuencoded file. To decode: uuencode OriginalFile DecodedFile
.hqx	MacBin hexed	Encodes a Macintosh file into 7-bit text so it can be safely transferred.

Other file extensions

As you can see, it is important to understand the meaning of file extensions. Here are some more:

.ps	Adobe's printer language, commonly used with Laser printers
.gif	CompuServe's Graphics Interchange Format, used for images
.jpg	an image compression format developed by the Joint Photographic Experts group
.tiff	tagged image file format, a not-so-compact file format for images
.bmp	Windows bitmap format
.mpeg	full-motion images in a file, similar to JPEG
.avi	Microsoft's full-motion video format
.dvi	another full-motion video standard
.wav	Microsoft's format for sound file
.sbi	Sound Blaster Instrument sound file format for single instruments

Finding out more

More information on file extensions and compression utilities is available at these URLs:

Common internet file formats and utilities	http://www.matisse.net/files/formats.html
Internet multimedia file formats	http://ac.dal.ca/~dong/contents.html
Cross platforms page, includes links to utilities	http://www.mps.org/~ebennett

Filenames

FTP servers often use UNIX as an operating system. One of the things to look out for is that UNIX filenames have no limit on length. DOS and Windows 3.1 or lower allow filenames of up to 8 characters. Windows 95 has done away with this limitation. When you transfer a file from a UNIX system to your PC you may find that the original filename has been truncated.

Chapter 9

Connecting to a remote computer: Telnet

What is Telnet?

Telnet is a program that allows you to connect to a remote computer and interact with it from your home. The computer on your desk becomes a terminal or extension of the remote computer. To use a remote computer you often need a username and a password. After you have connected to the remote computer you "log-in" using the username and password, this ensures that only authorized users have access to the computer. Many public services such as those supported by libraries will supply the username and password automatically when you first make the connection. Telnet allows you to use an application that is installed on a remote computer. For instance, you can use Telnet when:

• you want to access an Internet service, such as Gopher, IRC or MUDs, but don't have a program that manages the connection for you (a so-called client) on your computer;

- you want to perform some work on a remote computer, such as searching a database or library catalogue;
- you are away from home and you want to check your mail or look at some of your files.

Graphical Telnet clients for dial-up IP/graphical accounts

Telnet uses the by now familar client-server mode used by many Internet services. If you have a dial-up IP/graphical account, then a graphical Telnet client will make the job of connecting to a remote computer a little easier. Graphical Telnet clients have additional features such as a point-and-click interface to connect with the remote computer; they often remember the computers you have connected to before; you can keep a record of your Telnet session; and you can select from a number of different terminal emulations. The terminal emulation specifies the way that your computer responds and formats data sent by the remote computer. An indication that you haven't chosen the right terminal emulation is that the information displayed on your computer doesn't seem to appear in the right spot or commands you type don't have the desired effect. You can also customize your screen appearance by choosing font type, font size etc. There are a number of Telnet clients for Windows 3.1 and Windows 95 such as CRT or NetTerm. Windows 95 has a simple inbuilt Telnet client, that you can access by going to the MS-DOS prompt and typing Telnet. A good choice of Telnet client for the Macintosh is NCSA Telnet.

Here are the URLs for some graphical Telnet clients.

NetTerm 16-bit http://starbase.neosoft.com/~zkrr01/netterm.html
CRT   http://www.vandyke.com/vandyke/crt/
NCSA Telnet
     http://hyperarchive.lcs.mit.edu/HyperArchive/Archive/comm/inet/ncsa-telnet-27b4hqx

Chapter 8 explains how to obtain software. Most software comes in compressed form and chapter 8 also explains how to decompress it.

Using CRT on a PC

I have chosen CRT as a Telnet client because it's straightforward to use and not expensive. It has a few extra features: for instance it can be customized more easily than the Telnet client that comes with Windows 95. There are several other PC-based Telnet clients. They can usually be obtained by FTP and used for a trial period. You can always experiment with different available Telnet clients and choose the one you like best.

Let's assume you have installed CRT. Before you can use CRT you need to be connected to your ISP using a dial-up IP/graphical account. Once you are connected to the Internet, you can double click on the **CRT** icon to start it up. An empty window will appear. The empty window is your workspace once you are connected to the remote computer. Let's connect to a remote computer.

1. Select **connect** from the **File** menu. A further window appears. In this window you specify the protocol, and address of the remote computer. Select **Telnet** as your protocol in the box titled **Protocol**. Enter the address of the computer you want to connect to in the box titled **Hostname**. If the address includes a port number, enter that in the box titled **Port**; otherwise, keep this box empty. The port number is the number that occurs immediately after the hostname, e.g. archie.au:23. The port number allows different services to be run on a single computer. If you click on the box next to **Save new entries**, the program will remember the entries you have just made. Click on the **OK** button to start the connection process.

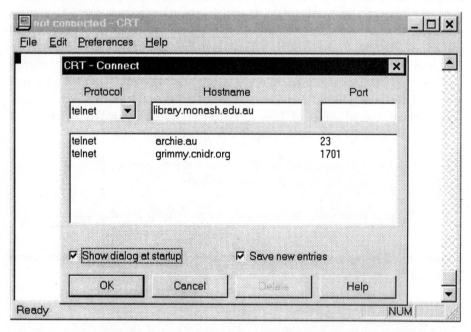

2. After a few moments you will be connected. How you proceed from here depends entirely on the remote computer. Usually there will be a help screen or a menu that will assist you in driving the remote computer. Here is the screen displayed when I connected to the Monash University library.

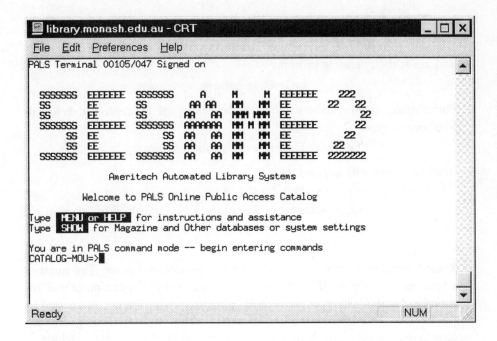

3. When you want to disconnect from your remote computer, choose **Disconnect** from the file menu.

Using NCSA Telnet on a Macintosh

NCSA Telnet is the popular Telnet client for Macintoshes. It can be obtained from many Macintosh ftp sites. It is straightforward to use. Let's assume you have successfully installed NCSA Telnet. This is what you do to use it:

1. Connect to your Internet service provider.

2. Click on the **NCSA Telnet** icon to start the program.

3. Observe how the menu along the top has changed. Select **Open connection** from the **File** menu.

4. A dialog box appears. Enter the address of the computer you want to connect to in the box next to **Host/Session Name**. Leave the rest of the dialog box empty and click on **Connect**.

5. Your computer will now contact the computer at the address you have specified. When the connection is established, a text window will appear. This is the window through which you communicate with the remote computer.

6. To end your Telnet session, select **Close** from the **File** menu. A dialog window will ask you if you are certain. Click on the **OK** button.

Using Telnet with a dial-up shell account

1. Dial into your Internet service provider and type `Telnet` and the computer's address at the operating prompt:

    ```
    telnet address
    ```

    For instance if you want to contact the library of Monash University in Melbourne, type:

    ```
    telnet library.monash.edu.au
    ```

    Your computer will respond with

    ```
    Trying 130.194.1.160...
    Connected to library.cc.monash.edu.au.
    Escape character is '^]'.
    Trying 21...Open
    ```

    Your computer is trying to connect to the remote computer. The number appearing after the word `trying` is the IP address of the computer you are trying to contact. This number uniquely identifies each computer connected to the Internet. Because humans find names easier to remember, computers are also given names. Just before the computer calls the remote machine it performs a translation between the host computer address and the IP number.

2. Next you will see:

    ```
    PALS Terminal 00100/285 Signed on


    SSSSSSS   EEEEEEE   SSSSSSS      A      M     M   EEEEEEE    222
    SS        EE        SS         AA AA    MM    MM  EE         22  22
    SS        EE        SS         AA   AA  MMM  MMM  EE             22
    SSSSSSS   EEEEEEE   SSSSSSS    AAAAAAA  MM M MM   EEEEEEE        22
         SS   EE             SS    AA   AA  MM    MM  EE             22
         SS   EE             SS    AA   AA  MM    MM  EE         22
    SSSSSSS   EEEEEEE   SSSSSSS    AA   AA  MM    MM  EEEEEEE    2222222

              Ameritech Automated Library Systems

          Welcome to PALS Online Public Access Catalog

    Type  MENU or HELP  for instructions and assistance
    Type  SHOW  for Magazine and Other databases or system settings

    You are in PALS command mode -- begin entering commands
    CATALOG-MOU=>
    ```

3. How you proceed from here depends entirely on the remote computer. Usually a help screen or a menu will assist you in driving the remote computer.

4. You can disconnect from the remote computer with the **Cntrl]** sequence of keys. Press both keys at the same time. This will disconnect you from the remote computer and return you to the Telnet program. To leave the Telnet program type:

quit

Telnet Command Summary

Here are some useful commands for Telnet

close	ends a Telnet session
display	shows the parameters used in the current session
mode	line by line or one character at a time
open hostname	connects to a remote site
quit	exits Telnet
set	allows you to set parameters
set?	gives you a list of possible parameters
set escape	defines the character used to disconnect from remote host
return or enter	takes you out of command mode and brings you back to the Telnet connection level of the remote computer
status	gives you some information about the connection
toggle	moves between opposing parameters
z	returns temporarily to the local connection
fg	takes you back to the remote computer.

Chapter 10

Privacy, anonymity and security on the Internet

The Internet is one of the least private means of communication, especially if you use email. Email is like a postcard: whoever handles it en route to its destination can read its contents. Email is especially vulnerable at the point where it is sent or received. Systems administrators have unrestricted access to all files on networked computers and can read all email received or sent.

Most of us don't imagine we have any sensitive material to hide. You may think you don't have to worry about issues of privacy and security when using the Internet. Perhaps you don't, but what about the time you sent an email to a friend (during work time and using your work account) describing your boss in no uncertain terms and your company's products as faulty. Or the time you complained (via email) about a colleague's standard of dress, habits of hygiene, or worse. More seriously, you might be working for an organization which deals in sensitive documents and information. Maybe you work for a women's refuge and regularly send co-workers sensitive addresses and names. Leaked information can endanger lives. People might decide to read your email because they have a personal vendetta against you. Industrial espionage is also increasingly common.

Most computers used at work or educational institutions are joined together to form a network (also called a LAN, for local area network). One of the reasons for networking computers is that files can be stored together on a special computer called a file server. Files on file servers are regularly backed up, which means even when you have deleted an email or any file it may still exist somewhere on a back-up tape. Remember also that if you are using your company's computer to send private email the company may have the right to inspect this email because it was written on company time using company equipment.

 Be aware that when your email doesn't reach its destination (perhaps you made a typo in the email address or you have the wrong address) it goes to a postmaster, either at your site or the site you were trying to send the message to. Invariably, the postmaster will glance at your message.

Is there privacy on the Internet?

Discussions on privacy usually centre on the absence of it. Is my privacy invaded or not? Did someone disclose information about me I don't want made public? This may be a seemingly small thing like whether or not I am a vegetarian, what country I was born in, or what colour my eyes are. On the Internet privacy also refers to my exclusive use and access to my account and the data stored on it and directed to it, e.g. email.

Using the Internet gives us the illusion of privacy. As you type on your keyboard there are no cues about who might be watching you or who might be recording your keystrokes. In most electronic forums (email lists, Usenet News and other types of bulletin boards) there are always many more people watching (so-called lurkers) than interacting. This gives participants the illusion that the forum is much more private and intimate than it actually is.

Computer in/security starts as soon as my computer becomes part of any network. System administrators (the people who look after the running of the network) generally have access to any and all parts of a system. That means all my email and all my files. Additionally many networked computer systems keep details of when I logged in, where I logged in from, for how long, and what I did. Of course, this is done for legitimate purposes of accounting and systems maintenance. Some of this information is needed to solve system problems or to detect "suspicious" logins. But this privileged access granted to system's administrators is easily abused. There are plenty of examples of system administrators overstepping the privacy boundary. Some lost their jobs for invading the privacy of their users without official sanctions; others operated under the direction of their company or law-enforcement officers and were helping to unmask and trap real or imagined criminals.

Programs which log your every keystroke are usually hidden and not accessible by a user. The information is stored in databases which belong to your service providers or company. Many Internet services such as FTP servers also log your activities. Sometimes the information is stored without reference to you in particular and is used only for statistical purposes; at other times your user name can be clearly linked to whatever activity is recorded. Some programs scan for certain types of behaviour, e.g. whether you are downloading very large files which may indicate they are pornographic in nature.

Other programs are able to "learn" your preferences and habits in a certain area. Indeed a program that learns to sort my mail into important and unimportant messages could be very useful. Another program that observes and "learns" my taste in music and then suggests new music to listen to may be fun and helpful. The downside is that such programs can also provide valuable marketing information about me.

Increasingly, marketing people are interested in this kind of statistical and personal data. But whose data is it? Does it belong to you or to your ISP? Or does it belong to the educational institution that provides a particular Internet service? Should you give your consent before this data is sold to the highest bidder, or is your consent implicit because you didn't say no? Some commentators predict that people will increasingly "pay" for the use of a particular Internet service by allowing service providers to record and sell marketing information about them. Possibly advertising will also increasingly be part of an Internet service and you might have to pay to exclude advertising.

Who are you on the Internet?

Identity is a fluid concept on the Internet. As you move to a new city, finish your education, change company, country or Internet provider, you seemingly acquire a new identity. This is because mostly your identity is determined from your email address. This is your user name plus your host name address (see chapter 5 for an explanation of email addresses). From an email message, additional information may be gleaned about you, such as your full name, the company you work for, the educational institution you study at, and the country you sent the message from.

Sometimes an email address does not reveal much at all about you, or it might even give a slightly wrong impression. For instance if Virginia Woolf worked for a company in London called Lighthouse Inc., her email address might be: v.woolf@lighthouse.com.uk. She decides to get her own Internet account with an ISP and gets 67.3456@compuserve.com as an additional email address. A year later, she decides to study part-time at the Open University and there her email address is woolf5@openuni.edu.uk. Only the first and last email addresses tell you that Virginia is in Great Britain (uk); the second one may or may not indicate the country of origin. In this case the Internet provider originated in the USA and now has branches overseas. Many US email addresses have no country code attached. This might give people the impression that Virginia is sending her email from the USA.

I think email addresses will be different in the future. People will be given either universal addresses or at least addresses that do not change as long as they continue to reside in a particular country. Some commentators predict that there will be a convergence between the Internet, the telephone service, and all other media. The Internet will be used not only to send messages and files but also to make telephone calls, watch videos and listen to music. If this occurs, you may be given only one number to cover phone and email, and the "system" will figure out where and in what form to send a given message.

Who is this message from?

It is surprisingly easy for people to intercept your email. There is no assurance that the message you have just received from me is truly from me. Somebody can intercept my email message en route and change its content, or forge a message entirely. If somebody obtains my password, they have access to my account, and any message sent looks as if it was sent by me. Luckily, these scenarios occur rarely.

Undoubtedly, Internet communications will become more secure. Security of communication is a prerequisite for commerce to do business on the Internet. Banks and many other commercial enterprises are working hard on solving problems associated with security.

Can I remain anonymous on the Internet?

When you buy a newspaper from a coin-operated box, and when you vote, you are anonymous. Nobody can trace your identity. When you hand over cash to buy a book, a cup of coffee or a car, nobody can trace the origin of the money handed over (unless you have been set up with marked money).

On the Internet anonymity means the absence of an identity. You have a number of choices: you can acquire a pseudonym (or "handle" in Internet jargon), you can hide where or to whom you are sending a message, or you can be truely anonymous. If you choose to be anonymous, it is still possible to have an email address; this is useful when you want to participate in two-way discussions but be "untraceable".

Anonymity can be useful. You may not want people to know who you really are when you contribute to a particular electronic forum. Maybe you are a celebrity or perhaps your private opinion conflicts with that of your employer. Maybe you want to report on government abuses or disclose some other potentially sensitive or damaging information. Maybe you are a lesbian and don't want your employer to know of your sexual orientation.

The idea that you can remain anonymous is frowned upon by many service providers, institutions and governments. Anonymous accounts (unlike public telephones) are at present rarely available or supported. To enable anonymity on the Internet we all need access to strong encryption techniques such as public key cryptography (see below). Public key systems that provide for anonymous two-way messages, digital signatures, secure and fraud-resistant pseudonyms and electronic cash are becoming increasingly available.

Anonymous mail and postings

You can make your email messages or postings to Usenet News anonymous by sending your mail message via an anonymous remailer. It will strip out your email address and any other identification information and replace it with an "anonymous ID". There are three types of anonymous remailers: pseudo-anonymous remailers, cypherpunk remailers and Lance Cotrell's "mixmaster remailers".

When you use a pseudo-anonymous remailer, you open an account with the operator of the remailer. This has the advantage that people can reply to your anonymous address. But this also means that the operator knows your real email address. Your anonymity is protected only as long as the operator keeps it secret. There have been cases where the police have forced an operator to reveal a person's identity. Anon.penet.fi is one of the best-known anonymous remailers. It has over 400,000 users on its database, offers anonymous email, and can deliver your anonymous Usenet News postings via email. In February 1995 the Finnish police forced anon.penet.fi to reveal the identity of one of its users. The police wanted to find the person who had allegedly stolen confidential information from a Church of Scientology computer and posted it on the Internet. The administrator of the remailer had two choices: reveal the person's name, or have the entire user list taken into police custody. He chose to reveal the name in order to protect the other users on the list. A somewhat more secure remailer is Alpha.c2.org. This remailer uses encryption, rather than a database of users. This ensures that the administrator doesn't know who uses a certain address.

Pseudo-anonymous remailers give you an anonymous alias. Cypherpunk remailers take your message, strip off all information that could identify a user and send it to the intended recipient. This is much more secure, especially if the message gets chained through several cypherpunk remailers, but it also means that no one can reply to you. There are several World Wide Web interfaces that you can use to send messages through cyperpunk remailers.

Mixmaster remailers are the most secure. They use advanced encryption techniques and a special message format to make it all but impossible to trace a remailed message. To use a mixmaster remailer, you need to obtain a special program (premail) that formats your message. Unfortunately this program runs at present only under UNIX, but should be available soon for PCs and Macintoshes. Check for an update on the situation at the remailer resource home page (the address is at the end of this chapter).

Using the World Wide Web to send anonymous mail

The easiest way to send anonymous mail is by using a World Wide Web interface (see chapter 7 to find out what the Web is and how to use it). Don't use this for extremely sensitive stuff, though, because it isn't quite as secure as running premail yourself (in particular, the connection between your Web browser and the gateway is not encrypted). Once you have connected to the Web address you can fill in your mail message and select the anonymous remailer you want to use. Practise using a remailer by sending a message to yourself. I used the Community ConneXion's Web-premail gateway at:

http://www.c2.org:80/remail/

This Web site uses premail, a UNIX-based program that manages all the details of using anonymous remailers. It automatically encrypts and signs outgoing email, and decodes incoming email with a single command. Once you have entered the delivery address and your message, you can select through which remailers you want your message sent or you can select "chain several remailer together", if you want your message to go through several remailers. This is how it looks:

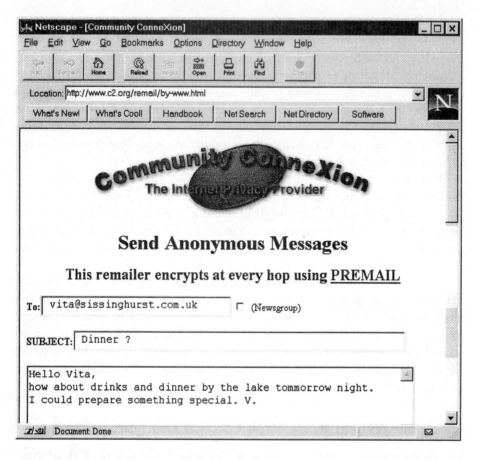

Here are the URLs of some anonymous remailers:

The Community ConneXion	http://www.c2.org:80/remail/
Michael Hobbs Web-premail	http://miso.wwa.com/~dochobbs/premail.html
Noah's place	http://noah.pair.com/anon.html

If you are using Windows 3.1 or Windows 95 and have a copy of PGP, you might want to get Joel McNamara's Private Idaho software (it's free). This is an interface to PGP encryption, Usenet News gateways and anonymous remailers. You can get the latest version at:

http://www.eskimo.com/~joelm/#Tools

Encryption and digital signatures come to the rescue!

If you weren't worried about the privacy of your Internet communications before, you probably are by now. Fortunately, there are ways to ensure privacy and security on the Internet: encryption and digital signatures. The encryption algorithm is a mathematical process that uses an encryption key (a word, number or phrase) to encode and subsequently decode a message. Digital signatures make sure that the message enclosed by a digital signature is truly from the sender and cannot be tampered with.

Many methods for encryption have evolved over the centuries. Today encrypting a message typically renders the original message incomprehensible by using a mathematical algorithm. Encryption can be compared to inserting a key into a lock (the algorithm) to make the text inaccessible. The "strength" of the lock (the algorithm), together with the length of the key, determines how hard it is to break the system.

For many centuries the most commonly used method for encryption was so-called private or secret key cryptography. In this method the secret key is known to both sender and recipient and hence must be kept private. This method is somewhat awkward as I personally have to give the secret key to you, so that when I send you an encrypted message you can decode it. Additionally one key is needed for each pair of people communicating. If more than two people want to communicate using private key cryptography, the distribution of the different keys soon becomes a problem. The more people are involved, the more keys are needed. For instance if there are 20 friends who regularly communicate with each other privately they would need to think of 165 different keys.

Public key cryptography

In the 1970s a mathematical breakthrough occurred which resulted in public key cryptography. It works like this. A mathematical process generates two related keys: one to encrypt a message (the public key) and one to decrypt the message (the private or secret key). The public key locks up the message, but cannot be used to unlock it again. The secret key is used to unlock the message. Hence only the secret key needs to be kept secret. The public key can be known by everyone, even strangers. So if I want to send you a secret message, I can use your public key to lock up the message and only you can unlock it using your secret key. Obviously it is important that I keep my private key very secret and store it securely. The public key, however, can be placed on a public key server. This is a database that holds people's public keys and anyone can use it to obtain someone's public key. Adding your public key to the end of your email messages is another way of distributing it.

Figure 10 Sending a secret message using public key cryptography

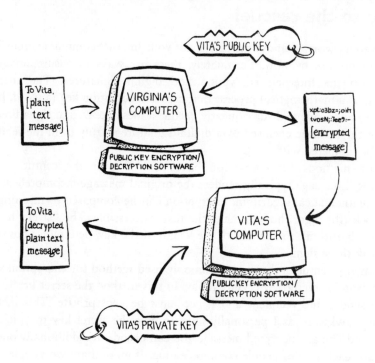

Introducing PGP

The most easily available and free encryption program using public key cryptography is PGP (pretty good privacy). Versions are available for PCs, Macintoshes, UNIX, VAX/VMS and other computers. Using PGP you can encrypt your email and files, compress your files before encryption and generate a digital signature.

There is a fair bit of controversy surrounding PGP (for a good coverage of this topic see Garfinkel 1995). Most governments treat encryption programs as ammunition and prohibit export. Through the centuries many battles and wars have been lost because the enemy managed to decrypt military communications. Many governments believe that their citizens should not have access to a secure method of encryption. They believe encryption should be illegal or at least that the government should have a way of breaking the key if necessary. Governments claim that this is necessary for the protection of its citizens from law-breakers, drug dealers and terrorists. However, governments have an inherent tendency to wish to control their citizens. Some governments believe their people must be actively surveyed and controlled in order for society not to fall apart. Privacy, or my right not to have certain information disclosed about me, is seen in this context as a threat to social order.

How to verify public keys

How can you verify that the public key printed at the bottom of my message is really my public key and not the key of an impostor? PGP uses the concept of "web of trust" to overcome this problem; other public key systems advocate the use of an authentication authority instead. In a "web of trust", people sign each other's key certificates and build a library of validated public keys. This signature is a promise that the person believes the key to be authentic and from the person it claims to come from. The other option is to entrust a single, centralized registry of public keys, controlled by an authentication authority, with this function. Some people go even further and propose that this authentication authority could dispense both the public and the private key. Personally, I find an authentication authority somewhat unappealing. It can be more easily subverted and if it dispenses both keys, can its trustworthiness be fully guaranteed?

Obtaining PGP and PGP front-ends

PGP can be obtained by using FTP from many sites around the world. Be aware, however, that it is illegal to export PGP from the USA, except to Canada, unless

you have a licence. If you want to use PGP commercially, check to see if you need a licence to use the IDEA algorithm embedded in PGP (USA, Canada and some European countries). Try to get the latest version of PGP (Version 3.0). PGP comes in compressed form (see chapter 8 for information on how to decompress files). Follow the instructions in the ReadMe file on how to install PGP on your system.

It is very important to read the manual that comes as part of PGP. Alternatively buy a book (e.g. Garfinkel, 1995) explaining it. PGP is not a complicated program, but you need to be clear in your mind how it operates, so you can be sure that your encryption works.

Here are some URLs for sites where you can obtain PGP:

WWW site
http://www.ifi.uio.no/pgp
http://world.std.com/~franl/pgp/pgp.html

Ftp sites in Australia
ftp://ftp.cc.adfa.oz.au/pub/security/pgp26i
http://hyperarchive.lcs.mit.edu/HyperArchive/Archive/cmp/mac-pgp-kit-171-as.hqx

Ftp sites in Europe
ftp://ftp.ox.ac.uk
ftp://ftp.informatik.uni-hamburg.de

Ftp sites in the USA
ftp://ftp.csua.berkeley.edu
ftp://net-dist.mit.edu

Email site
address: pgp@hypnotech.com
subject: HELP

Using PGP by itself can be clumsy and time-consuming, but there are numerous PGP front-ends that make it easier to use. A front-end is a program that manages the interaction between you and another program. Graphical front-ends are used to make the interaction between you and a text-based program such as PGP easier and more convenient. There are numerous PGP front-ends available for different operating systems.

The URLs for DOS (menu-driven) interfaces are:

PGPShell	ftp://ftp.ifi.uio.no/pub/pgp/pc/msdos/pgpshe33.zip
PGP Menu	ftp://ftp.ifi.uio.no/pub/pgp/pc/msdos/pgpmnu30.zip
PGP Shell	ftp://ftp.ifi.uio.no/pub/pgp/pc/msdos/pgs099h.zip
PGPfront	ftp://ftp.ifi.uio.no/pub/pgp/pc/msdos/pgpfront.zip
PGP for Idiots 3.0	ftp://ftp.ifi.uio.no/pub/pgp/pc/msdos/pgp4id30.zip

Here is a selection of PGP interfaces for Windows:

PGPClip http://ourworld.compuserve.com/homepages/michael_p_meyer/
sign and encrypt using the clipboard

PGP Win Shell http://www.aegisrc.com/utils2.htm
Windows front-end for PGP.EXE

PGP WinFront 3.1 http://www.netaccess.on.ca/ugali/crypt/winfront.html
Windows front-end for PGP.EXE

PGP for Windows 1.0g ftp://ftp.ifi.uio.no/pub/pgp/pc/windows/pgpwind.zip
Windows shell for PGP

PGP Windows 1.1 ftp://ftp.ifi.uio.no/pub/pgp/pc/windows/pgpwin11.zip
shell that includes key management and clipboard integration

Private Idaho 2.6b http://www.eskimo.com/~joelm/#Tools
PGP/anonymous remailer utility for Windows e-mail

Open Encryptor Interface for PGP 1.1 http://web.aimnet.com/~jnavas/winpmail.htm
for Pegasus Mail for Windows

WinPGP 4.0 http://www.vmedia.com/alternate/vvc/onlcomp/pgp/software/index.html
Windows front-end for PGP

MacPGP does not really need a front-end, but a Macintosh-friendly user interface
is available:

MacPGP Control	http://www.deepeddy.com/pgp

For a complete and current list of PGP front-ends, visit the International PGP
home page at http://www.ifi.uio.no/pgp

Using PGP with a graphical interface (WinPGP)

WinPGP is a Windows front-end for PGP which allows you, with the click of a
button, to encrypt and decrypt messages and manage your keys. WinPGP is
shareware and not expensive. It certainly makes using PGP a lot easier and faster.
After you have obtained a copy through FTP, you can keep it for 30 days to
evaluate. I have found WinPGP fairly easy to use.

To get the program started, double click on the **WinPGP** icon. A row of large buttons will appear that permit you to perform encryption and decryption and key management.

If you click on the **Preference** button the program will take you to a screen that allows you specify how you want encryption/decryption to be handled. Read the PGP help file to find out more about each parameter. You can also configure your **Launch** buttons from here.

The **Launch** buttons on the main menu bar enable you to start up specified programs, and set and reset file names.

As we go through the process of key management, encryption and decryption, I will explain how to use WinPGP for each purpose. Here is a preview of WinPGP's screen for key management.

WinPGP(tm) 4.0 - Key Management Routines		☒
-kg Create Keys	**-ke** Edit User ID or Pass Phrase	
-ka Add Key(Public or Private) to Key	**-kr** Remove a Key or User ID	
-kx Extract a Key from your keyring	**-ks** Sign and Certify Another's Public Key	
-kv View Keyring Contents	**-krs** Remove Selected Signatures	
-kcv View Key Fingerprint	**-kd** Revoke Your Own Key	
-kc Check Certifying Signatures	✗ Cancel ? Help	

Using PGP with MacPGP

MacPGP is an implementation of PGP for Macs. While not quite as graphical as WinPGP, it gives you access to PGP via easy-to-use menus. It is available from all major PGP sites and it is free.

To start the program, open your MacPGP folder and double click on the **MacPGP** icon (a man that looks vaguely like a comic-book version of a secret agent). MacPGP will start up and display the PGP Message window. You can check the version number of MacPGP and the current Greenwich Mean Time. This window is used to give you information and warning messages in response to your commands. You will never need to type anything in this window.

Notice how the menus along the top have changed. MacPGP is entirely driven by these menus. Click anywhere in the Message window to start. The first time you start MacPGP, it will also complain that it can't find your secret keyring. Don't worry: just click on the **OK** button.

Key management: creating a pair of keys for PGP

Now that you have installed PGP, it's time to create your very own pair of public and private keys.

Using PGP under DOS

1. If you are using Windows, select the **MS-DOS** icon in the Main Window and double click on it. If you don't have Windows, go to the directory of your choice by typing `cd c:\directoryname`. You will now be in the c:\ directory.
2. To create a pair of keys type:

    `pgp -kg`

3. PGP starts up and you are asked to pick the size of your key. Choose military grade for the highest level of security. Remember, the longer your key, the higher the level of security.

Using WinPGP

1. Start WinPGP by double clicking on the **WinPGP** icon.
2. Press the button with the **key** on it. The key management window appears.
3. Press **-kg** button, next to the bar that says **Create** keys. WinPGP calls up PGP. Now you need to pick your key size.
4. Whether you use PGP for DOS or PGP with a front-end, you need to select the size of your key. Choose military grade for the highest level of security. Remember, the longer your key, the higher the level of security.
5. PGP will ask your for a user ID. The preferred form is your name and then your email address enclosed in angled brackets:

    `userID <emailaddress>`

    For example:

    `Virginia Woolf <v.woolf@lighthouse.com.uk>`

Using MacPGP

1. Choose **Generate key...** from the **File** menu.
2. A dialog box asks you to select your key size by clicking on one of the three buttons or to pick your own key size by typing a number between 384 and 1024. Choose **military grade**. Key size is a trade-off between security and convenience. The larger the key, the longer it takes to encrypt a given message. If you have a Macintosh Plus or SE, choose a small key, especially if you intend to use PGP a lot.
3. Enter your User ID into the text field at the bottom of the window. The preferred form is your name and then your email address enclosed in angled brackets:

    `userID <emailaddress>`

    For example:

    `Virginia Woolf <v.woolf@lighthouse.com.uk>`

4. Finally, press the **OK** button.

Picking your pass phrase (Mac or PC)

Now, it is time to pick your pass phrase to protect your secret key. A pass phrase provides another layer of security for messages encrypted with PGP. It protects your secret key from being used by anyone but you. This is how it works: the pass phrase is used to decrypt your secret key and then your secret key is used to decrypt the message.

You will be asked to enter the pass phrase twice. Your typing will be invisible. Make sure to choose a password that is hard to break.

- Don't make it easy or obvious e.g. I work in Melbourne.
- Don't use names of family, friends or pets e.g. Zero is my cat.
- Don't use a well-known quote e.g. Women need men like a fish needs a bicycle.
- Make it easy to remember, but hard to guess.
- Remember if you forget your password you will not be able to decrypt your messages.
- Finally, do not write down your pass phrase.

After you have chosen a pass phrase, PGP is ready to generate your keys. PGP uses random numbers to generate the actual public and private key. A good way of generating truly random keys is by asking a person to perform a standard task e.g. typing random letters.

PGP will now ask you to type any key sequence you feel like typing until you hear a beep. Then after a couple of minutes PGP will have generated your private and secret key. The keys are placed in the public (pubring.pgp) and the secret (secring.pgp) keyring files.

Key management: viewing your keys

After you have gone through the key generation process you will find that PGP has generated two files:

secring.pgp (your secret keyring)

pubring.pgp (your public keyring)

Your keys are contained within these two files.

Using DOS PGP

You can view the content of your keyrings by typing:

```
pgp -kv userID keyring
```

If you do not specify userID or keyring PGP will display the last key generated. For example, if Virginia wanted to view her key she would type:

```
pgp -kv Virginia pubring
```

Using MacPGP

1. Choose **View keyring..** from the **Keys** menu.
2. A dialog window will ask you which keyring you want to view. Scroll along the window until you find your public (**pubring.pgp**) or secret (**secring.pgp**) keyring and click on it.
3. The keyring preview dialog window pops up. If you want to view all the keys, click the **OK** button. Otherwise type in your userID into the text box provided and click the **OK** button. The selected key will then be displayed in the PGP **Message** window.
4. If you want to see the signature of the displayed key, then check the **Show signatures also** box.

Using WinPGP

1. Press the **key management** button on the main screen.
2. Press the **-kv** button (View Keyring Contents).
3. WinPGP will prompt you for the **userID** and **keyring**. If you leave these fields empty, it will get the last key used.

This is what Virginia sees after issuing the **kv** command in DOS, MacPGP or WinPGP:

```
Pretty Good Privacy (tm) - Public Encryption for the masses.
(c) 1990-1995 Phil Zimmerman, Phil's Pretty Good Software.
7 May 95 International Version - not for use in the USA. Does not use
RSAREF. Current time: 1996/01/24 12:45 GMT


Key ring: c:\pgp\pubring.pgp
Type    bits/key/keyId  Date                 UserID
pub    1024/IEA1181E   1996/091/24     Virginia Woolf
                                <v.woolf@lighthouse.com.uk>
```

Key management: Giving your public key to someone

For others to be able to send you secret messages, they need to be in possession of your public key. You can either give them your public key personally on a floppy, place it for all to see at the end of your email, or put it on a public key server. Whichever method you choose, you need to extract your public key from your keyring.

Using DOS PGP

To extract your public key from your public keyring, type:

```
pgp -kxa userID filename
```

Virginia would type: `pgp -kxa Virginia Woolf virg`

This will place Virginia's public key into a file called virg.asc. The -a option specifies that the file will be in plain text, rather than unreadable binary format.

Using MacPGP

1. To extract a key select the **Extract Keys..** option from the **Keys** menu.
2. A dialog window will ask you which file to extract the key from. Click on the appropriate file and then on the **Open** button.
3. Single click on the keys you want to extract. Notice the checkmark appearing next to the selected key. If you change your mind about extracting a particular key, you can click on it again and deselect it.
4. When you are ready to extract the keys, click on the **OK** button.
5. MacPGP will now ask you for a filename to place the extracted keys in.

Using WinPGP

1. Press the **key management** button on the main screen.
2. Press the **-kx** button (extract a key from your keyring).
3. You will see a window that contains a **ListNames** button, and space to type the name of the file you want your public key placed in. The **ListNames** button brings up a list of names associated with the keys held in the public or secret keyring. If you want the output file to be in readable format, make sure to set **ASCII Armor On** in the **Preferences** window. When you click the **OK** button, WinPGP sends the following command to PGP:

```
pgp -kx userID filename
```

The effect of extracting a key

The key extraction command non-destructively copies the key specified by the user ID from your public or secret key ring to the specified key. This is what Virginia's public key looks like:

```
-----BEGIN PGP PUBLIC KEY BLOCK-----
Version: 2.6.2i

mQBNAzEGh8AAAAECAPbbE93loIbR+EDGsqSQ+tcrjcKehXDpJnUxfI3l89NRjw
O8Fp0wU7vuGd3yHYxXcajzMFXr+tR1T8p5EBAowxUABRG0I1ZpcmcgV29vbGY
gPHYud29vbGZAbGlnaHRob3VzZS5jb20+
=1WD9
-----END PGP PUBLIC KEY BLOCK-----
```

There are many more key management commands besides the ones discussed here. The PGP help file is excellent and will give you all the relevant information. Using a graphical front-end to PGP makes it easy to explore all the different options.

The key management commands for PGP DOS are as follows. In this list, the words in square brackets are optional. The default is the last UserID used and the associated public key.

pgp -kg	generates a pair of keys
pgp -ke [userID] [keyring]	edits the specified keyring
pgp -ka [userID] [keyring]	adds a key to keyring
pgp -kr [userID] [keyring]	removes a key
pgp -kv [userID] [keyring]	views a key (short form)
pgp -kvv [userID] [keyring]	views a key (long form)
pgp -kc [userID] [keyring]	checks what's in the keyring
pgp -kcv [userID] [keyring]	views and checks the keyring
pgp -krs [userID [keyring]	removes your key signature from userID's public key
pgp -kx [userID] [keyfile] [keyring]	copies userID's keyring into a specified file (prompting for necessary input)
pgp -kxa userID [keyring]	extracts a key in ASCII format
pgp -kd userID [keyring]	revokes or disables key

Decrypting Email

Now that you have created your keys and sent out your public key to all your friends, it's time to decrypt your first message. First you need to save the encrypted message to a file.

Using DOS PGP

1. Once the message is saved to a file you can decrypt it. Type:

   pgp filename

   PGP automatically looks up your secret key and decrypts the message for you. During this process PGP will ask you for your pass phrase. If you have entered your pass phrase correctly, PGP will put the decrypted message into another file, and tell you the new filename.

2. If you want to read the message without saving it to a file then type:

   pgp -m filename

   The file will be displayed on the screen, but not saved to disk.

Using MacPGP

1. First, save your message to a file. Select **Open/Decrypt ...** from the **File** menu.
2. The decryption dialog window will appear. Select the first option (**Depending on type of file decrypt, verify ....**) and let PGP worry about what to do.
3. Enter the name of the file in the **Name of output file** textbox.
4. Finally click on the **Do it** button.

Using WinPGP

1. Once the message to decrypt is saved in a file, press the **Decrypt** button on the main screen of WinPGP.
2. Enter the name of the file to decrypt or press the **browse** button to have a look at your directories. Press **OK**, when you have selected a file or filled in the file-name yourself.
3. WinPGP now hands over proceedings to PGP itself. PGP will ask you for your pass phrase and then decrypt the file.

Encrypting email

If you have obtained somebody's public key, you can send them an encrypted message. Here is how it's done.

Using DOS PGP

1. First create your email using a word-processor package and save the file as plain text or ASCII format. For instance if you use Microsoft Word, choose the **Save as** option and specify **Text only with line breaks** as your file type. If you are worried about people reading messages you have written on your computer, make sure to delete this file permanently, once you have encrypted the message. Once the message is created, encrypting it is easy.
2. Encrypt your message by typing:

```
pgp -eat filename NameOfPublicKeyFile
```

   If you want to get rid of the unencoded message at the same time, type:

```
pgp -eatw filename NameOfPublicKeyFile
```

   For instance, Virginia has written a message to Vita, which she saved in a file called letter1. Vita's public key is in a file called vita.pgp. Virginia now types:

```
pgp -eat letter1 vita
```

   Note Virginia does not need to type vita.pgp, because PGP knows to look for a file with that extension.

4. Now that the message is encrypted you need to open up your email package and send it to its recipient. There are as many different ways of getting this message into an email as there are email packages. Because your encrypted message is a file, you need to find out how to upload this text file into your email.

Using MacPGP

1. First create your message using a word-processor package and save the file as plain text or ASCII format. For instance if you use Microsoft Word, choose the **Save as** option and specify **Text only with line breaks** as your file type.

2. To encrypt the file choose **Encrypt/Sign ...** from the **File** menu. A file selection dialog box appears. Select the file you want to encrypt by clicking on it.

3. Now click on the **Open** button. Alternatively you can encrypt text from the clipboard by clicking on the **Clipboard** button.

4. The key selection dialog box will pop up and ask you to select the public key of the recipient of your file. Single click on the desired public keys (there can be several) then click on the **OK** button.

5. The encryption dialog box will pop up. Select **Encrypt**.

6. Unless you are sure the recipient also uses a Macintosh, select the **Treat source file as text** option. You may also want to select the **Wipe out source file** option by clicking on it. This option makes sure that the original unencrypted file will be overwritten and deleted for all time.

7. Finally press the **Do it** button.

8. Now you can import the encrypted file into your email program. The encrypted file has exactly the same name as the unencrypted file, except the last four characters are **.pgp**.

Using WinPGP

1. Using WinPGP you can use your word-processor to create a message, or you can choose one of the file creation options the program provides. Pressing **Notepad** in the main options window opens the Notepad program; pressing **MS-Write** opens the MS-Write program. Probably the best option for creating email is to press the **Clipboard** button. You can either compose a message if you are going to create an ASCII armored message, or you can cut and paste an ASCII armored message from another application like Eudora and decrypt it. ASCII armor is a system used by PGP to turn binary encoded information into a printable file. WinPGP always saves the text in the window as the filename **winpgpg1.txt**.

2. If you want to encrypt the message, but not sign it, click on the -ea option. This creates a message that is ASCII armored encrypted, but unsigned. You

will need to select a recipient's name by clicking the **ListNames** button and selecting a name from the list of public keys on your keyring. Click the **OK** button after you have made your choice. If you want the message to be encrypted and signed, click on the -esa option. Select a name from the public keyring by clicking on the **ListNames** button, then click **OK**.

3. Now click the **Encrypt** button. PGP will exit and upon return, you will have a new edit window. This time however, you will have the ASCII armored digital signature message, or an unsigned ASCII armored message, or an ASCII armored signed message. Now you can copy and paste the message into your mail program. If you wish to save the output for later use, select **Save as** from the **File** menu and save the message by a name other than winpgpg1.asc. If you do not choose this option, WinPGP automatically removes the file.

If you want to add options such as pass phrase, verbose, wipe, and eyes only (these are explained fully in the help file) to your encryption you need to set them in the **Preferences** window before you start the encryption process.

What does the -eat stand for? The -e option tells PGP that you want to encrypt something. The -a option tells PGP to encrypt in ASCII, the format email messages are sent in. And -t option specifies that you are encrypting a text file. The -w option tells PGP to wipe the file from memory after encryption.

What does an encrypted message look like?

Here is what a small encrypted message looks like. The message I encrypted was: "Hello how are you. Would you like to have lunch?"

```
-----BEGIN PGP MESSAGE-----
Version: 2.6.2i

hEwDT8p5EBAowxUBAgC0NWU21EneZKNizw3LqHs9qDtoyI8Fq8WmoC7UWlHDBQw0
u8OlVwL4XmxO4wtRfIzlhZwgv4LiAe8cestPJJVmpgAAAEbfN0EyNEBd8Y7Qej+f
941SdaKDADwy1xlg2lgF0Y44zuG8KH3p49csfVJOl2XNopKAbiosdPurP2bLURn6
I7uvNm6ab7D2=yuK3
-----END PGP MESSAGE-----
```

If you try to encrypt the same message twice, you will notice that the encrypted messages look different. This is because PGP uses random session keys for extra protection.

Digital Signatures

You will not always want to send encrypted messages. Often you will want to send messages or files that people can read straight away. Using a digital signature, you can make sure that people who read your message know whether it was really you who sent the message and whether or not it has been tampered with.

Figure 10.1   Sending a signed message using a digital signature

VIRGINIA USES HER PRIVATE KEY TO
CREATE A DIGITAL SIGNATURE

Virginia's Private Key

To Vita,
message
[signed by
Virginia]

VIRGINIA'S
COMPUTER

PUBLIC KEY ENCRYPTION/
DECRYPTION SOFTWARE

To Vita
message
[digital
signature]

To Vita
message
[signed by
Virginia]

VITA'S
COMPUTER

PUBLIC KEY ENCRYPTION/
DECRYPTION SOFTWARE

Virginia's Private Key

VITA USES VIRGINIA'S PUBLIC KEY
TO VERIFY THE DIGITAL SIGNATURE

Digital signatures work in the reverse order from encryption/decryption. You use PGP and your secret key to sign the message. Anybody can then use PGP and your public key to verify that the message is really from you and that it has not been tampered with.

Signing a message using DOS PGP

1. Create a message with your favorite word-processor and save it as a text file. Then type:

        pgp -sta filename

    The **-s** option tells PGP to sign the message, the **-t** option tells PGP to expect text, and the **-a** option tells PGP to write the message in text format.

2. PGP will ask you for your pass phrase, so it can access your secret key. The digitally signed message will be in a file called filename.asc.

3. Now you can add the signed message to your mail message.

Using MacPGP

1. Create the message you want to sign and save it in a file. Make sure to save the file in text format with line breaks.

2. Select **Sign only...** from the **File** menu.

3. A file selection dialog box appears. Select the file you want to encrypt by clicking on it. Now click on the **Open** button.

4. The **encryption options** window will appear with **Sign only** option already selected. Make sure that you select the **Append clear** signature option; otherwise, the message will look like alphabet soup to the recipient.

5. Click on the **Do it** button.

6. PGP will now ask you for your pass phrase. Type it into the text box and press the **OK** button.

Using WinPGP

1. Press **Clipboard** in the main window. Create your file and save it by choosing **SaveExit** from the **File** menu.

2. A window will appear that is divided into two areas. The left side is devoted to Encryption, the right side to Decryption. Press the **-sta** button to add an encrypted digital signature to your message. Press **Getnames** to select the secret key to use, then **Encrypt** to call up PGP. PGP will ask you for your **pass phrase** and, if it's correct, wrap a digital signature around the message. Your text will remain in plain text form.

Here is what a digitally signed message looks like:

```
-----BEGIN PGP SIGNED MESSAGE-----

Hi Vita,
It's been a while since we have seen each other. Would you be available
for a "private" al fresco lunch by the lake tomorrow? Please let me
know asap, so I can arrange something sumptuous ..... Love Virginia

-----BEGIN PGP SIGNATURE-----
Version: 2.6.2i

iQCVAwUBMH1bM1wTuVEeoRjhAQFgIAP9FWSoWohoozROQFK3o2W1OeMcuiS8vLcyC/fuVyh
IEPcVcCui6ScPKkVIKgNY3ma+xnG1KG3iS88dL8dmzYTkXArM101iC1InuayQrGOUv0Yces
bNHNBcXJx4/3yT2OU1pjPHL+pIpFtKrUCk8dNv96UvIoAj7oenludEC28xdAw==TDW1
-----END PGP SIGNATURE-----
```

Verifying a digitally signed message

Using PGP with DOS

Verifying a message that is digitally signed is straightforward.

1. Save the message to a file.
2. Make sure the public key of the person who signed the message is in your public key file. Then type:

```
pgp filename.asc
```

Using MacPGP

Verifying a message that is digitally signed is straightforward.

1. Save the message to a file.
2. Follow the instructions for decrypting a file above.

Using WinPGP

1. Press **Clipboard** in the main window. Create your file by copying and pasting the message you want to verify into the window. Save the file by choosing **SaveExit** from the **File** menu.
2. A window will appear that is divided into two areas. The left side is devoted to Encryption, the right side to Decryption. Make sure you have the public key of the person who signed the message in your public key file. Check the -p option, then press the **Decrypt** button.

PGP checks the digital signature of the file and informs you whether or not the digital signature matched the information in the public key file.

Commands for digital signatures

Here are the commands you will need. The command -u myID specifies the secret key to use (if you have several).

pgp -s message [-u myID]	signs the message
pgp -sb message [-u myID]	creates a signature that is separate from the message
pgp -se message [-u myID]	signs the message with my secret key and encrypts it with my public key
pgp -sea message userID	signs and encrypts the message using ASCII
pgp - seat message userID [-u myID]	uses ASCII and text to sign and encrypt the message
pgp -seaw message userID	signs and encrypts the message with ASCII then wipes the original message from memory.

Keeping your files safe and private

System administrators make regular back-ups of all files, which is handy if you have deleted something by mistake, but not so handy if you want something to disappear forever. In any case, many operating systems allow you to undelete deleted files. You have to use special commands to delete a file permanently, even on a system that is not connected to a network. If you type del or rm, or drop the file that you want to delete into the rubbish bin icon, the name of your file is removed from the file administration list, but the actual data still remains. There are various programs to recover deleted files such as the undelete command in UNIX or you can click on the recycle bin (Win 95) or the trash can (Mac) and retrieve the deleted files. If you want to delete a file permanently, you need to use one of the file wipe utilities (see Table 10.1). These utilities overwrite the data in your file several times and often also permanently delete the file name and related information from the administration table of your hard disk.

Table 10.1 Utilities for wiping files

Name of utility	What it does	Where to get it from
Real Delete(DOS)	intercepts DOS delete calls, overwrites files completely	ftp://ftp.demon.co.uk/pub/ibmpc/security/realdeal.zip http://www.ensta.fr/internet/dos-windows/Real_Delete.html
Nuke 1.1	overwrites as often as you want, DOS only	ftp://info.nic.surfnet.nl/mirror-archive/software/simtel-msdos/dirutil/nuke111.zip
Wipe Util	DOS and Windows file wiper	http://www.sky.net/~voyageur/
Burn 2.2 (Mac)	Overwrites, removes file administration info	ftp://ftp.nic.surfnet.nl/mirror-archive/software/info-mac/disk/burn-22.hqx
Flamefile1.38 (Mac)	Similar to Burn	http://www.umich.edu/~archive/mac/util/security/ http://ftp.cdrom.com/pub/mac/umich/util/security/

Protecting your files with PGP

If you store any sensitive information on your computer it is a good idea to encrypt the files containing this information. PGP uses conventional encryption for this. Only one key is necessary.

Using DOS PGP

1. To encrypt a file type:

```
pgp -w filename
```

2. PGP will ask you for a pass phrase, and then encrypt the file. Choose a pass phrase that is different from the pass phrase you use for your secret key.
3. Once the file is encrypted you need to get rid of the old file. If you use DOS or Windows you could use the **del** command, but the file can be brought back with the **undel** command. Other operating systems have similar shortcomings. Hence it is always best to use the -w option when you encrypt a file. PGP will delete the file permanently and securely after it has created the encrypted version.

4. To decrypt the file type:

```
pgp filename
```

Again PGP will ask you for your pass phrase and then if you have typed the correct pass phrase, decrypt the file for you.

Using MacPGP

Follow the instructions given for encrypting an email (above), and use your own public key to encrypt the file.

Using WinPGP

1. You can encrypt a whole directory using WinPGP. Press the **Dir.Encrypt** button on the main window.
2. The next window asks you to specify the directory path, then the same pass phrase twice. Press **OK** and the directory will be encrypted.

More Information on Anonymity and Security

Here are some URLs you might find useful:

Remailers Resource Pages:
http://www.cs.berkely.edu/~raph/remailer-list.html
http://www.stack.urc.tue.nl/~galactus/remailers/
http://www.well.com/user/abacard/remail.html

List of the type-1 remailers:
http://kiwi.cs.berkeley.edu/pgpkeys

Web page for Mixmaster remailers:
http://kiwi.cs.berkeley.edu/mixmaster-list.html

Anonymity on the Internet FAQ:
ftp://rtfm.mit.edu/pub/usenet/news.answers/net-anonymity

Privacy and anonymity FAQ:
ftp://rtfm.mit.edu/pub/usenet/news.answers/net-privacy/part1-3

A helpful book is *PGP: Pretty Good Privacy*, by Simon Garfinkel. O'Reilly and Associates, CA. (1995).

Women working in women's refuges, the environmental movement, feminist or lesbian activism, or other areas which may be viewed as subversive by mainstream society, should be especially aware of issues of privacy and security when using computers and Internet facilities. It is up to you whether you take the time to install programs such as PGP, but it could be a wise move if you are dealing with matters of a private and sensitive nature. Encryption provides you and your clients with the necessary protection.

Chapter 11

Resources

The World Wide Web

Many women with access to the Internet find email communication sufficient for their needs and regard other Internet services like the World Wide Web as time wasters. Friends of mine have attended short Internet training courses and been given such a limited view of the resources they have come away thinking the information on the Internet is simply trivial. This view couldn't be further from the truth. The Web is now regarded by many women in all walks of life as one of the most useful resources for acquiring and circulating up-to-date information. Lawyers, who have been reluctant to use the Internet for security reasons, are now coming to realise that the best source for legal information is the World Wide Web. Educators find the Web has much to offer in the way of inspiration for themselves and their students. Feminists are integrating the Web into their activities by operating their own Web pages or utilising the resources of others.

A nursing friend who visited us while attending a conference on Dementia in Melbourne was curious to know what all this Internet "hype" was about. I asked her if there was a subject that interested her. "How about Alzheimers disease" she said, no doubt suspecting we'd be wasting our time. A quick search using the Lycos search engine (http://www.lycos.com) revealed numerous resources on the topic and we soon tracked down recent scientific papers. Our friend found a research paper of particular relevance to her work which had not yet been published in a medical publication, and I could tell she was just a little impressed. The next day at the conference this very paper was referred to and our friend was able to say that she had already read it on the Internet. She was surprised, and secretly pleased, that she was the only person who had utilized the Web to keep up to date with recent research in the field. An instant convert, our friend prevailed upon her nursing colleagues to plug in their modems and make use of the new technology for the benefit of their patients, to further increase their knowledge and to communicate with each other.

The World Wide Web is now the most useful launching place for tapping into Internet resources. To get you started, I've put together a list which covers interests as varied as women's engineering organizations, breast cancer, Women's Studies resources and lesbian activism. Not all of the Web sites chosen are women specific, for example alternative medical resources, environmental groups and educational sites. The list is by no means complete but will give you a taste of the infinite resources available to you. By using search engines it is possible to find information on every topic imaginable. There are numerous sites aimed specifically at women which, quite frankly, are as lightweight as the women's magazines commonly found in supermarkets, providing little more than fashion tips and gossip. I have tended not to include such sites, however occasionally they represented the only women-specific sites in a particular geographical location, and therefore provide useful links of specific interest to the region. Some Web sites were in the early stages of their construction when I visited them, so their content and usefulness may have changed. The views put forward may not coincide with my own, nor yours. Web sites, unlike books do not remain static.

The information you will find on the Internet should be treated with the same discretion as that written in books and magazines located in your local libraries, newsagents and bookstores. If you're after medical information, for example, you should check that what you find is from a legitimate source. However, it's up to you to decide what you regard as a legitimate source – the testimony of a woman who is herself suffering from breast cancer may be more valuable to you than a scientific paper taken from an esteemed medical journal. The beauty of the Internet is that you'll find both. Just as you might browse through books, rejecting certain writers and searching until you've found something which is helpful, you should treat the Internet in the same way. If you have a particular interest, focus on it. The Internet is not in itself a time waster, used sensibly it should actually save you immense amounts of time.

One of the problems with providing such a list of resources is that Web addresses do change. While you can be assured that at the time of writing the addresses listed are correct and I've visited each one of them, I can give no guarantee that they will remain so. When addresses are changed you are usually automatically notified when you go to the original site. Sometimes though the site just seems to disappear into the ether without trace. All is not lost. If you have an idea what the site was called and/or the subject matter you can use a search engine to relocate it.

When you go surfing on the Net you must be prepared to spend time investigating. Some Web pages are not very well organized and on the surface don't appear to contain much useful content. Be inquisitive, just click onto those highlighted bits of text and see where they lead you. You may be pleasantly surprised. Be patient, remember the information is travelling all around the globe to get to you – why not do some knitting while you wait.

Activism and Politics

ACLA Pornography and Anti-Pornography Ordinance Information Center
Part of Nikki Craft's Always Causing Legal Unrest organization, which works against pornography. Features articles on sexual harassment, Prostitution and Post Traumatic Stress Disorder, The Harm of Pornography, Exposing Paedophilia within American Nudists associations, identifying hate crimes against women and more.

http://www.igc.apc.org/nemesis/ACLU/Porn

See Nikki's own home page for more articles on Andrea Dworkin, Feminism and the Women's Movement and more:

http://www.igc.apc.org/nemesis/ACLU/Nikki

Amnesty International On-line
Their manifestoes, campaigns and publications can be found at this excellent site. Amnesty International is spotlighting women as the "invisible victims of the 90s".

http://www.io.org/amnesty

Anarcha Feminism
Bibliographies of historical anarchist feminists, including some of the papers and writings of Volarine de Cleyre, Emma Goldman and Lucy Parsons. Links to feminist organizations and texts.

http://www.wam.umd.edu/~ctmunson/afem_kiosk.html

Andrea Dworkin Web Site

An excellent resource for Andrea Dworkin admirers and researchers. Online are excerpts from her novels and short stories and texts of her most powerful speeches, articles and interviews (including the text of the anti-pornography civil rights ordinance she co-authored). You must obtain permission in writing before reproducing any of the texts. A very well explained and organized site.

http://www.igc.apc.org/womensnet/dworkin

A Tribute to Tibetan Women's Association

Contains the full National Report on Tibetan Women from August 1995, submitted to the Beijing Conference, which reported on the abuses of women in Tibet and the continued violations of human rights by the Chinese authorities. Comprehensive and horrifying reading.

Canadian based with extensive links to Tibetan Buddhist sites.

http://www.grannyg.bc.ca/tibet/tibet.html

Catt's Claws

US based feminist newsletter and mailing list covering abortion issues, euthanasia and censorship.

http://worcester.lm.com/women/is/cattsclaws.html

Femina Borealis

A feminist activist activity, education and research project on women and development in Northern Europe (Finland, Norway, Sweden, Russia, and the Sami region). Research into women's needs and creating networks. Administered by the Northern Feminist University, Bodo, Norway.

http://www.luth.se/research/irp/borealis.html

Feminist Activists on the Net

An as yet small but potentially useful index of women's activist activities on the Internet.

http://www.igc.apc.org/women/activist/

Feminists for Animal Rights

A publication which appears twice yearly in print and on-line, dedicated to abolishing all forms of abuse against women and animals. FAR seeks to raise the consciousness of the feminist community, the animal rights community and the general public regarding the connections between the objectification, exploitation and abuse of both women and animals in patriarchal society. As ecofeminists they promote vegetarianism and are vegan in orientation.

http://envirolink.org/arrs/far/newsletter/index.html

Guerrilla Girls

"The Guerrilla Girls are a group of women artists and arts professionals who make posters about discrimination", dubbing themselves "the conscience of the art world". They use humour to provoke discussion, and wear gorilla masks to "focus on the issues rather than our personalities". Visit their site and see some of their work.

http://www.voyagerco.com/gg/gg.html

Lesbian Avengers (London Chapter)

The Lesbian Avengers are a non-violent direct action group committed to raising lesbian visibility and fighting for lesbian survival and lesbian rights. The group organizes actions, demonstrations, protests and parties. A good place to find out more about lesbian activism in the UK. Also has links to other lesbian sites, virtual salons, publications and literature, lesbian-owned businesses, products and services, humour, film reviews, travel and much more. A great site!

http://www.cs.ucl.ac.uk/students/zcacsst/LA.html

Network for East-West Women

A communications network for women's rights activists. Active since 1990, based on women's responses both in the east and the west, to the radically altered conditions of the post-cold-war world. Aims to generate activities, alliances and to strengthen women's social and political objectives. You can also subscribe to their mailing lists.

http://www.igc.apc.org/neww

PAWS Online

The Progressive Animal Welfare Society based in Seattle, US. You'll find advice on adopting, choosing, animal shelters, local volunteers and other animal rights links on the Web.

http://www.paws.org/

Peacenet – On-line for Peace and Justice

Computer network dedicated to peace, social and economic justice, human rights and the struggle against racism.

http://www.econet.apc.org/econet/

The Tibetan Nuns' Project

The project was started in 1987 in order to channel assistance to the many hundreds of Tibetan nuns who are victimized for their beliefs and practices, particularly in China. It organises fundraising and provides an efficient system of communication and administration for nuns' assistance and development. Visit their Web site to find out how you can assist .

http://www.manymedia.com/tibet/TibetContactsNuns.html

The Vegan Society

Promotes living entirely free of animal products for the benefit of people, animals and the environment.

http://catless.ncl.ac.uk/veg/Orgs/VeganSocUK/

Web Active – What's new in activism online

A weekly WWW publication enabling people to keep up-to-date on the latest activism and progressive politics on the Internet. Helps you to navigate the Web and plug you into activist opportunities. Reviews activist sites worldwide.

http://www.webactive.com/

Women for Women in Bosnia

Representatives who operate within existing relief teams in Bosnia and Croatia work to identify those who are in most need of assistance. Find out how you can volunteer your help.

http://embassy.org/wwbosnia/wwbosnia.html

Women Leaders Online

US based, dedicated to stopping the Radical Right agenda.

http://worcester.lm.com/women/women.html

Astrology

Wemoon (We of the Moon)

Wemoon is an astrological moon calendar and ecofeminist appointment book, which gives a daily guide to natural rhythms and a lunar perspective through the thirteen moons of the year. It includes art and writing and is described as a "goddess inspired network for womyn sharing around the planet". Order your calendars via the net.

http://www.teleport.com/~wemoon/

Art, Film and Music

Coalition of Women Improvisors and Composers

Encouraging women to play music, communicate with others and become involved with the Coalition.

http://www-personal.umich.edu/~katt/cwic.html

Cybergrrl Goes Surfing – Musical Sites

A regularly updated site where you'll find, lyrics, stories, tour schedules (and more) relating to some of your favourite female artists.

http://www.cybergrrl.com/cool/music.html

K12 Resources for Music Educators

Created by Cindy Shirk, this is a great boon for music teachers and musicians. There's information on every instrument featured in bands and orchestras, lesson plans, mailing lists to join, newsgroups to visit. Of special interest to women are the sites on women composers of the past, including composers of early music. Another great feature is the option of downloading sheet music.

http://www.isd77.k12.mn.us/resources/staffpages/shirk/cindys.page.k12.link.html

Tandanya

A beautiful, award-winning site with artwork and culture from the National Aboriginal Culture Institute

http://www.webmedia.com.au/tandanya

The Varo Registry

An online registry of artwork by international, contemporary women artists. Each artist is provided with her own web site and can be contacted by email. Artists are categorized under medium, genre, nationality and movement.

http://199.4.94.46/registry/list.html

The World's Women On-line

A registry of women artists on-line, covering so far the US, Canada and the UK. This site was developed as a project incorporated into the Beijing Conference on Women and aims to utilize the Internet as a global exhibition format.

http://wwol.inre.asu.edu/intro.html

WIFT (Women in Film and Television, NZ)

Based in Christchurch, Aotearoa/New Zealand, this is a professional organization which aims to ensure that the interests of women are recognised and supported throughout the film and TV industry in NZ. WIFT is also established in the UK, US, Canada and Australia.

http://www2.chch.planet.org.nz/~montage/wift.html

WIFT (Australia)

An Australian professional organization encouraging, mentoring and networking traditions among women in the field. Missions and goals and information on WIFT's advocacy and information services.

http://www.deakin.edu.au/arts/VPMA/wift.html

Books and Writing

A Celebration of Women Writers

Includes biographies and entire books online! Including works by Andrea Dworkin, Willa Cather, Petra Kelly, Gertrude Stein (Tender Buttons), Virginia Woolf, Beatrix Potter and many classics.

> http://www.cs.cmu.edu/Web/People/mmbt/women/celebration.html

A Guide to Feminist Science Fiction Resources, in print and on the Net

Bibliographies, indexes, electronic sources, print sources.

> http://nickel.ucs.indiana.edu/~hwhipple/rg.html

Chicken Soup for the Women's Soul

A compilation of stories and anecdotes about women, contributed by readers. You can send in your submissions and read some of the stories on-line.

> http://www.cgim.com/chiksoup/

Distinguished Women, Past and Present

Very comprehensive site for biographies of women.

> http://www.netsrq.com:80/~dbois/

Feminist Bookstores Worldwide

A useful directory for travelling women although many well known stores are not listed. The site has links to Gay and Lesbian bookstores.

> http://www.igc.apc.org/women/bookstores/

Feminist Science Fiction – Fantasy and Utopia

Lists authors and books by categories. Provides interesting biographies.

> http://www.uic.edu/~lauramd/sf/femsf.html

Newspapers Online

This is a listing of newspapers throughout the world which publish online. Not all of the articles a particular newspaper publishes are available online, only those considered particularly newsworthy.

> http://www.intercom.com.au/intercom/newsprs/index.htm

Notable Women

A database of over 500 women (past and present) including their name, birth place and date and a few lines on why they are famous.

> gopher://gopher.emc.maricopa.edu:70/11/library/notablewomen

Sisterhood Bookshop

Books by and for women, located in Los Angeles, founded in 1972 by three women active in the Women's Liberation Movement. The entire inventory is on-line. You can order by mail, books, music and videos.

http://www.labridge.com/sisterhood/

Spinifex Press Home Page

Melbourne's own women's press extraordinaire. Includes catalogue of books with short reviews, lists distributors and agents worldwide, and has a handy order form so you can order your books on-line – or just make comments.

http://www.publishaust.net.au/~spinifex

The Kassandra Project

A series of Web pages which aim to be an introduction to German women writers, artists and thinkers from around 1750 to 1820. Calls to attention those who have been too long ignored and overshadowed by the big [male] names in German history.

http://www.reed.edu/~ccampbel/tkp/project.html

The Library of Congress

The largest library in the English-speaking world which has facilities for searching its data base and retrieving information on books on-line. Also allows access to government information and historical archives. Useful for researchers.

http://lcweb.loc.gov/homepage/lchp.html

The National Library of Australia

Not as comprehensive as the Library of Congress but also useful for researchers.

http://www.nla.gov.au/

The On-line Book Page

Index of books available online.

http://www.cs.cmu.edu/Web/books.html

Business and Legal Resources

Green Market – A World Guide for Sensible Living

What makes a company green? Who are the leaders and the losers? Whose watching corporate behaviour and what do they see? You'll find the answers to these questions and more at this site which also lists companies which are ecosensitive, innovative and offer inexpensive products.

http://www.greenmarket.com/

Her House Home Page

A project of Habitat for Humanity which seeks to eliminate poverty housing and homelessness in the world. Her House is a coalition of individuals and corporations helping women achieve home ownership. It builds housing and renovates, with women's needs in mind, and gives work to women builders. Based in Washington DC but visitors to this site will be encouraged by their achievements.

http://www.herhouse.org/house.htm

Internet Resources for Women's Legal and Public Policy Information

Advice and resources compiled by the University of Michigan, USA.

http://asa.ugl.lib.umich.edu/chdocs/womenpolicy/feminist.html

Maori Women's Business Resource and Employment Centre

Maori women in Christchurch, Aotearoa/New Zealand, have access to a resource centre which offers business advice and employment information targetted at their needs. Offers also mentoring, support, referrals and training.

http://www.chch.planet.org.nz/green/community/anya1.html

National Women's Justice Coalition

Providing links to women's legal information, law reform reference alerts, conferences, and up-to-date progress on law reform bills in Australia. It aims to influence policy and provide an effective voice on women's justice issues.

http://www.ozemail.com.au/~nwjc/

Women's Business Resource

Providing information, advice, wisdom, marketing and recommended reading. A well-organised potentially useful site.

http://www.athenet.net/~ccain

Education

Macarthur Girls' Technology High School

An excellent site for information and further resources for girls and children. Has an impressive selection of links throughout Australia and the world of the top educational sites, from aboriginal studies to music and theatre. You can also visit the school.

http://www.ozemail.com.au/~mghslib/mghsinfo.html

TAP – The Ada Project

TAP-Junior is a fantastic resource for young girls, teachers and parents. Has advice on computer software and games designed with girls in mind, links to other web sites for girls, visit the walk-through computer at the Boston Computer Museum and the

Family Math Home Page which encourages girls and minorities to pursue a maths career.

TAP is also a great site for grown-ups with excellent information for women about the world of science and technology. The site provides news on conferences, projects and programs relating to women and computer science and information on institutions where women have programs designed especially for their needs.

http://www.cs.yale.edu/HTML/YALE/CS/HyPlans/tap/tap.html

Teacher Talk

An online magazine written by a teacher for teachers, produced by the Center for Adolescent Studies at Indiana University, USA, however plenty of material would be useful in any country. Classroom methods and problems, discrimination, homophobia, gender bias, sex in advertising, cultural differences are all issues discussed. Many contributions are academic studies of students' interaction in high schools.

http://education.indiana.edu/cas/tt/tthmpg.html

Environmental concerns

Conservation International

Dedicated to conserving the earth's biodiversity

http://www.conservation.org/

EcoNet

Serves organizations and individuals working for environment preservation and sustainability. Builds coalitions and partnerships to develop the use of electronic communications mediums.

http://www.econet.apc.org/econet/

Friends of the Earth

Green campaigning worldwide.

http://www.foe.co.uk/

Greenpeace International

Protecting diversity, preventing pollution, ending nuclear threats, promoting peace – read about the good work done by Greenpeace worldwide.

http://www.greenpeace.org

Women and Environments

An online magazine based in Toronto, Canada that examines women's relationship to the environment from a feminist perspective. Also academic research and theory,

professional practice, community experience, ecology, feminist activism, housing, transportation, childcare, health and "breaking down barriers for women farmers".
http://www.web.apc.org/~weed

Health

Alternative Medicine

Your first stop for all alternative therapies with sites on the Internet, from music therapy to the Alexander Technique. Excellent!
http://www.pitt.edu/~cbw/altm.html

Alzheimer Web

For researchers and workers in the field, with information on counselling and advisory services, education and training materials, books, discussions, mailing lists.
http://werple.mira.net.au/~dhs/ad.html

Avicom's MED Guide – the Internet guide to modern medicine

A good source for medical information, covering "alternative" medicine such as Osteopathy.
http://montana.avicom.net/medguide/

Disabilities

The Disability Information and Resource Centre in South Australia has an excellent site with over 600 disability organizations listed throughout the country.
http://www.dircsa.org.au

Endometriosis

A useful page providing links to research, medical reports, social support and personal home pages of sufferers.
http://www.ivf.com/endohtml.html
Another good site with articles on diet and communicating effectively with your doctor etc.
http://www.webcom.com/~geomanda/endo/

Immune Web Site

Articles and information for people with all kinds of immune system problems like chronic fatigue syndrome, candida, lupus, etc. Runs a mailing list as well.
http://weber.ucsd.edu/~cnorman/info.html

Medical Resources on the Net

Describes and evaluates resources available on the Internet. A first stop for medical professionals.

http://www.vifp.monash.edu.au/medical/eval.html

Menopause

For useful places to get information on menopause and related symptoms, like osteoporosis and urinary incontinence.

http://www.ivf.com//meno.html

Repetitive Strain Injury

You can find very comprehensive information about injuries related to typing and technology on the net. Ergonomics, keyboards, research papers, safe furniture, occupational safety and medical information are just some of the areas covered. There are too many resources to list them all. Here are two good sites which also provide links to other related resources on the Internet.

http://www.alumni.caltech.edu/~dank/typing-archive.html
http://www.cs.princeton.edu/~dwallach/tifaq/

The Candida Yeast Answer Wellness Program

You can have a free copy of the program sent to you by email (only if you live in the US and Canada at present), though some of the information is available online.

http://bellnet.com/cwc.htm

WHAM – Women's Health Action and Mobilization

"Demanding, securing and defending absolute reproductive freedom and quality health care for all women." Has a mailing list you can subscribe to.

http://www.echonyc.com/~wham/

Women's Resources on the Internet

An excellent listing of places to go to find women's health resources, from breast cancer to female urinary incontinence. It also points you to a host of other women related resources on the Internet.

http://sunsite.unc.edu/cheryb/women

Breast Cancer Web Sites

Avon's Breast Cancer Awareness Crusade

Set up in the USA with funding from Avon's world-wide fund for women's health. Provides plenty of online information, support groups and chat lines.

http://www.pmedia.com/Avon/avon.html

National Breast Cancer Centre

Under development but still worthwhile, especially for Australian readers. Resources, statistics, research. There are plans to include a section on women's writing and their experiences with breast cancer.

http://www.nbcc.org.au

The Breast Cancer Information Clearinghouse

Produced by the New York State Educational and Research Network, the Clearinghouse provides links to a large range of online sites where detailed information for breast cancer patients and their families can be located.

http://nysernet.org/bcic/

Lesbian, Bisexual and Gay Resources

D.Y.K.E

UK-based Web site for lesbians. An imaginative design makes up for rather confusing organization. There's some interesting stuff, if you can find it. It's unpredictable but fun. *The Cruise Me Now Cafe* is an, as yet, limited guide to lesbian venues around the globe, but it's sure to get better as readers contribute their own favourite spots. Useful if you're planning to visit London, Glasgow and Amsterdam. Links to the latest lesbian icons (like k.d. lang of course!).

http://dspace.dial.pipex.com/town/square/ad454

Euro-Sappho

A list for sapphic discussion of interest to European lesbians. Open to all lesbians but maintains an International/European flavour. Includes an extensive list of lesbian centred European films – mouth watering!

http://www.helsinki.fi/~kris_ntk/esappho.html

Foundation Group 7152 – Dutch Organization for Lesbian and Bisexual Women

A support network for women during the awakening of their feelings and acceptance of those feelings towards women. The group meets regularly and also publishes a magazine. Its a well organized site which is available in both English and Dutch.

http://www.cybercomm.nl/~lonys/engels.html

Gay and Lesbian Star Trek

Trekkie fans have been sorely disappointed that the death of the show's creator, Gene Rodenberry, has seen their favourite sci-fi losing its original focus – a future where war, poverty, racism and sexism are all things of the past. This site aims to set things right!

http://ccnet4.ccnet.com/gaytrek/

Labrys – Lesbians in Yugoslavia

A very interesting site highlighting the status of lesbians living in the former Yugoslavia. Describes a revealing survey of ordinary citizens in Belgrade regarding their attitudes towards lesbianism. Information also on healthcare, the law, harassment, employment and child custody.

http://www.igc.apc.org/neww/ceewomen/labrys.html

Lesbian.org

This is a non-profit organization run by Amy Goodloe, dedicated to promoting lesbian visibility on the Internet and empowering women online. Lesbian.org offers free webspace, 550k in size, to lesbian orientated, non-profit organizations as well as online web design and layout assistance (for a fee). Amy also hosts moderated lists including internet-women-help, mac-women (help for women using Macintosh computers), women-online-news, lesac-net, ba-cyberdykes, and lesbian studies. You'll find many links to other useful sites. (For more information see chapter 2).

http://www.lesbian.org/

Lesbian Buddhists online

An informal mailing list for lesbians involved in all areas of Buddhism. Currently the group is small, friendly and mostly has US participants.

http://www.cpsc.suu.edu/users/henderso/lzg.html

LL – Organization of Lesbians in Slovenia

LL is part of the Students Cultural Centre of the University in Ljubljiana. Operating closely with Lilit (a feminist group), they look at lesbian culture, movements and lifestyles.

http://www.kud-fp.si/~zoran/QRD/ll.html

Queer Resources – Aotearoa (New Zealand)

New Zealanders and visitors can keep up-to-date with issues relevant to the lesbian and gay community at this helpful resource. It profiles gay friendly accommodation, mailing lists to join in New Zealand, and includes a country wide calendar of events and festivals. Has links to the gay media including magazines and periodicals. Information regarding human rights legislation in NZ is a useful addition. Plenty here of interest to lesbians.

http://nz.com/NZ/Queer

Roz Mov – Gay and Lesbian Life and Organizations in Greece.

Bars and meeting places in the cities as well as the countryside listed. Also has gay and lesbian literature in Greek.

http://www.geocities.com/WestHollywood/2225/index.html

For the lesbian movement in Greece

http://www.geocities.com/WestHollywood/2225/lmgr.html

Russian Gay Life Pages

Not a lot of lesbian content but this site is very new so hopefully the lesbian presence grow. It provides a mailing address for the Moscow Lesbian Pink Candle group. Otherwise this site is put together by men, for men, and mostly it's in Russian.

http://www.vmt.com/gayrussia/

Magazines Online for Women

Allegra – German Women's Magazine

A useful site if you're planning to visit Germany, and you are able to read German. Has a calendar of cultural events and a section on the media, as well as links to other German based online magazines.

http://www.allegra.de/allegra.html

Geekgirl

Australian webzine by Rosie Cross. Interviews, art, fancy graphics online. See chapter 2.

http://www.geekgirl.com.au/

Herspace

A non-threatening US based zine dedicated to "building a women's gateway" to the Internet. Deals with issues in the home, work, health, social issues, culture, fashion. Interesting graphics. Has useful links.

http://www.herspace.com/herspace

Sojourner

Sojourner is a women's newspaper published by MIT since 1975. It provides feature articles, interviews, reviews, fiction and poetry by and for women. Some articles are online.

http://www.tiac.net/users/sojourn/

The Women's Room

Another non-threatening, US based, lightweight online magazine. "Our aim is to make this site a refreshing stop on the Net – an oasis of female oriented conversation, advice, ideas and information." Visually nice.

http://www.inlink.com/~womensrm/

Webgrrls

Sacramento-based Web site with many links including women and sport.

http://www.yolo.com/~asw/webgrrls/

Webgrrls Aotearoa

Part of the worldwide Webgrrls project, this one is based in Wellington, New Zealand. It aims to provide a non-competitive environment for women working with the Internet.

http://www.netlink.co.nz/~brendal/index.html

Web Weavers on the Web

An amusing and imaginative site put together by Sage Lunsford, with stories, advice and more links.

http://www2.best.com/~tyrtle/women.html

Parenting

CTI – Centre for Nursing and Midwifery – England

For nurses and midwives involved in teaching. Gives advice, workshops, demonstrations and an exchange of information.

http://www.shef.ac.uk/uni/projects/ctinm

Hunter Valley Midwives Association

History of how the organization started in Australia. General support for midwives.

http://www.efn.org/~djz/birth/HVMA/HVMA.html

Midwives in Private Practice in Victoria, Australia

Information from their brochure. Lists midwives in private practice in Victoria and has useful links to other midwifery organisations around Australia and the US.

http://www.efn.org/~djz/birth/add695/mipp.html

Mom's Space

Accumulated Web Wisdom on Motherhood, offering support and sharing for parents. Also has useful links to other sites, books and videos.

http://www.cs.cmu.edu/afs/cs.cmu.edu/user/jeanc/mom/space.html

Online Birth Centre

Pregnancy/Midwifery/Breastfeeding/Birth Resource Centre. News items about home births, massage, articles and links to resources worldwide.

http://www.efn.org/~djz/birth/birthindex.html

Recipes

Epicurious

For those who like to cook with style or can only afford to read about it. Recipes and tidbits compiled from the magazines Epicurious, Gourmet and Bon Appetit.

http://www.epicurious.com/epicurious/home.html

Mimi's Cyber Kitchen

Claims to be the best and largest food site on the Internet. Healthy eating, ethnic delights, allergy free food, Mimi's special recipes plus many more.

http://www.cyber-kitchen.com

Vegan Cooking – see Activist section for details.

Vegetarian Cooking

The Australian Vegetarian Society explains the benefits of a vegetarian diet and includes articles from its magazine New Vegetarian. Includes a shopping guide and links to other sites world-wide.

http://www.moreinfo.com.au/avs/

WWW Culinary Resources

Books, food, wine, beverages, schools, herbs, gardening, Japanese cooking classes, professional resources, regional fare, recipes and restaurants of the world – and that's not all!

http://www.webcom.com/~gumbo/food-www.html

Spirituality and Religion

Lesbian Buddhists online – see Lesbian section for address and description.

Starlady's Spirituality, Meditation and Prayer Centre

Information and links for women on Christianity, the Bahai Faith, Buddhist Studies, Witchcraft and Wicca.

http://www.efn.org/~djz/religion.html

The Feminist Theology Page

Here you'll find bibliographies of some well known feminist theologians including those from Christian, Islamic, Judaism, Pagan/Wican and women-centred traditions.

http://www2.gsu.edu/~reoldc/feminist.html

Sport and Recreation

Gardening
The Society for Growing Australian Plants publish articles from their magazine. Of interest to those keen on the native flora. Provides a listing of other Internet resources of interest to gardeners.
> http://www.ozemail.com.au/~sgap/index.html

The Case
If you like to solve mysteries visit The Case. Each Tuesday night, a new mystery to solve is posted on the Web and can be sent to your email address. The solution is available on Thursday evening.
> http://www.thecase.com/

US National Women's Martial Arts Federation
Information about the organization, relevant books, women's sports pages and other useful links.
> http://galaxy.tradewave.com/editors/weiss/WomenMA.html

Wombats on the Web
Home page for the Women's Mountain Bike and Tea Society with news relevant to female bikers. Browse Wombat online art gallery.
> http://www.wombats.org/

Women's Soccer Foundation
A non-profit organization in the USA dedicated to promoting women's soccer.
> http://www.cris.com/~Jg189/wsf/

Women's Sports Page by Amy Lewis
Extensive index of women's sports pages. From flying to soccer, from tennis to volleyball.
> http://fiat.gslis.utexas.edu/~lewisa/womsprt.html

Another good source for sporting events based in the US can be found at:
> http://www.yolo.com/~asw/skywomen/

Travelling on the Cheap

Internet Guide to Hostelling
A world-wide data base of hostels, travel information, backpackers hotels, with a useful bulletin board for travellers.
> http://www.hostels.com/hostels/

Lonely Planet Online

Pick any spot in the world and zoom around at your leisure. Readers of Lonely Planet's essential guides and handbooks, and newcomers, will enjoy this site.

http://www.lonelyplanet.com.au/

Shoestring Travel

Described as the e-zine of inexpensive travel. Hotels, restaurants, airfares, room exchange. The list of sites is enormous and no country or form of travel is left untouched.

http://www.stratpub.com/

The Akiko Tour of New Zealand/Aotearoa

I couldn't resist including this one. Tour New Zealand on the Internet, visit major holiday destinations, learn about the history and politics, enjoy the pretty pictures, then buy a ticket.

http://nz.com/NZ/NZTour/

Travelling Women

Unfortunately for some of us, all of these are based in the USA.

Adventure Travel for Women

Female guides, women only travel tours including Hawaii and sailing in Fiji and the Bahamas.

http://www.gorge.net/business/adventure/women/

Earth Wise Journeys

"Earth friendly travel for discovery of our global community." They emphasize the environment, wilderness settings, involvement with local culture world wide. Destinations include North America, Latin America, Asia, Africa, the Pacific, Europe.

http://www.teleport.com/~earthwyz/women.htm

Olivia Cruises for Women

Women only cruises to the Caribbean, Alaska, Mediterranean, Mexico, Tahiti and Colorado.

http://oliviatravel.com/

Wild Women Adventures

"Dedicated to the proposition that you can restore, energize and empower yourself while exploring the world." Includes Mexico, "Retreat for Mommies", Florence.

http://www.wildwomenadv.com

Women Power Enterprises

Supporting wildlife, conservation, ecotourism. Includes Kenyan safaris.
http://www.mm.com/womanpower/

Women's Studies

Diotima – Women and Gender in the Ancient World

Materials for study about patterns of gender around the ancient Mediterranean. Provides a forum for collaboration amongst teachers in the field.
http://www.uky.edu/ArtsSciences/Classics/gender.html

Fawcett Library – National Research Library for Women's Studies in London

Lists articles and books available in the library, very extensive and up-to-date.
http://www.lgu.ac.uk/phil/fawcett.htm

Feminism and Women's Studies

Excellent site for finding published works from feminist writers online.
http://english-www.hss.cmu.edu/feminism/

Feminist Studies Aotearoa

An electronic journal for feminists.
http://www.massey.ac.nz/~wwwms/FMST/Info.html

Resources for Women's Studies

This site has a very extensive selection of files online including a paper entitled *Women and Sexual Slavery in Japan* submitted by the Korean Council, and others covering: violence and harassment of women, discrimination, the "glass ceiling", politics and women's health. Instructions on how to submit papers are included.

Also online are feminist film reviews, a picture gallery of notable women, details on conferences around the world (and calls for papers) relevant to women, government documents as well as useful links for finding information about Women's Studies worldwide. An excellent site.
http://inform.umd.edu:86/Educational_Resources/AcademicResourcesByTopic/WomensStudies

University of Wisconsin Women's Studies Librarian's Office

A full directory of books and publications which can be ordered by mail through the library service. Bibliographies are available for free on request by email. Links to gopher sites where further publications are catalogued. Another excellent site.
http://www.library.wisc.edu/libraries/WomensStudies/

Usenet FAQ's – soc.feminism

Useful information of interest to feminist studies.

http://www.cis.ohio-state.edu/hypertext/faq/bngusenet/soc/feminism/top.html

Women's Studies – Aotearoa/New Zealand

For course outlines and details about the staff at Victoria University, Wellington, visit:

http://www.vuw.ac.nz/academic/prospectuses/womens-studies.html

The **Women's Studies Homepage** at Massey University provides information about courses, tutors etc. as well as employment opportunities within feminist studies, advertised throughout NZ.

http://cc-server9.massey.ac.nz/%7Ewwwms

Women's Studies/Women's Issues

Good links to relevant sites from Joan Korenman.

http://www-unix.umbc.edu/~korenman/wmst/links.html

Women in Science and Technology

Ada Project – A web resource for women in computer science.

For a fuller description see the Education section.

http://www.cs.yale.edu/HTML/YALE/CS/HyPlans/tap/tap.html

Social Science Information Gateway

A gateway to feminist resources in the social science field.

http://sosig.esrc.bris.ac.uk/Subjects/feminism.html

Society of Women Engineers

Based in New York. This site aims to stimulate women to achieve their full potential as engineers and leaders. Expands the image of the profession and demonstrates the value of diversity.

http://www.swe.org/

WITI – Women in Technology International

An online campus where women can expand their knowledge of technology. You'll find expert advice, the latest news and exciting developments in technology. WITI's mission is to "increase the number of women hired and promoted to management and executive level positions, help women become more technology literate and financially independent, and to encourage young women to choose careers in technology and science."

http://www.witi.com/

'Yellow Pages' for women in science groups

Mostly relevant to those at US university campuses. Local and national resources.
http://www.columbia.edu/~jrf3

Women's Organizations

American Association of University Women

Advice on education and equality, research, grants, legal advocacy.
http://www.aauw.org/

NOW (National Organization for Women)

US based "Feminization of Power". Concerns are equality, laws, abortion rights. Organizes marches.
http://www.now.org/

The Housing for Women Trust

Based in Christchurch, New Zealand, the Trust is supporting women in finding accommodation alternatives to enable them to change the circumstances which disempower them. The Trust believes that women in poor housing face physical violence, sexual exploitation and other abuse and is working to reduce these risks.
http://www.chch.planet.org.nz/green/community/women.html

The United Nations Division for the Advancement of Women

Responsible for servicing the Commission on the Status of Women (CSW), the main UN policy-making body for women and the Committee on the Elimination of Discrimination against Women (CEDAW).
http://www.undp.org/fwcw/daw.htm

Official documents relating to the Fourth World Conference on Women can be found at http://www.undp.org/fwcw/fwcw2.htm including the final version of the Beijing Declaration and Platform for Action, statements by governments, the United Nations, inter-government organizations and NGOs.

Photographs from the Conference can be downloaded from the file and reproduced.

United Nations Information Services

Index to UN document searching and related links. Information on conferences. Gopher services on UN affiliated organizations including the World Bank, the World Health Organization, the UN Security Council etc.
http://www.undcp.or.at/unlinks.html

WEDO – Women's Environment and Development Agency

Aims to foster leadership and advocacy skills to transform women's concerns about the environment, development, population and gender equity into actions, programs and policies.

gopher://gopher.igc.apc.org/11/orgs/wedo

Women in International Trade

US organization dedicated to enhancing the visibility's and opportunities for women in the field of international trade.

http://www.embassy.org/wiit/

Women's Online Networks

Canadian Women's Internet Association

Containing mostly useful links. Of interest were the Internet Help for Women links, quirky health and fitness links, women's spirituality and a collection of sites relating to global awareness. They have two Web addresses.

http://www.women.ca and http://www.helix.net/women/

Cybergrrl Webstation

"Your first step on the Web" – indeed this is probably the most extensive resource for women on the Internet. It amply covers activism, green politics, health, music and more. Especially useful is their Safety Net Domestic Violence Resource (see relevant section on women's abuse and domestic violence for more details).

http://www.cybergrrl.com/

Feannex

Canadian based, non-profit women's online resource network. A women's based society aiming to create an easily accessible information system. Providing information, a mentor program and a virtual market place.

http://raven.ritslab.ubc.ca/feannex.html

Femina – A World Wide Web Directory for Women

An off-shoot of the Cybergrrl Web Station, Femina provides a comprehensive searchable directory of links to women centred sites. Has a huge data base and a powerful, intuitive search engine.

http://www.femina.com/

Feminist.com Directory of Resources

Information from non-profit organizations (both in-house and online) and links to women's sites all over the Internet. Aims to make networking for women, on and off the Internet, easier. Includes the usual issues – activism, health, politics, children, reproductive rights. Look no further for the perfect quotation from a notable woman.

http://feminist.com

Feminist Web Page

Links for people interested in women's issues regarding social justice, human rights and the law.

http://www.geocities.com/capitolhill/2995

Links for the Discriminating Web Diva

More useful places to go on the Web for women involved in activism and to meet some interesting women who've played a part in shaping the Internet.

http://www.rpi.edu/~schmel/gender.html

Mailing lists for women

Describes 70 mailing lists connected to feminist or gender issues, with instructions for joining and submitting messages to lists.

http://women-www.uia.ac.be/women/roadmap/women/w000000a.html

Modem Grrls

Discover more women on the Web. Good music links and a special feature on girl heroes.

http://www.gnofn.org/~jbourg/grrls

Monash University Feminist Resources

Australian based, this is a good place to find feminist mailing lists and Usenet groups.

http://www.monash.edu.au/cc/staff/phi/dey/WWW/fem.html

Pleiades Networks – An Internet Resource for Women

A focal point for women's information and dialogue on the Web, aiming to encourage women's access. Discussion forums on politics, relationships, food, the arts, science and technology, money, health, books and movies.

http://www.pleiades-net.com/

Rain Network's Women's Internet Council

A clearing house for women working with the Internet.

http://www.rain.org/wic.html

Russian Feminist Resources

An excellent resource for women from post-communist states, for researchers and those of us who are just interested in this region. It provides "links and information relating to Russian women and the development of independent grassroots feminism in Russia in recent years." Large sections relating to the arts (from music to ballerinas), articles from the Russian press, health, politics (including a discussion of Western feminism and how it relates to post-communist regions), activism, sport, literature and academic writing. Plus links to individual women's home pages. This is a real find and should keep readers occupied for hours.

http://www.geocities.com/Athens/2533/russfem.html

For sites relating to women in Albania, Armenia, Croatia, Kosova, Latvia, Poland, Romania, Serbia, Slovenia and the Ukraine visit:

http://www.geocities.com/Athens/2533/russfem4.html

The Female Equation

A good site for links to women's resources online.

http://www.getnet.com/women.html

The Feminist Majority On-line – Women's Webworld

Up-to-date news comments from US newspapers. Information on where you can write to express your views on media coverage. Excerpts and broadcasts of conference papers etc. and a directory of jobs of interest to feminists.

http://www.feminist.org

WOM – Women's Online Media Project

Japanese, non-profit women's network. Access to women's studies, health, issues on the net and information about Japanese women's concerns. Mostly in English.

http://vcom.suehiro.nakano.tokyo.jp/WOM/

Women Online

Providing quality, affordable computer and Internet training for women. For more information see Chapter 2.

http://www.women-online.com

WomensNet – Online Newsletter

Computer services, Internet and Information Resources for Women. A non-profit network for women, activists and organizations using computer networks for information sharing and increasing women's rights. Provides email accounts, Internet access, Web publishing, consulting and training. They have unique information resources such as data bases and electronic conferencing not found on the Internet.

http://www.igc.apc.org/womensnet/

Women'space

"Aims to promote accessibility to the internet, its information, tools and resources; enhance the effectiveness of women's organising through national global connections; bring global online resources to local community actions; support and exchange of experiences and ideas amongst women's groups." See Chapter 2 for details.

http://www.softaid.net/cathy/vsister/w-space/womspce.html

Women'sWire

American oriented, with news items from US newspapers, profiles of prominent women, surveys which readers can participate in (including the proposed online rating for Web sites) and useful links.

http://www.women.com/welcome/

Women WebWorks

US based site which aims to build a web of sites to enhance women's growth and creativity. Good information on education.

http://www.konnect.com/

Womenznet

A network of newsgroups, conferences and weblinks from Spider Redgold of Pegasus Net, Australia. Has good links to Australian sites of interest to women.

http://www.womenz.net.au/

Women's Abuse and Domestic Violence

Assault Prevention Information Network

Provides links to self-defence and martial arts sites. Information on strategies, protection, and courses.

http://galaxy.einet.net/galaxy/Community/Safety/Assault-Prevention.html

Donna Riley's Domestic Violence Page.

Very extensive listing including information published by the American Psychological Society which, amongst other things, profiles the perpetrators of violence.

http://www.epp.cmu.edu/~riley/domestic.html

Family Violence Prevention Fund

Taking steps to help address abuse and aid battered women. Links to other domestic violence groups.

http://www.igc.apc.org/fund/

Safety Net Domestic Violence Resources

Part of the Cybergrrl project this is an extremely useful resource. You'll find statistics from the USA as well as the UK and Australia, projects and organizations and a special section reporting on the ACT's (Australia) Community Law Reform Committee on Domestic Violence.

http://www.cybergrrl.com/dv.html

Writers' Resources

Acronyms and Abbreviations
Have an acronym or abbreviation expanded and submit some yourself if they're not on file already.

> http://www.ucc.ie/info/net/acronyms/acro.html

Andy's Anagram Solver
Available in English, Dutch and French.

> http://www.ssynth.co.uk/~gay/anagram.html

Quotations – Find a quote for all occasions.

> http://www.xmission.com/~mgm/quotes

Reference Dictionaries
Online Dictionaries and Thesaurus. Includes Chinese, English, French, German, Greek, Italian, Japanese etc. Also history, philosophy and computer related dictionaries.

> http://www.arts.cuhk.hk/Ref.html#dt

There's a more extensive dictionary at:

> http://math-www.uni-paderborn.de/HTML/Dictionaries.html

Mailing Lists

Mailing lists are a wonderful invention for those of us who like to communicate with others about our interests, be they seriously philosophical or recreational amusements. That must be just about all of us! It's exciting to meet someone new and discover that they also share the same obsession. Conversely, it can be frustrating to feel that you're the only woman who cares about a certain subject. With the invention of electronic mailing lists there's a good chance you'll find at least one other person who enjoys or studies the same things you do. It may seem unnatural to be divulging your thoughts to women you've never met, who live in places you've never visited. When first subscribing to a mailing list you may chose to spend a while getting a feel of the threads of conversation and the general tone of the current discussions. This is known as "lurking" and is quite acceptable behaviour. If you don't like what you're reading you can simply unsubscribe.

When you send a posting to a mailing list remember that your message will go out to all list members. Members may include people located all over the globe and it could be easy to give offense even inadvertently. Women-only mailing lists will usually expect you to confine yourself to certain behaviours – that means no "flaming" or offensive language. Heated discussions are expected, but so is sensitivity to others.

Mailing lists which are of potential interest to women probably number in the thousands. The following selection is compiled from various sources and is only a small sample of the diverse subjects being discussed via the Internet. It wasn't possible for me to subscribe to and revue each of the lists I have included. The lesbian-oriented lists originate mainly from Amy Goodloe's excellent **Lesbian.org** Web site. For more detailed information about these mailing lists and to discover more for yourself, I suggest you visit **http://www.lesbian.org**. The lists relating to feminism were mostly compiled by Joan Korenman (**http://www-unix.umbc.edu/~korenman/wmst/**)and are part of the WMST-L mailing list file collection. If you know of any omissions, additions or changes, Joan asks that you notify her by email at: **korenman@umbc2.umbc.edu.**

Other feminist lists come from Dey Alexander's Philosophy in Cyberspace Internet resource which can be found on the Web at

        http://www.monash.edu.au/cc/staff/phi/dey/WWW/phil.html

The rest I've picked up myself via the World Wide Web, from Internet publications, or from friends.

I have included email addresses and instructions on how to subscribe to each mailing list. Most mailing lists operate using a list processing service, common ones are **Majordomo**, LISTSERV and **Listproc**. In Chapter 6 you'll find instructions on subscribing and unsubscribing to each of these list processing services, along with information on how mailing lists actually work.

Where I have used [ ] around the words **your name** you should leave the brackets out. Your name always refers to your first and last names. Where I have used < > around the words **your email address**, these brackets should stay. For example:

        subscribe fmst-talk [your name] <your email address>

would read:

        subscribe fmst-talk Netty Brown <n.brown@apana.daemon.org.au>

General List in alphabetical order

ABIGAILS-L

A feminist activist discussion list dedicated to gaining full and equal women's rights through immediate actions. Your subscription request will be forwarded to the listowners for approval.

    To subscribe email: LISTSERV@NETCOM.COM.

    Message reading: SUBSCRIBE ABIGAILS-L [your name]

Association of Women in Slavic Studies

Moderated list serving professional and academic needs. Concerned with the status, achievement and problems of women in the region.

To subscribe email: **listserv@msu.edu**

Message reading: **subscribe AWSS-L [your name]**

AUSTEN-L

A list for discussion of the work and time of 19th-century British novelist Jane Austen and her contemporaries.

Send subscription messages to: **LISTSERV@VM1.MCGILL.CA**

BEIJING-CONF

A moderated list supported by the United Nations Development Programme. It includes subscribers from 55 countries, including 28 developing countries. As a result, the list emphasizes discussion of the Beijing UN Women's Conference issues as they affect developing countries as well as industrialized ones. The list hopes to continue beyond the Conference, focusing on implementation of the Women's Conference and the Social Summit agreements.

To subscribe email: **MAJORDOMO@CONFER.EDC.ORG**

Message reading: **SUBSCRIBE BEIJING-CONF [your name] <your email address>**

BIG-MOMS

"Is primarily for large moms (be they tall or obese or both), and large women who want to be moms", as well as other people who are supportive of big moms. Topics include social issues, fertility issues, gestational diabetes, parenting issues, etc.

To subscribe email: **BIG_MOMS_LIST-REQUEST@BUTLER.HPL.HP.COM**

Message reading: **SUBSCRIBE <your email address>**

BKSYSNET (BlackSystersNetwork)

A list for all Black women. It addresses issues related to women of African descent anywhere in the world.

To subscribe email: **BKSYSNET-REQUEST@AVNET.CO.UK** .

Message reading: **SUBSCRIBE**

BOOKFIENDS

A list for feminist, lesbian, gay, and other alternative editors, publishers, booksellers, distributors, and the like.

To subscribe, write to Felice Newman at Cleis Press: **CLEIS@ENGLISH.HSS.CMU.EDU** giving her your name, the name of your company, and your email address.

BRONTE

Devoted to discussion of the three Brontë sisters' lives and works.

To subscribe email: MAJORDOMO@WORLD.STD.COM

Message reading: SUBSCRIBE BRONTE [YOUR NAME] <YOUR EMAIL ADDRESS>

CATTSCLAWS

US based feminist mailing list covering abortion issues, euthanasia, censorship. They also have a Web site.

To subscribe email: listserv@netcom.com

Message reading: subscribe catts-claws [your name]

CCOAR, sponsored by the Coalition of Campus Organizations Addressing Rape

A moderated discussion list for activists, educators, and researchers working against rape. Conference and action announcements, job listings, and discussion of rape education, activism, or research are all appropriate for the list. All subscribers must be approved by the listowners.

Send subscription requests to eribet@orion.oac.uci.edu or to u54232@uicvm.uic.edu.

In the subject heading, write "subscription".

In the message, include your **name**, **email address**, and the **password** you want to use (4–8 letters), and specify whether you want to receive the list in digest form.

CCWEST

Is a list (and a site of resources) for women and girls in science and technology in Canada.

To subscribe email: LISTPROCESSOR@CUNEWS.CARLETON.CA

Message reading: SUB CCWEST [your name]

CHILDFREE

Provides information, discussion, and a supportive environment for those who have actively chosen to be child-free as well as those in the process of so choosing or who have been forced, for various reasons, to remain child-free. The list encourages the child-free lifestyle; it is not for those trying to find ways out of it, nor for those wishing to criticize it.

To subscribe email: MAJORDOMO@PETROGLYPH.CL.MSU.EDU

Message reading: SUBSCRIBE CHILDFREE <your email address>

CITNET-W (The Healthy Cities Women's Network)

A list for people interested in women's health issues and healthy cities issues.

Send subscription messages to LISTSERV@INDYCMS.IUPUI.EDU

COSWA-L

Is designed to promote the participation and recognition of women in archaeology and anthropology. It provides a forum for anyone interested in discussing gender issues relevant to these disciplines.

To subscribe email: LISTSERVER@RELAY.DOIT.WISC.EDU

Message reading: SUB COSWA-L [your name]

CRONE

Is intended primarily for women of maturity who wish to explore alternative approaches to the spirituality and health needs of the pre-and post-menopausal woman. The lists welcomes women and men of all ages but asks that postings deal with "the issues involved with the concept of the crone as expressed in the elder wisdom."

To subscribe email: LISTSERV@LISTSERV.AOL.COM

Message reading: SUBSCRIBE CRONE [your name]

CYBER-SISTERS

An unmoderated list for women artists, performers, and writers who wish to use the Internet and WWW to explore their art, express their creativity, and network with other women.

To subscribe email: MAJORDOMO@PMEDIA.COM

Message reading: SUBSCRIBE CYBER-SISTERS [your name] <your email address>

ECOFEM

Ecofem is an unmoderated list which is a forum in which a variety of viewpoints concerning women and the environment can be discussed. These include the wide-ranging views of feminism (liberal, radical, socialist, postmodern, and yours) and the multi-hued "environment".

To subscribe email: listserv@csf.colorado.edu

Message reading: subscribe ecofem [your name]

EDUCOM-W

This is an unmoderated list to facilitate discussion of issues in technology and education that are of interest to women.

To subscribe email: listserv@bitnic.educom.edu

Message reading: subscribe educom [your name]

EE-WOMEN

An unmoderated list for discussion of women's issues related to Central and Eastern Europe.

To subscribe email: LISTPROC@CEP.NONPROFIT.NET

Message reading: SUBSCRIBE EE-WOMEN [your name]

For more information about the list please contact: CEP@MINERVA.CIS.YALE.EDU

EFA-WOMEN

A moderated list open to women in Australia. A project of the Electronic Frontiers Australia women's subcommittee, the list has been established to provide a safe space where women's online concerns can be addressed and where women can share advice, support, and suggestions.

To subscribe email: EFA-WOMEN@EFA.ORG.AU

Message reading: SUBSCRIBE EFA-WOMEN

EKATERINA-L

Devoted to the scholarly discussion on the life, times and impact of Catherine the Great, Empress of Russia (1729-96), in English, Russian, German and French.

To subscribe email: listserv@uhccvm.its.hawaii.edu

Message reading: subscribe ekaterina-l [your name]

EMWEB

A list for discussion of the lexical play of words in Emily Dickinson's poems, though other topics concerning Dickinson are also welcome.

To subscribe email: MAJORDOMO@LAL.CS.BYU.EDU

Message reading: SUBSCRIBE EMWEB [Your Name] <your email address>

EWM – European Women in Mathematics

To subscribe email: LISTSERV@VM.CNUCE.CNR.IT

Message reading: SUBSCRIBE EWM [your name]

FAB – Feminist Approaches to Bio-Ethics

The list's purpose is to provide a forum for the exchange of information and discussion on research related issues. Calls for papers, references, job postings and the like are welcome. The list was initiated by a few members of the Network for Feminist Approaches to Bio-ethics. Anyone interested in joining the network should contact Anne Donchin at ista100@indycms.bitnet.

To subscribe email: fab-request@phil.ruu.nl with information about why you'd like to join.

FAH – Feminist Art History list

A list for researchers, curators, art historians, faculty, students, and all those interested in discussing research issues and sharing resources of women artists throughout history. Although this is an email list, you subscribe by submitting a request at the list's web site. Those without Web access should write to Robin Masi: MASI@SONOMA.EDU, who will add you to the list.

FAVNET – Feminists Against Violence Network

Run by a feminist attorney working in the field of violence against women. Subscribers include survivors, social workers, shelter workers, lawyers and students.

To subscribe email: **mdubin@ix.netcom.com** requesting to be added to the list.

F-EMAIL

A British list whose purpose is to "facilitate discussion and information exchange on gender differences in use of computer communication", noting that while internetworking is a predominantly male domain, "females may in fact be better suited to computer-mediated communication."

To subscribe email: **MAILBASE@MAILBASE.AC.UK**

Message reading: **JOIN F-EMAIL [your name]**

FEM-ALERT – Feminist Alert Network

An informational mailing list established by the Feminist Majority to inform people about key feminist issues and about major additions to the Feminist Majority's World Wide Web site.

To subscribe email: **MAJORDOMO@FEMINIST.ORG**

Message reading: **SUBSCRIBE FEM-ALERT [your name] <your email address>**

FEMALE-L – FEMinistische ALternativE

A German-language Women's Studies list based in Austria. Messages in German or English are invited about feminist research and teaching, information about conferences, new books, and other announcements, other online sources of Women's Studies materials, etc. It is hoped that people from many countries and continents will participate.

To subscribe email: **LISTSERV@ALIJKU04.EDVZ.UNI-LINZ.AC.AT**

Message reading: **SUBSCRIBE FEMALE-L [your name]**

FEMECON-L – Feminist Economists

To subscribe email: **LISTSERV@BUCKNELL.EDU**

Message reading: **SUBSCRIBE FEMECON-L [your name]**

FEMEDIT

A list for editors of feminist journals and periodicals.

To subscribe email: **LISTPROC@WHEATONMA.EDU**

Message reading: **SUBSCRIBE FEMEDIT [your name]**

FEMJUR – Feminist Legal Theories

The list provides a forum for discussing theories and issues regarding feminism and women and law. Sharing research questions, scholarship, calls for papers, job announcements, and support.

Moderated by Prof. Leslie Bender: lbender@suvm.syr.edu
To subscribe email: listserv@suvm.syr.edu
Message reading: **subscribe femjur [your name]**

FEMINIST –
The Feminist Task Force of the American Library Association

It deals with issues such as sexism in libraries and librarianship, pornography and censorship in libraries, and racism and ethnic diversity in librarianship.
To subscribe email: LISTSERV@MITVMA.MIT.EDU
Message reading: **subscribe feminist [your name]**

FEMINIST MOTHERS AT HOME

A list "for thinking women who choose to stay at home with their children and do something more than watch Regis and Kathie Lee." The list, which limits the number of subscribers, offers "a positive feminist voice to the issues that surround mothering." More information can be found at the list's Web site.
To subscribe, contact Ann Allen at: AMALLEN@MILLCOMM.COM

FEMISA

A list for discussion of feminism, gender, women and international relations.
To subscribe email: LISTSERV@CSF.COLORADO.EDU
Message reading: **SUBSCRIBE FEMISA [your name]**

FEMMENT-L

A list for discussion of feminist mentoring, especially in academic fields that are still male-dominated. Topics include defining feminist mentoring, mentoring strategies, types of mentoring and their effectiveness, and anything else related to examining the role of mentoring within a feminist context.
To subscribe email: FEMMENT-L-REQUEST@WIZARD.UCR.EDU
Message reading: **SUBSCRIBE FEMMENT-L <your email address>**

FEMPED-L

A feminist pedagogy list, has been designed for discussing issues of power and positionality in the classroom and how feminist pedagogy can be used to challenge patriarchal models and methods that silence and intimidate women in educational settings.
To subscribe email: LISTSERV@UGA.CC.UGA.EDU

FEMSW-L

An unmoderated Feminist Social Work list.
To subscribe email: LISTPROC@LIST.UVM.EDU
Message reading: **SUBSCRIBE FEMSW-L [your name]**

FGM-L

Is dedicated to discussion and research about Female Genital Mutilation in the United States and internationally.

To subscribe email: MAJORDOMO@HOLLYFELD.ORG

Message reading: SUBSCRIBE FGM-L <your email address>

FIST (Feminism in/and Science and Technology)

An unmoderated list for discussion of feminism and science and technology.

To subscribe email: FIST-REQUEST@NIESTU.COM

Message reading: SUBSCRIBE

FMST-L

A moderated list in Aotearoa/New Zealand "for those interested in feminist theory, feminist perspectives in philosophy, contemporary feminist debates, publications and research, book and film reviews, and debates on issues with a Pacific-Rim modality."

To subscribe send a two-line e-mail message to:

UOTAGO@STONEBOW.OTAGO.AC.NZ

The first line should read: SUBSCRIBE FMST

The second line should read: END

FMST-TALK

This is an unmoderated list for subscribers to FMST (Feminist Studies in Aotearoa Electronic Journal). The list offers the opportunity to give feedback on FMST journal articles, make comments on its topic areas, communicate with other subscribers, and make your views and research known.

To subscribe email: majordomo@massey.ac.nz

Message reading: subscribe fmst-talk [your name] <your email address>

FRENCH FEMINISM

This list, sponsored by the Spoon Collective, is for the discussion of French feminism.

To subscribe email: majordomo@jefferson.village.virginia.edu

Message reading: subscribe french-feminism [your name] <your email address>

GEN-MUS

A list for discussion of music in relation to women, gender, and sexuality.

To subscribe email: MAJORDOMO@VIRGINIA.EDU

Message reading: SUBSCRIBE GEN-MUS [your name] <your email address>

GEOGFEM

Devoted to "feminist/gender issues in Geography."

To subscribe email: LISTSERV@UKCC.UKY.EDU

Message reading: SUBSCRIBE GEOGFEM [your name]

GIRL

A private, unmoderated list for and about girls, grrrls, young women, lesbian and feminist youth, etc. (female and approximately 25 and younger). To subscribe, send a brief bio (100 words or more) including your age, interest in the list, your background, work, experiences, or commitments, and anything else you want list members to know (bios are posted when your subscription is accepted, you must request otherwise or this will be done automatically).

To subscribe email your bio to: GIRL@UCI.EDU

GRANITE

Aims to stimulate research in the field of gender and new information technologies and to provide a platform for discussions about theories and research from a feminist/women's studies perspective.

To subscribe email: LISTSERV@NIC.SURFNET.NL
Message reading: SUBSCRIBE GRANITE [your name]

HDSOC-L

A list for the exchange of information on the works of the poet HD (Hilda Doolittle). The list is affiliated with the Hilda Doolittle Society.

To subscribe email: LISTSERV@UCONNVM.UCONN.EDU
Message reading: SUBSCRIBE HDSOC-L [your name]

HELWA-L

A list for Malaysian women in the USA and Canada.

To subscribe email: LISTSERV@PSUVM.PSU.EDU
Message reading: SUBSCRIBE HELWA-L [your name]

HILLEL-WOMEN

A low-volume Jewish women's issues discussion list sponsored by Hillel (a campus-based Jewish students organization).

To subscribe email: LISTPROC@SHAMASH.NYSERNET.ORG
Message reading: SUBSCRIBE HILLEL-WOMEN [your name]

H-STATE

A list for scholars of the welfare state, social welfare history, and policy history, including issues such as mother's assistance and protective legislation for women and children.

To subscribe email: LISTSERV@MSU.EDU
Message reading: SUB H-STATE [your name, your school]

H-WOMEN
A forum for scholars and teachers of Women's History.
    To subscribe email: LISTSERV@MSU.EDU
    Message reading: SUBSCRIBE H-WOMEN [your name]

IAWM
A list for members of the International Alliance for Women in Music (formerly International League of Women Composers). Discussion focuses on women composers and women-in-music topics. There are regular postings of composer opportunities. Non-member participation on the list is permitted.
    To subscribe email: IAWM-REQUEST@ACUVAX.ACU.EDU
    Message reading: SUBSCRIBE

ICWP-L International Center for Women Playwrights
Giving women in theatre, especially playwrights, the opportunity to converse with one another concerning all aspects of their craft. While ICWP-L is for members and its supporters, those wishing to subscribe to this list for 3 months before deciding on membership may do so.
    To subscribe email: LISTSERV@UBVM.CC.BUFFALO.EDU
    Message reading: SUBSCRIBE ICWP-L [your name]

INTERNET-WOMEN-HELP
A women-only list designed to provide women with a forum for asking questions and receiving help on a wide variety of Internet-related functions and issues. It is for questions and answers ONLY.
    To subscribe email:
INTERNET-WOMEN-HELP-REQUEST@LISTS1.BEST.COM
    Message reading: SUBSINGLE or if you prefer the digest version: SUBSCRIBE

INTERNET-WOMEN-INFO
Designed to complement INTERNET-WOMEN-HELP by providing a space for women to share information of relevance to women and the Internet. This list is not a forum, it's for information posts only.
    To subscribe email:
INTERNET-WOMEN-INFO-REQUEST@LISTS1.BEST.COM
    Message reading: SUBSINGLE or if you prefer the digest version: SUBSCRIBE

INTVIO-L
Devoted to discussion of "all areas of family violence" including spousal abuse, child abuse, and "any other areas of intimate violence that subscribers may wish to explore."
    To subscribe email: LISTSERV@URIACC.URI.EDU
    Message reading: SUBSCRIBE INTVIO-L [your name]

IRWMST-L

Set up by the Irish Higher Education Equality Unit for people involved or interested in Women's Studies in Ireland. It is hoped that the list will facilitate discussions of teaching and research, exchanges of information and advice, and increased contact.
To subscribe email: LISTSERV@IRLEARN.UCD.IE
Message reading: SUB IRWMST-L [your name]

IWIDG

A list for discussion of Iranian women's issues.
To subscribe email: LISTPROC@U.WASHINGTON.EDU
Message reading: SUBSCRIBE IWIDG [your name]

MAC-WOMEN

Macintosh help forum for women only, designed "to provide women who are Mac experts a chance to share their knowledge, and to provide women who are Mac users a comfortable, low-volume forum for learning more about all things Macintosh."
To subscribe email: MAC-WOMEN-REQUEST@LISTS1.BEST.COM
Message reading: SUBSINGLE or if you prefer the digest version: SUBSCRIBE

Maiden L

"This list is designed for women who are new to the Internet, who need a helping hand."
To subscribe email: majordomo@women.ca
Message reading: subscribe maiden-l [your name] <your email address>

Materialist Feminism

Materialist feminism represents a powerful theoretical/activist perspective which brings together feminists from all disciplines, united in their desire to build a feminist project for the 21st century. It considers the ways class, divisions of labour, state power, as well as gendered, racial, national, and sexual subjectivities, bodies, and knowledges are all crucial to local and global social production.
To subscribe email: listproc@csf.colorado.edu
Message reading: subscribe matfem [your name]

MEDFEM-L

An unmoderated list for discussion of feminist approaches to medieval studies.
To subscribe email: LISTPROC@U.WASHINGTON.EDU
Message reading: SUBSCRIBE MEDFEM-L [your name]

MINERVA

For discussion of women and the military and women in war.
To subscribe email: LISTSERV@GWUVM.GWU.EDU
Message reading: SUBSCRIBE MINERVA [your name]

MUJER-L

A list for those who share an interest in Chicana and/or Latina issues.
    To subscribe email: LISTPROC@LMRINET.GSE.UCSB.EDU
    Message reading: SUBSCRIBE MUJER-L [your name]

MWCF – Metro Women Chemists Forum

A list (sponsored by the American Chemical Society) giving women (and men) in the chemical professions an opportunity to discuss and share information on job and personal issues such as dealing with advisors and co-workers, harassment on the job, unemployment, and managing career and family.
    To subscribe email: juzak@aecom.yu.edu
    Message reading: "subscribe MWCF" (include the quotation marks)

NAISTUTKIMUS – Finnish Women's Studies

The postings are in Finnish, although announcements can also be posted in other languages.
    To subscribe email: LISTPROC@UTA.FI
    Message reading: SUBSCRIBE NAISTUTKIMUS [your name]

Network of East-West Women

Based on the responses of women, from both the East and West, to the radically altered conditions of the post cold-war world. To generate activities, alliances and strengthen women's social position and political objectives.
    To subscribe email: majordomo@igc.apc.org
    Message reading: subscribe women-east-west [your name] <your email address>

OWS-L – Oz Women's Studies

A women's/gender list based at the University of South Australia. It welcomes subscribers from all countries.
    To subscribe email: MAILSERV@MAGILL.UNISA.EDU.AU
    Message reading: SUBSCRIBE OWS-L [your name]

PAR-L

A bilingual (English/French), moderated list for exchanging information about policy, action, and research on issues of concern to women in Canada. Set up by the Canadian Advisory Council on the Status of Women (CACSW), PAR-L is intended as a support for the community of feminist researchers and activists in Canada.
    To subscribe email: PAR-L-SERVER@UNB.CA
    Message reading: SUBSCRIBE PAR-L [your name]

PERSONALIST-FEM

This discussion list is a place for feminist-minded people to exchange ideas, work, and experiences having to do with the place of the "personal" in feminist work/lives. The list will discuss autobiographical theorising, pedagogy, personal experience, life-writing, literary criticism, theory, and tell stories about the contributors' own lives, work, writing, and teaching. Challenging the view that "academic" work and "personal" experience are radically different things.

To subscribe email: **majordomo@qiclab.scn.rain.com**

Message reading: **subscribe personalist-fem [your name] <your email address>**

Pleiades Networks

Discussion forums on politics, relationships, food, arts, science and technology, money, health, music and movies.

For information on how to subscribe, email: **admin@pleiades-net.com**

POWR-L

The Psychology of Women Resource List is co-sponsored by Division 35 of the American Psychological Association and the Association for Women in Psychology. Its purpose is to facilitate discussion of current topics, research, teaching strategies, practice issues, and public policy, and to publicize relevant information.

To subscribe email: **LISTSERV@URIACC.URI.EDU**

Message reading: **SUBSCRIBE POWR-L [your name]**

PSYCWOMEN

A list for any students interested in discussing issues related to the psychology of women.

To subscribe email: **PSYCWOMEN-REQUEST@FRE.FSU.UMD.EDU**

Message reading: **SUBSCRIBE PSYCWOMEN [your name]**

Questions should be emailed to the list owner, Pat Santoro: e2pysan@fre.fsu.umd.edu

PWINET-L

Established by Division 35, the Psychology of Women Division of the APA, to enhance discussion among feminist psychologists interested in international research or practice.

The list is not automated; if you wish to subscribe, send a note with your email address to: **FRIEZE@VMS.CIS.PITT.EDU** (Irene Hanson Frieze, Ph.D.).

SASH – Sociologists Against Sexual Harassment

A moderated list focusing on sexual harassment.

For more information or to subscribe, write to Phoebe M. Stambaugh: azpxs@asuvm.inre.asu.edu

SAWNET – South Asian Women's Net

A discussion group for women from the south Asian countries (Bangladesh, Bhutan, Burma, India, Nepal, Pakistan, and Sri Lanka) as well as women from other parts of the world interested in the concerns of south Asian women. This forum is open only to women.

To subscribe email: SAWNET@CS.CONCORDIA.CA

Message reading: SUBSCRIBE

SEAC+WOMYN

A US women's environmental activist list run by the Student Environmental Action Coalition.

To subscribe email: LISTPROC@ECOSYS.DRDR.VIRGINIA.EDU

Message reading: SUBSCRIBE SEAC+WOMYN [your name]

SISS – Sisters in Sobriety

A closed email women's meeting of Alcoholics Anonymous.

To join the group, send an email message to: SISS-APPROVAL@WORLD.STD.COM stating your adherence to the Third Tradition of AA: "The only requirement for membership is a desire to stop drinking."

Society for Women in Philosophy

Mainly providing information, this moderated list calls for papers in feminist philosophy, has announcements of SWIP meetings and other conferences and requests for references or information. A SWIP-L file of course syllabi in feminist philosophy is maintained and is retrievable by the list members. An appropriate place for discussion of issues and controversies within feminist philosophy.

To subscribe email: listserv@cfrvm.cfr.usf.edu

Message reading: subscribe swip-1 [your name]

SPIDERWOMAN

A high-volume list for women who manage and/or design World Wide Web sites. It supports women Web designers by providing a supportive atmosphere to deal with Web development and consulting, including such issues as HTML coding questions, developing standards for Web pages, integration of business and social responsibility, networking, being a female computer consultant/Web developer, etc.

To subscribe email: MAJORDOMO@LISTS.PRIMENET.COM

Message reading: SUBSCRIBE SPIDERWOMAN [your name] <your email address>

STOPRAPE

A sexual assault activist list.

To subscribe email: LISTSERV@BROWNVM.BROWN.EDU

SYSTERS

Designed for professional women in computer science. Topics vary, but include introductions, job listings, book reviews, discrimination, "what should I do" situations, and setting up systers meetings at conferences. It is also a place to organize efforts to change or influence policies affecting women in computer science.

   To subscribe email: SYSTERS-ADMIN@SYSTERS.ORG

   Message reading: "subscribe"

SYSTERS-STUDENTS

A student-oriented version of the SYSTERS list (see above), for female graduate and undergraduate students in computer science.

   To subscribe and for more information, email a brief introduction to:
   SYSTERS-STUDENTSREQUEST@MARIA.WUSTL.EDU

T-AMLIT (Teaching the American Literatures)

A moderated list for teachers and scholars interested in discussing innovative and effective ways to teach a radically expanded American literature. Literature by women and by others under represented in the traditional curriculum plays a vital part in this discussion.

   To subscribe email: LISTPROC@LIST.CREN.NET

   Message reading: SUBSCRIBE T-AMLIT [your name]

THIRD WORLD WOMEN

Discusses issues related to the representations of "Third World Women," including interrogating the construction of identities as TWW and the effects of those identities on personal and professional lives, etc. A list where academic and nonacademic discussions intersect.

   To subscribe email: MAJORDOMO@JEFFERSON.VILLAGE.VIRGINIA.EDU

   Message reading: subscribe-third-world-women [your name] <your email address>

TW-WOMEN

Addresses various feminist issues faced by Taiwanese women. It advocates equality between genders, solicits the involvement of male feminists, and seeks to establish links between TW-WOMEN and other Women's Movement groups in Taiwan.

   To subscribe email: MAILSERV@UTARLG.UTA.EDU

   Message reading: SUBSCRIBE TW-WOMEN [your name]

UHURA

A collaborative research project online, for women researching some aspect of the net who wish "to discover more about our purposes for using this technology . . . in an emergent and collaborative way." Moderated by Fiona Sanderson, the group is closed and promotes connections between members in order to "situate our knowledge of each other's research in a personal context too."

   To subscribe email: Majordomo@mail.rmplc.co.uk

Message reading: subscribe uhura [your name] <your email address>
Or email Fiona for more information: fionas@rmplc.co.uk

VS-ONLINE-STRAT

This is a moderated list which "provides a place to link up globally with women (and men) to discuss issues directly related to our struggles and successes in getting women's information, ideas, and perspectives online." It is supported by Virtual Sisterhood (see Chapter 2 for details).
 To subscribe email: majordomo@igc.apc.org
 Message reading: subscribe vs-online-strat [your name] <your email address>

WAM

Helping members of Women and Mathematics keep in touch and share information.
 To subscribe email: MAJORDOMO@MYSTERY.COM
 Message reading: SUBSCRIBE WAM [your name] <your email address>

WEBWOMEN-TECH

A list for women involved in the technical side of managing web sites.
 To subscribe email: WEBWOMEN-TECH-REQUEST@NIESTU.COM
 In the subject field write: SUBSCRIBE

WHIRL – Women's History in Rhetoric and Language

The list focuses on all kinds of women's rhetorical activities (argumentation, debate, public speaking, oration, fiction, non-fiction, etc.) from ancient times to the present.
 To subscribe email: listserv@cmsa.berkeley.edu
 Message reading: subscribe whirl [your name]

WIG-L

A list sponsored by the Coalition of Women, focuses on the feminist study of German literature, culture, and language. In German.
 To subscribe email: LISTSERV@CMSA.BERKELEY.EDU
 Message reading: SUBSCRIBE WIG-L [your name]

WIML-L (Women's Issues in Music Librarianship).

For more information contact Laura Gayle Green:
 LGREEN@IUBVM.UCS.INDIANA.EDU

Windows-Women

This list is a companion list to mac-women. It is a women-only list to ask questions about Windows 3.1, Windows 95 and Window's NT. It is a safe place where you can ask questions that might get you flamed on another list.
To subscribe email: Majordomo@blob.best.net
Message reading: subscribe windows-women <your email address>

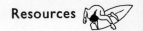

WIPHYS

A moderated list for issues of concern to women in physics.
> To subscribe email: LISTSERV@APS.ORG
> Message reading: SUBSCRIBE WIPHYS [your name]

WISA

A mainly US-based list focusing on issues relating to women in Student Affairs, specifically, and higher education in general.
> To subscribe email: LISTSERV@ULKYVM.LOUISVILLE.EDU
> Message reading: SUBSCRIBE WISA [your name]

WISENET

This list is for the discussion of women's issues/feminist issues in science, mathematics, and engineering.
> To subscribe email: listserv@uicvm.uic.edu
> Message reading: subscribe wisenet [your name]

WISHPERD

Focusing on women in sport, health, physical education, recreation, and dance.
> To subscribe email: LISTSERV@SJSUVM1.SJSU.EDU
> Message reading: SUBSCRIBE WISHPERD [your name]

WISP-L

Providing a forum for discussion among members of Women in Scholarly Publishing (WISP) and restricted to WISP members. Membership in WISP is open to all who work in scholarly or university press publishing or in related professions who actively support equal rights and equal opportunity for women and minorities.
> To subscribe email: LISTSERV@IUBVM.UCS.INDIANA.EDU
> Message reading: SUBSCRIBE WISP-L [your name]

WMST-L

An academic list devoted to discussion of Women's Studies teaching, research, and program administration. It also distributes relevant job and conference announcements and calls for papers, and maintains online collections of syllabi, bibliographies, and other relevant files.
> To subscribe email: listserv@umdd.umd.edu
> Message reading: subscribe wmst-1 [your name]

WOAH-HERSTORY – Women of Achievement and Herstory

A daily posting by Irene Stuber (irenestuber@delphi.com) about the achievements and lives of women throughout history.
> To subscribe email: LISTSERV@NETCOM.COM
> Message reading: SUBSCRIBE WOAH-HERSTORY [your name]

WOMAN PLUS

Moderated by Julia Kachalova from Moscow for "the dissemination of positive experiences."

To subscribe email: **Owl@udn.msk.su**

Message reading: **subscribe womplus.zhif**

WOMCOLLIB

A list established to share information among those working in libraries at women's colleges and to share scholarly inquiry dealing with women's colleges or women's education. Examples of issues include ways in which women access and process information, ways library facilities may be best designed to serve women, and scholarly resources valuable to the study of women's education.

To subscribe email: LIST-REQUEST@CATT.COCHRAN.SBC.EDU

In the subject header write: SUBSCRIBE WOMCOLLIB [your name]

WOMEN

A general purpose list for all women's groups and areas of interest for women and their friends.

To subscribe email: **women-request@athena.mit.edu**

To post messages email: **women@athena.mit.edu**

WOMEN – Women's Issues in Turkey

Women aims to be a communication medium for people interested in women's issues in Turkey, in developing countries, and all over the world. The list accepts messages in English and Turkish, and is intended, primarily, to serve the academic and professional needs of people involved in women's issues and gender as researchers, librarians, or program administrators, particularly in developing countries.

Moderated by Hatice Kubra Bahsisoglu (**kubra@hun.tr**) and Mujgan San (**msan@hun.edu.tr**)

To subscribe email: **listproc@bilkent.edu.tr**

Message reading: **subscribe WOMEN** [your name]

WOMEN-CLINICDEFENSE

A list for information, discussion, and analysis of "the escalating war against women, particularly regarding reproductive rights and abortion access". Anyone fighting the Right is welcome to participate; abortion providers, clinic workers, and pro-choice escorts and defenders are especially encouraged to join.

To subscribe email: MAJORDOMO@IGC.APC.ORG

Message reading: **subscribe women-clinicdefense** [your name] <your email address>

WOMEN-L

Welcoming women from all backgrounds to discuss women's issues, with a particular focus on the Internet, new technologies, and Internet culture.

To subscribe email: MAJORDOMO@HELIX.NET

Message reading: SUBSCRIBE WOMEN-L [your name] <your email address>

WOMEN-LIST

A moderated, announcement-only list "where you can post announcements about women-related information, events, news – anything that is for and about women either online or in the "real world".

To subscribe email: MAJORDOMO@CGIM.COM

Message reading: SUBSCRIBE WOMEN-LIST [your name] <your email address>

WOMENS-CYCLING

An unmoderated list for those interested in the issues of women on self-powered cycles, especially bicycles.

To subscribe email: LISTSERV@NETCOM.COM

Message reading: SUBSCRIBE WOMENS-CYCLING <your email address>

WOMENS-STUDIES

Designed for members of the Women's Studies Network Association (UK) and for academic staff and researchers in Women's Studies. The list provides a forum for the exchange of information and a noticeboard for conferences, recent publications, etc.

To subscribe email: MAILBASE@MAILBASE.AC.UK

Message reading: JOIN WOMENS-STUDIES [your name]

WOMEN20S

A list for issues pertaining specifically to women in their 20s. For example: issues of safety, professional/ educational issues, relationship/marriage issues, economic issues, etc.

To subscribe email: LISTSERV@SJUVM.STJOHNS.EDU

Message reading: SUBSCRIBE WOMEN20S [your name]

WOMENWORK

Dealing with the issues of women and work in the context of economic empowerment of women in developing countries or areas of economic hardship and crisis.

To subscribe email: MAJORDOMO@HUMANISM.ORG

Message reading: SUBSCRIBE WOMENWORK [your name] <your email address>

WORKING-CLASS-LIST

A list designed primarily for working-class academics. It deals with issues related to a working-class background and focuses especially on the intersection of race, class, and gender.

To subscribe email: MAJORDOMO@SOL.ACS.UWOSH.EDU

Message reading: SUBSCRIBE WORKING-CLASS-LIST [your name] <your email address>

WRAC-L – Women's Resource and Action Centers

Focusing on issues and resources of significance to women's centres. The list is open to the staff and affiliates of women's centers, whether community-based or associated with schools, colleges, or universities.

To subscribe email: LISTSERV@DARTMOUTH.EDU

Message reading: SUBSCRIBE WRAC-L [your name]

ws-1 – Women's Studies

This list provides a focal point for Women's Studies students and staff discussions, book notices, queries about research, assignments, contacts, issues and syllabi at Massey University, NZ. Moderated by Lynne Alice (l.c.alice@massey.ac.nz)

To subscribe email: majordomo@massey.ac.nz

Message reading: subscribe ws-1 [your name] <email address>

WSST

This list operates as a Women's Studies bulletin board with a particular emphasis on teaching and resourcing Women's Studies. Based in Otago, New Zealand.

For more information email: Sarah Williams
(sarah.williams@stonebow.otago.ac.nz)

To subscribe email: uotago@stonebow.otago.ac.nz

Message reading: subscribe wsst

WTP-L

The Women and Theatre Program discussion list which is a forum for scholars and artists interested in feminism, sexualities, race, class, and gender as they relate to theatre and performance. People can exchange information about current research, production methodologies, teaching or rehearsal strategies, funding sources, useful texts/films, the availability of performers as guest artists, new plays.

To subscribe email: LISTSERV@UHCCVM.UHCC.HAWAII.EDU

Message reading: SUBSCRIBE WTP-L [your name]

WWP-L

Set up by the Women Writers Project to discuss the project and women writers from pre-Victorian periods.

To subscribe email: LISTSERV@BROWNVM.BROWN.EDU

Message reading: SUBSCRIBE WWP-L [your name]

XXANDLAW

A list for women law students open only to women. The list's purpose is to provide a forum for discussion of women's status as "outsiders" in legal culture. Messages about any subject of concern to women in the law are welcome.

To subscribe, email your name and email address to:
OWNER-XXANDLAW@LAW.WISC.EDU

Gender, Equity and Sexuality

BITHRY-L

"A list for the theoretical discussion of bisexuality and gender issues. It is neither a social group, nor a support group, nor an announcement or news forum."

To subscribe email: LISTSERV@BROWNVM.BROWN.EDU .

Message reading: SUBSCRIBE BITHRY-L [your name]

DIOTIMA

Women and gender in the ancient world. Ahahita is an unmoderated list for discussion amongst teachers in the field.

To subscribe email: listserv@ukcc.uky.edu

Message reading: subscribe ahahita [your name]

EDEQUITY – Educational Equity Discussion List

Encourages discussion of educational equity in schools, colleges, etc. among teachers and other educators, equity practitioners, advocates, parents, policymakers, counsellors and others interested in equity. The list serves as a forum to discuss how to attain equity for males and females; and how gender equity can be a helpful construct for improving education for all. The participation of both women and men is welcomed.

To subscribe email: MAJORDOMO@CONFER.EDC.ORG

Message reading: SUBSCRIBE EDEQUITY [your name] <your email address>

FEMSUPREM

Has been set up to discuss "the idea that perhaps women are superior to men, whether in a few ways, or in everything." Both women and men may join and participate.

To subscribe email: FEMSUPREM-REQUEST@RENAISSOFT.COM

Message reading: SUBSCRIBE FEMSUPREM

GENDER

A moderated forum for exploring the role of communication (including media) in how ideas of masculinity, femininity, androgyny, and other concepts of gender are negotiated.

To subscribe email: COMSERVE@CIOS.LLC.RPI.EDU

Message reading: JOIN GENDER <your name>

GENDER

A second list called Gender, this one based in Norway, is for "discussing all aspects of gender and (biological) sex issues." One of the list's primary concerns is "to provide an open-minded forum for discussion of gender stereotypes vs. individuality, gender roles, and particularly how people can get beyond these restrictions."

To subscribe email: **MAJORDOMO@IFI.UIO.NO**

Message reading: **SUBSCRIBE GENDER <Your email address>**

GENDER-SET

A list for discussion of research on gender, science, technology, and engineering (SET).

To subscribe email: **MAILBASE@MAILBASE.AC.UK**

Message reading: **JOIN GENDER-SET [your name]**

GENED

A list where teachers, parents, researchers, and others can discuss gender and education, especially in K-12. Topics may include gender issues for schools and in the K-12 curriculum; gender equity; gender identity formation; gender and health; and similar topics.

To subscribe email: **MAJORDOMO@ACPUB.DUKE.EDU**

Message reading: **SUBSCRIBE GENED [your name] <your email address>**

SSSSTALK

A sexuality discussion list where "professional researchers, clinicians, educators, and students in the field of sexuality can communicate freely, professionally, and efficiently."

To subscribe email: **LISTSERV@TAMVM1.TAMU.EDU**

Message reading: **SUSCRIBE SSSSTALK [your name]**

Health

Bereavement Support

Online service for death and dying, bereavement, major losses – physical and emotional. Offers support, discussions and counselling information.

To subscribe email: **rivendell@rivendell.org**

Message reading: **subscribe rivendell [your email address]**

Breast Cancer Mailing Lists

To subscribe email: **Listserv@morgan.ucs.mun.ca**

Message reading: **SUBSCRIBE BREAST CANCER**

Cancer Mailing Lists

To subscribe email: **Listserv@wuvmd.wustl.edu**

Message reading: **Subscribe Cancer.L**

CANCERNET

List for cancer sufferers and their families.
    To subscribe email: **cancernet@icicb.nci.nih.gov**
    Message reading: **help**
    Within ten minutes you'll be sent information about the list.

CANDIDANEWS

An open and unmoderated forum for the exchange of ideas on Candida research, intended for academics, researchers, students and clinicians.
    To subscribe email: **listproc@stonebow.otago.ac.nz**
    Message reading: **subscribe candidanews [your name]**

C+Health

Computers and Health – technology causing injuries.
    To subscribe email: **listserv@iubvm.ucs.indiana.edu**
    Message reading: **subscribe c+health [your name]**

CULTURE-AND-NURSING

A list where nurses and other health care professionals can discuss the political, economic, and demographic issues affecting health care today. Provides a network with others in the field of cross cultural and transcultural nursing.
    To subscribe email: **MAJORDOMO@ITSSRV1.UCSF.EDU**
    Message reading: **subscribe culture-and-nursing [your name] <your email address>**

GYN-DOCS

An unmoderated list for discussion of academic topics in gynecology by health care professionals.
    To subscribe email: **MAJORDOMO@OAC1.OAC.TJU.EDU**
    Message reading: **SUBSCRIBE GYN-DOCS <your email address>**
    For more information send message reading: **INFO GYN-DOCS** to the above address.

IMMUNE

A high-traffic list for people with immune system related ailments. Web page section has details.
    To subscribe email: **immune-request@weber.ucsd.edu**
    Message reading: **subscribe immune**

MEDS-AT-LARG

A list for discussion of articles posted on the Women's Medical Health Page (Web address: **http://www.best.com/~sirlou/wmhp.html**), as well as general questions and concerns relating to women's health. Physicians, medical students, lay women, and others interested in women's health are encouraged to join.

To subscribe email: **MAJORDOMO@SPECTER.USA.NET**

Message reading: **SUBSCRIBE MEDS-AT-LARGE [your name] <your email address>**

MENOPAUS

A list for discussion of menopause, and the sharing of remedies and personal experiences related to menopause. Note the 'e' of menopause is not included in the address.

To subscribe email: **LISTSERV@PSUHMC.HMC.PSU.EDU**

Message reading: **SUBSCRIBE MENOPAUS [your name]**

NURSENET

Focusing on nursing administration, nursing education, nursing practice, and nursing research.

To subscribe email: **LISTSERV@VM.UTCC.UTORONTO.CA**

Message reading: **SUBSCRIBE NURSENET [your name]**

NURSERES

A moderated list for nurse researchers.

To subscribe email: **LISTSERV@KENTVM.KENT.EDU**

Message reading: **SUBSCRIBE NURSERES [your name]**

OB-GYN-L

An open, unmoderated list for obstetricians and gynecologists. Topics of discussion include practices, research, case studies and lifestyle.

To subscribe email: **LISTSERV@BCM.TMC.EDU**

Message reading: **SUBSCRIBE OB-GYN-L [your name]**

OVARIAN

An unmoderated discussion list for patients, family, friends, researchers, and physicians who wish to discuss issues relating to ovarian cancer or other ovarian disorders such as ovarian cysts. The list should not be used to discuss reproductive/fertility problems. Only subscribers may post messages.

To subscribe email: **LISTSERV@SJUVM.STJOHNS.EDU**

Message reading: **SUBSCRIBE OVARIAN [your name]**

RSI-UK

Great Britain's mailing list for people suffering from repetitive strain injury (RSI).

To subscribe email: **listserv@tictac.demon.co.uk**

Message reading: **subscribe rsi-uk [your name]**

SOREHAND
San Francisco based mailing list for people with RSI.
> To subscribe email: listserv@itssrvl1.ucsf.edu
> Message reading: subscribe sorehand [your name]

WHAM (Women's Health Action and Mobilization)
Demanding, securing and defending absolute reproductive freedom and quality of health care for women.
> To subscribe email: listproc@listproc.net
> Message reading: SUBSCRIBE WHAM [your name]

WHERE-L
The women's health education and research exchange list, provides a forum to discuss journal articles and exchange information on women's health issues. It originates from the Institute for Women's Health, Medical College of Pennsylvania, and is open to anyone interested in women's health issues.
> To subscribe email: MAILSERV@MEDCOLPA.EDU
> Message reading: SUBSCRIBE WHERE-L [your name]

WITSENDO
A list for discussion of endometriosis treatment and support.
> To subscribe email: LISTSERV@LISTSERV.DARTMOUTH.EDU
> Message reading: SUBSCRIBE WITSENDO [your name]

WMN-HLTH
A Women's Health Electronic News Line started by the Center for Women's Health Research.
> To subscribe email: LISTPROC@U.WASHINGTON.EDU
> Message reading: SUBSCRIBE WMN-HLTH [your name]

Lesbian and Bisexual Lists

ALFP
A moderated list for lesbian/bisexual/queer feminists who write poetry. Any and all poetic writing by queer women is welcome, regardless of topic, as well as discussions about famous and not-so-famous poets, literary theories, feminism, etc.
> To subscribe, send an email message to Leah Sheppard at:
> SHEPPARD@POBOX.UPENN.EDU

BA-CYBERDYKES
San Francisco Bay area dyke chat. Only for Northern Californian girls. Lesbian and bisexual women only.
    To subscribe email: **majordomo@queernet.org**
    Message reading: **subscribe ba-cyberdykes [your name] <your email address>**
    For information only write: **info ba-cyberdykes**

BIFEM-L
Providing a safe place for bisexual and bi-friendly women.
    To subscribe email: **listserv@brownvm.brown**
    Message reading: **subscribe bifem-l [your name]**

BOOKWOMAN
On-going discussions about the writing of women. A private list moderated by Dorsie Hathaway.
    To subscribe email: **majordomo@vector.cast.com**
    Message reading: **subscribe bookwoman [your name] <your email address>**

BYKER-DYKES
For lesbians who ride and love motorcycles. Open to all women who wish to participate.
    To subscribe email: **majordomo@lists.best.com**
    Message reading: **subscribe byker-dykes [your name] <your email address>**

DHARMA-DYKES
An informal mailing list for lesbians involved in all areas of Buddhism. Currently the group is small, friendly and mostly has US participants.
    To subscribe email: **majordomo@goonsquad.spies.com**
    Message reading: **subscribe dharma-dykes [your name] <your email address>**

DYKENET-L
A dyke-only flame free zone to post from the heart.
    To subscribe email: **LISTSERV@netcom.com**
    Message reading: **subscribe DYKENET-L [your email address]**

EURO-SAPPHO
For sapphic discussion on topics of particular interest to European dykes. Membership is open to all women and is restricted to women; postings may be in any of the major European languages.
    To subscribe email: **MAJORDOMO@SETA.FI**
    Message reading: **SUBSCRIBE EURO-SAPPHO [your name] <your email address>**
    If you encounter problems subscribing email:
EURO-SAPPHO-REQUEST@SETA.FI

GAYNET

A list focusing on gay and lesbian concerns on college campuses.

    To subscribe email: MAJORDOMO@QUEERNET.ORG

    Message reading: SUBSCRIBE GAYNET <your email address>

GGBB

Created for the discussion of issues facing gay and lesbian couples by people who will experience or have already dealt with these same issues. These issues include monogamy, sex, domestic partnership benefits, dealing with family members, anti-couple bias in the general g/l/b community, networking with other couples, etc.

    To subscribe email: MAJORDOMO@ABACUS.OXY.EDU

    Message reading: SUBSCRIBE GGBB [your name] <your email address>

INGENUE

A mailing list for k.d. lang devotees.

    To subscribe email your request to: ingenue-request@kai.rsmas.miami.edu

    Send postings to: ingenue@kai.rsmas.miami.edu

International Lesbian Avengers

A private list restricted to members. See Web resources for details.

    To subscribe email: majordomo@queernet.org

    Message reading: subscribe avengers [your name] <your email address>

LBJW

A discussion list for lesbian and bisexual Jewish women.

    To subscribe email: listserv@uci.edu

    Message reading: subscribe lbjw [your name]

LESAC-NET

A list for lesbian and bisexual women who are academics – graduate students, faculty members, and those "in-between" degree programs. The list's purpose is to enable women to connect with others who have similar research interests and to provide a space to discuss what it means to be a lesbian or bisexual woman in academia. It is NOT a general lesbian discussion list, nor is it limited to scholars of lesbigay studies.

    To subscribe email: majordomo@queernet.org

    Message reading: subscribe lesac-net [your name] <your email address>

    For more information write: info lesac-net

LESBIANS IN MATH

A list for women actively pursuing a maths career. "Giving advice and support, dealing with outness issues, two body problems and a generally chilly climate." An opportunity to "give first hand accounts of the atmospheres at various campuses. A network of professionals to make contacts."

    To subscribe email Nadine at: nadine@math.uchicago.edu

LESBIAN-STUDIES

Open only to women, this is an academic list for discussion of research in the field of lesbian studies. Not for general chat.

 To subscribe email: **majordomo@queernet.org**
 Message reading: **subscribe lesbian-studies [your name] <your email address>**
 For information only write: **info lesbian-studies**

LESBIAN-WRITERS

A professional networking, support, and discussion group for lesbians who are or aspire to be published writers of fiction, non-fiction, or poetry. A clearinghouse of information of interest to lesbian writers and a springboard for spin-off mini-lists that will function as "virtual writing" groups.

 To subscribe email: **majordomo@queernet.org**
 For information only write: **info lesbian-writers**

LEZBRIAN

A forum for discussing professional issues of interest to lesbian and bisexual women library workers. While the main focus of discussion will be on librarianship and library issues as they concern lesbians and bisexual women, the discussion on LEZBRIAN may also touch upon the broader and/or related fields of queer, gay, bisexual, and/or transgendered/ transsexual librarianship. We STRONGLY ENCOURAGE new subscribers to introduce themselves and state their interest in the list.

 To subscribe email: **listserv@listserv.acsu.buffalo.edu:**
 Message reading: **Subscribe LEZBRIAN [your name]**

LIFE

A spin-off from Euro-Sappho which discusses "real life vs cyber life" and the integration of both worlds into the formation of a cyber community. Discussions stress theory as well as stories and experiences and explore the nature of cyberspace with the possible goal of eventually making a book out of the postings.

 To subscribe email: **listserv@ls2.informatik.uni.dotmund.de**
 Message reading: **subscribe life [your name]**
 For more information email Ricki at: **wegner@ ls2.informatik.uni.dotmund.de**

LIS – Lesbians in Science

Lesbians in Science was born at the Michigan Women's Festival in 1990 and has grown into an international organization of lesbians practising, or interested in, diverse sciences. The list includes discussions, resources, information sharing as well as being a social network and support group. For lesbians in industry, universities, government labs, etc.

 To subscribe email: **LIS-REQUEST@KENYON.EDU**
 Message reading: **SUBSCRIBE LIS [your name] [your email address]**

LIVING

An unmoderated forum for lesbians with some sort of physical handicap. It is not limited to lesbians in wheelchairs, but is meant to be a support list for lesbians to talk about any sort of physically challenging situation that they are living in at the moment, be it temporary or permanent.

For subscription information email:
LIVING-REQUEST@QICLAB.SCN.RAIN.COM

L-PLUS

A list for lesbians 50 and over (think of the Roman numeral L).

To subscribe email: MAJORDOMO@VECTOR.CASTI.COM

Message reading: SUBSCRIBE L-PLUS [your name] <your email address>

If you have a signature file, write **END** on a line by itself after the subscription request line.

MLN – Malaysian Lesbian Network

Offering networking and social support for Malaysian lesbians

To subscribe email: LISTSERV@BROWNUM.BROWN.EDU

Message reading: **subscribe QAPA-L [your name]**

Post a message to QAPA-L specifying your wish to subscribe to **MLN**

MOMS

A list for lesbian mothers, co-mothers, and mom-wannabes. Only women may join; only subscribers may post messages.

To subscribe email: MAJORDOMO@QICLAB.SCN.RAIN.COM

Message reading: SUBSCRIBE MOMS [your name] <your emailaddress>

To contact the listowner directly email:
MOMS-OWNER@QICLAB.SCN.RAIN.COM

NICEJG – Nice Jewish Girls

A list for lesbian and bisexual Jewish women. It is "a social, political, cultural, and spiritual gathering place" for women only.

To subscribe email: MAJORDOMO@ZOOM.COM

Message reading: SUBSCRIBE NICEJG [your name] <your email address>

NOGLSTP

The National Organization of Gay and Lesbian Scientists and Technical Professionals.

To subscribe email: NOGLSTP-REQUEST@ELROY.JPL.NASA.GOV

OWLS – Older and Wiser Lesbians

A virtual meeting place for lesbians over 40 to gather to discuss ideas, concerns, developments and "discovering middle age". It is a high-volume list which is private and closed.

To subscribe email: MAJORDOMO@VECTOR.CASTI.COM

Message reading: SUBSCRIBE OWLS [your name] <your email address>
To contact the listowner directly email:
OWLS-OWNER@VECTOR.CASTI.COM

PNW-SAPPHO

Pacific North West Sappho list for organising get togethers in the area and announcing planned visits.

To subscribe email: **majordomo@qiclab.scn.rain.com**
Message reading: **subscribe pnw-sappho [your name] <your email address>**
The second line should read: **end**

POLITIDYKES

A virtual saloon dedicated to progressive, political discussion. Described as a friendly space for lesbians, bisexuals and queers to discuss things political – to question, challenge, converse, share and to push the limits of ones understanding.

To subscribe email: **majordomo@vector.cast.com**
Message reading: **subscribe POLITIDYKES [your name] <your email address>**

QSA – Queer Studies Aotearoa

Aims to connect scholars and activists working in the areas of feminism, queer studies, cultural studies, and gay, lesbian and bi-sexual rights. It will provide an opportunity for discussion in these areas and networking with those interesting in queer studies and activism outside Aotearoa.

To subscribe email: **MAJORDOMO@MASSEY.AC.NZ**
Message reading: **SUBSCRIBE QSA [your name] <your email address>**

ROGUE

A list for lesbian or queer women from Europe (or rooted in Europe in some way), with sapphic motivations, involved in the business of publishing or writing. To discuss the products and processes of writing prose which has its inspiration in the personal imagination (autobiographies and memoirs included). To generate intelligent and knowledgeable conversations about writing, to test ideas and to explore and develop new Internet specific writing cultures. Exploring the transformation of the role as writers from the printed word to cyber bytes (e.g. Web publishing).

For subscription information email: **rogue-request@seta.fi**

SAPPHO

A forum and support group for gay and bisexual women. Membership is open to all women and is limited to women.

For more information email: **SAPPHO-REQUEST@APOCALYPSE.ORG**

SISTAH-NET
A list for lesbians of African descent.

> To subscribe, email a brief bio to: SISTAH-REQUEST@FAMILY.HAMPSHIRE.EDU
> With a subject line labeled: Re: BIO

SOBERDYKES
Support for lesbians in recovery from alcohol and drug dependence (but not their dependents).

> To subscribe email: majordomo@vector.casti.com
> Message reading: subscribe soberdykes [your name] <your email address>

SUOMEN SAPFO
A Sappho list for Finnish lesbians, in finnish only.

> For information email: Eva.Isaksson@Helsinki.Fi

SYSTERS-OUT – Lesbians in Computer Science
An unmoderated private list for lesbian and bisexual women with degrees or studying in the area of computer science. To share experiences within the industry and academia and to raise the field's visibility. To share resources and information and offer mutual support. Aims for a narrow focus.

> To subscribe email: systers-out-request@illustra.com
> Message reading: subscribe [your name and email address]

UK-MOTSS
A lesbian, bisexual and gay network community based in the UK and Europe, offering support. There are two lists, one general and one for women only.

> To subscribe email: uk-motss-REQUEST@dircon.co.uk
> Message reading: request uk-motss-women (for the women only list)

WILD-LIST
A forum for information and discussion about lesbian studies from a European perspective. It's a closed list and for women only.

> To subscribe email: MAJORDOMO@HELSINKI.FI
> Message reading: SUBSCRIBE WILD-LIST [your name] <your email address>
> If you encounter subscription problems email:

WILD-LIST-REQUEST@HELSINKI.FI

Religion

BRIDGES

A moderated list that explores Jewish feminist identity and considers both Jewish and female existence and activism in relation to movements for change.
    To subscribe email: LISTSERV@ISRAEL.NYSERNET.ORG
    Message reading: SUBSCRIBE BRIDGES [your name]

CHRISTIAN-WOMEN

A women-only discussion forum "for Christian women who use the Internet for personal, domestic, business, and/or ministry activities."
    To subscribe email: MAJORDOMO@ICLNET.ORG .
    Message reading: SUBSCRIBE CHRISTIAN_WOMEN [your email address]

FEMINIST-THEOLOGY

An unmoderated forum for the academic discussion of Jewish and Christian feminist theology. Topics discussed include a feminist critique of traditional ways of doing theology and may cover all aspects of theological study.
    To subscribe email: MAILBASE@MAILBASE.AC.UK
    Message reading: SUBSCRIBE FEMINIST-THEOLOGY [your name]

FEMREL-L

Focuses on women and religion and feminist theology.
    To subscribe email: LISTSERV@LISTSERV.AOL.COM
    Message reading: SUBSCRIBE FEMREL-L [your name]

KOL-ISHA

A moderated list for halachic questions and issues concerning women's roles in Judaism.
    To subscribe email: LISTSERV@ISRAEL.NYSERNET.ORG
    Message reading: SUBSCRIBE KOL-ISHA [your name]

PHOEBE-L

Named for the biblical Phoebe who carried the letter to the church at Rome, is a list for all women seeking equality for women in the church: laywomen and clergy of all denominations. Its purpose is to provide a forum for the exchange of ideas, an avenue of mutual support, and and a way to share resources and information.
    To subscribe email: MAJORDOMO@MICH.COM
    Message reading: SUBSCRIBE PHOEBE-L [your name] <your email address>

SISTER-L

Focusing on "the history and contemporary concerns of Catholic women religious (sisters and nuns)." The list is open to scholars, practitioners, and others interested in these issues.

To subscribe email: LISTSERV@LISTSERV.SYR.EDU
Message reading: SUBSCRIBE SISTER-L [your name]

WOMENRAB

This is a multidenominational, international moderated discussion group for and by women rabbis and women rabbinical students, and is designed to provide supportive, accessible sanctuary in cyberspace to list members in which to discuss personal, professional, familial, emotional, spiritual, Halachic, and educational issues pertinent to women in the rabbinate.

Moderated by Ann Plutzer (**plutzera@ujafedny.org**)
To subscribe email: **listserv@jtsa.edu**
Message reading: subscribe womenrab [your name]

Spirituality

COE – Circles of Exchange

Provides a forum for women who want to share their spirituality through an exchange of correspondence and creativity.

To subscribe email: LISTSERV@LISTSERV.AOL.COM
Message reading: SUBSCRIBE COE [your name]

WMSPRT-1 – Women and Spirituality

This list is an open discussion list for women and men interested in goddess spirituality, feminism, and the incorporation of the feminine/feminist idea in the study and worship of the divine.

To subscribe email: **listserv@ubvm.cc.buffalo.edu**
Message reading: subscribe wmsprt-1 [your name]

FEM-BIBLIO

A list for discussing books related to women and/or spirituality.

To subscribe email: LISTSERV@LISTSERV.AOL.COM
Message reading: SUBSCRIBE FEM-BIBLIO [your name]

WWWW – Wild Wolf Women of the Web

This list purports "to serve as a communications channel for women, to discuss the wildish and archetypical nature of women, poetic and spiritual thoughts, and grow together as friends and pack mates."

To subscribe email: LISTSERV@HOME.EASE.LSOFT.COM
Message reading: SUBSCRIBE WWWW [your name]
More information can be found at the web site: **http://www.tir.com/~annie**

Bibliography

Here is a list of magazines that I have read during the writing of this book: *Australian Netguide, Internet Australasia, internet.au, .net, Wired, the Network Observer* (http://communication.ucsd.edu/pagre/tno.html).

I subscribe to the following mailing lists: efa-women, vs-online-strat, Red Rock Eater News Service (rre-request@weber.ucsd.edu, in the subject line type: subscribe firstname lastname) and spiderwoman.

These are some of the books we have read:

Busey, Andrew (1995). *Secrets of the MUD Wizards*. Indianapolis: SAMS Publishing.

Capel, Christene (1995, December 11). Email communication with the authors.

Capel, Christene (1996, March 2). Email communication with the authors.

Cross, Rosie (1995, December 11). Email communication with the authors.

December, John and Neil Randall (1994). *The World Wide Web Unleashed*. Indianapolis: SAMS Publishing.

Doreen (1996, January). Making Diversity Work. In Scarlet Pollock and Jo Sutton, *Women'space, 3*. http://www.softaid.net/cathy/vsister/w-space/womspce.html

Falk, Bennett (1994). *The Internet Roadmap*. San Fransisco: Sybex.

Farquhar, Diane and Lynn Mary-Rose (1989). *Women Sum It Up: Biographical Sketches of Women Mathematicians*. Christchurch, Aotearoa/New Zealand: Hazard Press.

Ford, Roger and Oliver Strimpel (1985). *Computers: An Introduction*. London: Orbis.

FrauenUmweltNetz (1995). *Computervernetzung fuer Frauen*. Bern: eFeF-Verlag.

Freed, Les (1995). *The History of Computers: A family album of computer genealogy*. Emeryville, California: Ziff-Davis Press.

Herring, Susan C. (1993). Gender and democracy in computer-mediated communication. *Electronic Journal of Communication 3* (2).

Garfinkel, Simon (1995). *PGP:Pretty Good Privacy*. Sebastobol: O'Reilly and Associates.

Gibson, William (1984). *Neuromancer*. New York: Ace.

Gilster, Paul (1995). *The New Internet Navigator*. New York: John Wiley and Sons.

Goodloe, Amy. *Women Online: Who Are We*. http://www.women-online.com

Grace, Margaret (1996, March 3). Email communication with the authors.

Guyer, Denise W. (1995, January). *Pioneering Women in Computer Science. Communications of the ACM, 38* (1).

Kiwanuka, Justine (1996, January). The Disability Network in Beijing. In Scarlet Pollock and Jo Sutton, *Women'space, 3*.
http://www.softaid.net/cathy/vsister/w-space/womspce.html

Lewis, Judith S. (1992). Princess of Parallelograms and Her Daughter: Math and Gender in the Nineteenth Century English Aristocracy. *Lewis and Clark Gender Studies Symposium*. Portland, Oregon: Lewis and Clark University.

Lowe, Sue (1996). *On-line in OZ*. Sydney: Addison-Wesley.

Michaud, Judy (1996, April/May). Why Run a Web Site? In Scarlet Pollock and Jo Sutton, *Women'space, 4*.
http://www.softaid.net/cathy/vsister/w-space/womspce.html

Miller, Robert and Elissa Keeler (1995). *Internet Direct: Connecting through SLIP and PPP*. New York: MIS Press.

Osen, Lynn M. (1974). *Women in Mathematics*. Cambridge, Massachusetts and London: MIT Press.

O'Leary, Barbara Ann (1996, January 29). Email communication with the authors.

O'Leary, Barbara Ann (1995). *Sea Change: Vsisters online newsletter*.
http://www.igc.apc.org/vsister/

Perl, Teri (1978). *Math Equals: Biographies of women mathematicians and related activities*. California: Addison Wesley.

Pollock, Scarlet and Jo Sutton. *Women'space*. Home Page.
http://www.softaid.net/cathy/vsister/w-space/womspce.html

Pollock, Scarlet and Jo Sutton (1996, January). *Women'space, 3*.
http://www.softaid.net/cathy/vsister/w-space/womspce.html

Pollock, Scarlet (1996, April/May). What Do Women Activists Do Online? In Scarlet Pollock and Jo Sutton. *Women'space, 4.* http://www.softaid.net/cathy/vsister/w-space/womspce.html

Rheingold, Howard (1993). *The Virtual Community: Homesteading on the Electronic Frontier.* Massachusetts: Addison-Wesley.

Seligsohn, I. J. (1967). Your Career in Computer Programming. In Julian Messner (Ed.), Simon and Schuster. Cited by Denise W. Guyer, (1995). *Pioneering Women in Computer Science. Communications of the ACM 38* (1) 47.

Sinclair, Carla (1996). *Netchick: A Smart-Girl Guide to the Wired World.* New York: Henry Holt and Company.

Shaz (1996, April 5). Email communication with the authors.

Spender, Dale (1995). *Nattering on the Net: Women, Power and Cyberspace.* Melbourne: Spinifex Press.

Sproul, Lee and Sarah Kiesler (1991). *Connections: New Ways of Working in a Networked Organization.* Massachusetts: MIT Press.

Stein, Dorothy (1995). *Ada, A Life and Legacy.* Massachusetts: MIT Press.

Turkle, Sherry (1995). *Life on the Screen: Identity in the Age of the Internet.* New York: Simon and Schuster.

Turnipseed, Kathryn (1996, January 7). Email communication with the authors.

Turnipseed, Kathryn (1996b, February 20). Email communication with the authors.

Turnipseed, Kathryn (1996c, February 20). Email communication with the authors.

Wiggins, Richard (1994). *The Internet for Everyone: a guide for users and providers.* New York: McGraw Hill.

Glossary

Anonymous FTP   A form of **FTP** that allows you to retrieve files without the need for an assigned user ID. "Anonymous" is used as the log-in word and your **email** address as the pass word.

Anonymous remailers   Strip **email** or **Usenet News** postings of information which identifies the sender, and then sends them on to their destination.

Archie   A tool used to search the data bases of **anonymous FTP** sites for files containing the words or character strings which you specify. Archie collects the names of files stored worldwide and adds them to a searchable data base.

Archiving   Provides a means for putting many files into a single file. This is useful for making back-up copies of files or for packaging up a group of files to move them to another system.

ASCII   American Standard Code for Information Interchange. A file which contains standard text characters as data. The term "flat ASCII" is often used to refer to a simple text file, with no special embedded code or data which are used to format the file.

Attachments   Files attached to **email**. The original format of the file is preserved, but you may need a decoding program to be able to read the attachment sent to you.

Bandwidth   The amount of data or traffic a network connection can carry at one time. The higher the network bandwidth the more carrying capacity it has and the faster the information will flow.

Binary   Any file that contains data outside the standard character set (**ASCII**), including **compressed** files, compiled programs and **archived** files.

Bit   A binary unit, the smallest unit of information used by a computer, either in the form of a 0 or 1.

bmp   Bitmap, a type of graphics file.

Boot Virus   A **virus** which invades and takes over the master boot and boot records of your hard disk, interfering with the correct running of the computer.

Bookmarks, Favourites and **Hotlists**   Names used by different **browser** programs which allow you to record the **URLs** of your favourite **Web pages**.

Bounced Mail   **Email** which has been incorrectly addressed and therefore reappears in your mailbox.

Bps   Bits per second, the data movement speed on modems.

Browser   See **Web browser**.

Bulletin Board System   A local computer system, originally independent of the Internet, where users can dial-in to **upload** or **download** files and chat. Many BBSs now have connections to the Internet and in many areas they are the cheapest way of accessing the Internet.

Case Sensitivity   The sensitivity of a program to the use of upper and/or lower case text.

Channel   An area on an **IRC server** which you can enter, which has a specific discussion topic operating at the time.

Client   A program residing on your computer. Its purpose is to request information and tasks from **server** programs, residing on other computers. See **client-server architecture**.

Client-Server Architecture   is used by Internet services – such as **email, FTP, Gopher, IRC** and the **WWW** to distribute computer transactions (using specified protocols) between the client software, located on the user's computer and the server software, located on the host's computer. A host could be a **UNIX** workstation, a mainframe or another type of computer.

Communications and Terminal Packages   Software packages which manage the communications between your computer and the packages on your **Internet Service Provider's** computer.

Com ports   Communications ports used by computers to link to and communicate with external devises such a printers, mice, scanners and modems.

Compression   The process of making a file smaller by removing all the **bits** not needed for storage and travel, e.g. data consisting of a string of fifty 0's would be altered so that the repetition of the 0's would be represented by a symbol, thus enabling only two symbols to be transmitted.

Content Provider   Any person or organization providing content on the **Web, FTP** or **Gopher**.

Control/Rating/Filtering Programs   Software programs which control the online access of certain offensive or unsuitable material. Some block offensive words and phrases while others remove specific **Usenet Newsgroups** and **Web sites**. Others classify sites and allow access only to those with a suitable classification. Examples are Netnanny, Surfwatch and Cybersitter.

Crossposting   A posting sent to several **Usenet Newsgroups** at the same time. Not a recommended practice.

Cyberspace   The imaginary place, essentially a place in your mind, which encompasses all of the services on the Internet.

Dialogue box   A small window that pops up when you are using graphical software applications. Its purpose is to ask for information or to confirm a decision.

Dial-up   To access the Internet through a **modem**.

Digital Signatures   Used by **public key encryption systems** such as **PGP** for signing **email** documents. Digital signatures guarantee a message is from the sender and has not been tampered with. Identifiable by a block of "nonsense" data appended to the end of a file.

DNS Domain Name System   The convention of naming computers and a directory service for converting the domain names into **IP addresses**.

Download   Transferring information from another computer to your own.

Electronic mailing lists   See **mailing lists**.

Electronic Market Place   A way of describing the Internet which emphasises its marketplace capabilities. Information becomes a commodity to be bought and sold, therefore the Internet is used to perform transactions of commerce.

Email   A system which allows people to send messages back and forth using computer networks via the Internet.

Emoticons   Little pictures made up of keyboard characters which indicate emotions used in Internet transactions. Also known as smileys. ;-)

Encryption   A method of encoding messages using mathematical algorithms. The message becomes incomprehensible to anyone who does not have access to the secret code.

Eudora   One of the most popular **email** software programs used on the Internet.

E-zines, zines and 'zines   Electronic magazines published on **the Web** or through **email**, usually by individuals or non-profit organizations.

FAQs   Frequently asked questions about the Internet, computing and other related topics. They are often stored publicly on the Internet and discussed in Internet magazines.

File extension   The three letter code used to label a file, found after the file name and the dot. Used to indicate the file format e.g. text, sound or video or the software package that was used to create the file.

Firewalls   Security programs used by companies connected to the Internet to keep private computer's activities secret from the outside world. Sensitive material is kept inside the firewall while information for public viewing is on the other side.

Flaming   Involves nasty messages being sent, either as **email** or posted on **Usenet Newsgroups** or to **mailing lists,** usually in response to a comment someone has made on the Internet. Often aimed at "burning" the recipient in a public way.

FTP   File Transfer Protocol, the technical name for the system which allows software and files to be transferred between computers linked through the Internet.

FTP sites are **servers** (computers) on the Internet which contain files which you can **download** onto your computer.

Gateway address   The address of a service which translates between different protocols or formats, e.g. between Internet style mail (**SMTP**) and Microsoft mail.

GIF   Graphics Interchange Format, a commonly used system on the Internet for storing and exchanging still-image pictures.

Gopher   A hierarchical information system for delivering documents (gopher files) over the Internet. **Web browsers** allow you to access gopher files also.

Helper Applications   Software programs linked to your **Web browser** which extend its capabilities allowing you to use the sound and/or video capabilities in a document. If a helper is needed in order to use such a facility, a window will pop up and ask if you want to proceed.

History Lists   Record the **links** visited in a current session on **the Web**.

Homepage   This is the entry point on **the Web** for access to a set of **Web pages**. A person will often refer to their title page as their homepage.

Host   The computer that you connect to to access the Internet.

Hostname   The name of a computer on the Internet.

HTML   Hyper Text Markup Language, refers to the document structuring tags used to prepare information and create designs for **Web pages**, including the text and **links**.

HTTP   Hypertext Transport Protocol is the protocol that **browsers** use to connect to and communicate with Web servers (computers that store **Web pages**) on **the Web**.

Hypertext   is a piece of text with **links** to other pages. Hypertext links allow you to move through information space in a non-sequential manner. The concept of hypertext is integral to the **World Wide Web**.

Hyperlink – see **link**.

Information Super Highway   A metaphor for the Internet which stresses the access and distribution of information. It defines the Internet as an extension of the current broadcasting model of information delivery.

Internet Service Provider   Often referred to as an **ISP**, the company or organization that offers access to the Internet to individuals or organizations.

IP   Internet Protocol, the protocol used by computers to define the structure of packets of data (see **packet switching**).

IP address   Your computer's address expressed in numbers on the Internet, distinguishing your computer as a separate entity. When connected by **modem** to the Internet this address will be temporary.

IRC Internet Relay Chat, a live conferencing service which works like a **real-time** telephone party line. As you type on a particular channel all the people connected to this **channel** see what you type, and can send messages back in return.

ISDN Integrated Services Digital Network uses digital telephone lines instead of analogue lines to connect to the Internet. It delivers multiples of 64 kbps capacity which is more than twice as high as an ordinary phone line's capacity, enabling video, voice and data to be delivered more efficiently. Instead of using a modem to connect to the line you use a device called a "codec".

Java A programming language which delivers small programs to your **Web browser** allowing animation, interactivity and games facilities to appear on **Web pages**.

JPEG Named after the Joint Photographic Experts Group which developed an image compression and display method for digital graphical images.

Kbps Kilobits per second, usually referring to **modem** speed.

LAN Local Area Network, two or more computers joined together in a network.

Link A highlighted item on a **Web page** which performs an action when its clicked on, e.g. it might take you to another site, display a graphic or **download** a file.

Listproc, LISTSERV and **Majordomo** Listprocessors which automate the tasks and processes associated with a **mailing list** management.

Log-on The act of connecting to a computer system by typing your **username** and your password. Sometimes these actions are automated.

Lurker Someone who watches **Usenet Newsgroup** discussions, **mailing lists** or visits **IRC channels** or MUDs without actually participating. This is a useful way of getting acquainted with these facilities before joining in the discussions.

Lynx A text-based **Web browser** which allows access to **the Web** using the curser keys on your keyboard. Lynx is not capable of bringing you any of the graphics or sound functions which might be embedded in a **Web page**.

Macro Virus A program **virus** associated with word processing packages or spreadsheets that permit users to make a single command (macro) out of a series of commands. It may be spread via the Internet as a result of people **attaching** infected documents to their **email**.

Mailing Lists A group of people with a special interest who all receive **email** messages sent to the group by other members. One-to-many communication.

Majordomo See LISTSERV.

Mb Mega byte.

Mbps Mega bits per second.

MIME Multi Internet Mail Extension, a standard that permits the transfer of sound and pictures by **email**.

Mirror site   A computer that contains an exact copy of the information found on another computer elsewhere on the Internet. Set up to reduce traffic on the Internet and to reduce **downloading** time.

Modem   Modulation/Demodulation. A device which allows Internet connection to take place. It converts digital data produced by your computer into analogue signals, which can be transmitted down a telephone line and then reconverted into digital data by the receiver's modem.

Moderator   The person who checks all contributions to a **Usenet Newsgroup** or **mailing list** for their suitability before posting them.

MUDs   Multi User Dimensions (or Dungeons) which are **text based** virtual environments consisting of rooms or areas which you can "move" about in and interact with others. Players take on characters and play out roles with other people in **real-time**. They are used recreationally as games but can be social spaces and educational tools as well. Various types of **MUDs** are known as **MOOs**, **MUSHes** and **MUSEs**.

Netiquette   The unspoken and spoken rules of acceptable behaviour when using the Internet to communicate with others.

Netscape Navigator   One of the most popular graphical Web browsers.

Network Computers   Cut-down versions of today's PCs. Still in the development stage, the main function of Network computers will be to access the Internet.

Newsgroups   The Internet version of discussion groups.

News readers   Programs that allow you to read and respond to messages posted in various **Usenet Newsgroups**.

Online   The act of being actively connected, via the Internet, to a remote computer. Also used to describe a type of magazine or **e-zine**, or other information, which is published on the Internet.

Packet Switching   A method for moving packets (small amounts of binary information), or parts of messages as independently routed units within the Internet. Packets which have the same starting point may follow different paths until they reach the same ending place.

PGP   Pretty Good Privacy is software that uses public key cryptography which you can utilise to **encrypt** files on your computer so no-one else can read them. You can also encrypt **email** messages so only the intended recipients can read them, and sign documents to make messages tamper proof.

PICS   The Platform for Internet Content Selection is a rating system which allows people to voluntarily rate or classify their **Web sites** according to standards of acceptability (self rating) and also attaches labels to the content of sites (third party rating).

Pine   One of the most common and easy-to-use **email** programs.

PK(un)zip   A well-known (de) **compression** utility.

Plugins   Extend **Web browser** capabilities, allowing additional features such as animation and sound. They are fully integrated into your browser and will automatically come into use when needed.

POP   Post Office Protocols are used by programs like **Eudora** to handle the storage of **email** messages until you are ready to collect them.

POP Server   The computer that holds **email** until you are ready to retrieve it.

Port Number   The number that occurs immediately after the hostname, e.g. archie.au:23. The port number allows different services to be run on a single computer.

Posting   A message sent to a **Usenet Newsgroup**.

PPP   Point to Point Protocol. The technology that allows a dial-up connection to the Internet via a modem and telephone line.

Program Viruses   invade an executable program, via infected floppy diskettes and/or infected software on the Internet. The virus is spread when you run the program.

Public Key Encryption   A technique for **encrypting** information in such a way that the key used to decrypt a message is different from the key used to encrypt it.

Private Keys   Used by **public key** cryptography systems for **encryption** and decryption.

Public Keys   Used to **encrypt** messages and verify **digital signatures**.

Real time   Happening right now, as opposed to asynchronously. IRC and MUDs happen in real time but **email** messages collect on a **server** and are read at a time suitable to the receiver.

RL   Real life as opposed to life as experienced through a computer screen. (An **email** friend might suggest "let's meet in RL").

RSACi   Recreational Software Advisory Council on the Internet. A voluntary content-labeling system.

Search Engines   Software tools which automatically search indexes of information on the Internet (e.g. **Web pages, Usenet News, postings** etc.), using key words to find what you are looking for. Examples are Lycos and Infoseek.

Secret Key   A key used by **public key** cryptography systems which is kept secret and used to decrypt messages that are **encrypted** with the corresponding public key. It's also used to sign documents with a **digital signature**.

Server   A computer that stores information on a large amount of hard disk storage and makes it available to other users.

Shockwave   Software which delivers Macromedia director files to a **Web page**. Macromedia director is a software package that creates multimedia files.

Signatures   Short quotes, phrases or pictures made up of screen characters, which are automatically added to the end of **email** messages.

Slip   Serial Line Internet Protocol, a **dial-up** connection to the Internet.

Slip emulator   A piece of software that "fakes" a **slip** connection between your computer and your ISP's computer. This is useful if you can only afford or set up a text-based/shell account.

SMTP   Simple Mail Transfer Protocol, the **email** protocol of the Internet. A **server** permanently connected to the Internet handles all incoming and outgoing **email** traffic.

Spamming   Sending hundreds of inappropriate **postings** to **Usenet Newsgroups**, **mailing lists** or to an individual's **email** address.

Subnet mask   A special number provided by your ISP which ensures that **packets** are correctly transferred from your computer to the **host** computer.

Surfing   Browsing the Internet, almost at random, spending time travelling but not really reading anything in depth. Witches have been known to "surf the Net".

Systems Administrator   A person who administers computer networks and looks after the applications that connect the network to the Internet.

TCP/IP   Transmission Control Protocol/Internet Protocol, software that enables computers to contact each other over the Internet.

Telnet   Allows your computer to log into another computer and for you to control it from your home. Your home computer becomes a terminal or extension of the remote computer.

Terminal Emulation   Software that translates any characters you type on your home computer into characters your host computer will understand and vica versa. Used when **Telnetting** to enable your computer screen to behave the way the remote computer expects.

Text-based   Text only data as opposed to graphics, sound and/or video (these are usually **binary**).

UNIX   An operating system used by many Internet hosts.

Upload   To send or contribute information from your computer to another computer (usually to an **FTP server**).

URL   Uniform Resource Locator. The addressing system used on the Internet to identify a resource on the **WWW**. The URL tells the **Web browser** which computer to connect to and where on the computer a required Web page is located.

Usenet News Also known as **Network news, Netnews** or **Newsnet** is the giant bulletin board and repository of thousands of discussion groups worldwide. Developed in the **UNIX** community but is now commonly carried as an Internet service.

Username You need a username to **log-on** to your **ISP**'s computer, and from there connect to the Internet. This name is usually allocated by your ISP, however you can sometimes choose one yourself.

Veronica Very-easy-rodent-oriented Netwide Index to Computerized Archives. A tool you can use to search for information on **gopher** sites.

Viruses A computer virus is a program which was designed to replicate itself. Some viruses eventually take up so much space on your computer that they bring it to a complete halt. Others can actually destroy files on your hard disk.

VRML Virtual Reality Modeling Language. A programming language for creating virtual worlds. With a VRML viewer you can tour a 3D model building or manipulate animations of 3D objects.

World Wide Web, also known as the **WWW** and **the Web**. A powerful Internet tool for retrieving and distributing information, which uses a system of linking pages of related information together (**hypertext**). It acts as a global publishing system.

Web browsers (also known as **Web clients**) Software programs used to access Internet tools. They reside on your computer and allow you to establish a connection to a remote computer and retrieve files.

Web page A Web page is part of the **WWW**. In order to be part of **the Web** all Web pages must be linked in some way to each other by **hypertext**.

Web servers Software programs that reside on computers and are permanently connected to the Internet. Servers respond to requests by **Web browsers** for particular **Web pages**.

Web of trust A technique used by **PGP** for building a library of validated **public keys**.

Winsock A standard that defines how **TCP/IP** connects to a Windows operating system.

Zine See e-zine.

Zipfile A compressed file.

Index

Notes

Nattering on the Net

by Dale Spender

Dale Spender promises to change the way we think about computers. She reveals that men are writing the road rules for the information superhighway subjecting women to new forms of sexual harassment and even "data rape". But Dale Spender is also excited about the possibilities of the new media. She asks will the Net create virtual sisterhood?

> "Almost singlehandedly [Dale Spender] was responsible for one of the most radical revisionings of contemporary education and now thankfully she has turned her hand to the new technology . . . She is hooked, she admits it, and she wants women to get in quick, to fully understand the Net, to use it and to name our space on the highway."
>
> – Carole Spedding,
> The Women's Book Club, UK

> "This book enriched viewshed (the way you look at the world). Dale playfully wrestles with the forces that are changing our ideas of authorship, intellectual property and community. *Nattering on the Net* is a book you must read."
>
> – David Cole,
> President, America OnLine Enterprises

ISBN 1-875559-09-4

The Silicon Tongue

by Beryl Fletcher

Alice is seventy. Abandoned in England at the age of seven, Alice is sent to New Zealand as a servant. At seventy, she tells her story into the tape recorder of a mysterious oral historian and discloses family secrets of rape and adoption. She discovers a kinship with teenage Nethead, Pixel, and learns that old women can fly in cyberspace along with the young. Meanwhile, Alice's daughter Joy, finds out that when it comes to family stories there is more than one version of the truth.

Commonwealth Award Winner, Beryl Fletcher's scope and her ability to unwind a tale are truly brought to life in this, her third novel.

ISBN 1-875559-49-3

Building Babel

by Suniti Namjoshi

A fabulous new book from a writer whose work spans continents and worlds. In the world of Babel, power and the discipline of love come under scrutiny. Filled with characters from fairy tales and myth, Suniti Namjoshi follows the trials and tribulations of well-known sisters, such as Little Red, Snow White, Crone Kronos, Queen Alice, Sister Solitude, Cinders and the Black Piglet.

She invites readers to contribute their speculations on the Spinifex Home Page about possible worlds that sisters might invent.

"Suniti Namjoshi is an inspired fabulist: she asks the difficult questions – about good and evil, about nature and war – unfailingly bracing her readers with her mordant humour and the lively play of her imagination."
– Marina Warner

ISBN 1-875559-56-6

If you would like to know more about Spinifex Press,
write for a free catalogue or visit our Home Page.

SPINIFEX PRESS
PO Box 212, North Melbourne,
Victoria 3051, Australia
http://www.publishaust.net.au/~spinifex